BIBLICA ET ORIENTALIA

(SACRA SCRIPTURA ANTIQUITATIBUS ORIENTALIBUS ILLUSTRATA)

19

ROMAE

E PONTIFICIO INSTITUTO BIBLICO

1967

JOSEPH A. FITZMYER, S.J.

THE ARAMAIC INSCRIPTIONS
OF SEFÎRE

ROME
PONTIFICAL BIBLICAL INSTITUTE
1967

IMPRIMI POTEST

Romae, die 14 iunii 1967
R. A. F. MacKenzie, S. I.
Rector Pontificii Instituti Biblici

IMPRIMATUR

Ex Vic. Urbis, die 3 iulii 1967
✠ A. Traglia, Card. Vicarius

TYPIS PONTIFICIAE UNIVERSITATIS GREGORIANAE - ROMAE

To
Professor William F. Albright
My Revered Teacher
In Gratitude

TABLE OF CONTENTS

PLATES

    I. Comparative Table of the Scripts of the Main Northwest Semitic Inscriptions of the 9th-8th Centuries B.C.

   II. Stele I — Diagram Showing the Relative Position of the Fragments

  III. Stele I — Face A, Upper Portion

  IV. Stele I — Face A, Lower Portion

   V. Stele I — Face B, Upper Portion

  VI. Stele I — Face B, Lower Portion

 VII. Stele I — Face C, Upper Portion

VIII. Stele I — Face C, Lower Portion

  IX. Stele II — Face A

   X. Stele II — Face B

  XI. Stele II — Face C

 XII. Stele III — Left Side

XIII. Stele III — Right Side

XIV. Stele I A (a-b) — Photographic Reproduction

 XV. Stele I B (b) — Photographic Reproduction

XVI. Stele II B — Photographic Reproduction

XVII. Stele III — Photographic Reproduction

XVIII. Map of the Ancient Near East with reference to the Sefîre Inscriptions.

PREFACE

This book represents a thorough revision of the two articles which I published at different times on the three Aramaic inscriptions from Sefîre in northern Syria dating from the eighth century B.C. The first article was entitled, " The Aramaic Suzerainty Treaty from Sefîre in the Museum of Beirut," and appeared in the *Catholic Biblical Quarterly* 20 (1958) 444-76. It was devoted to what has come to be called Sefîre Inscription III. The second article, similar in form, was entitled, " The Aramaic Inscriptions of Sefîre I and II," and appeared in the *Journal of the American Oriental Society* 81 (1961) 178-222 ; as its title indicates, it was devoted to the first two inscriptions of this group. Since these articles of mine a good number of further studies of the three inscriptions have appeared, commenting on or developing further points of interpretation. It has seemed good to rework the two articles, combining them into a unified treatment, and bringing the discussion of the inscriptions in them up to date by taking into account the subsequent observations of other writers. Our basic interpretation has not been altered much, but the reader will find the comments on various lines completely rewritten at times. This unified treatment of the three inscriptions has also necessitated the rearrangement of comments ; some of the commentary on the lines of Sf III was quite developed and in the later article on Sf I and II I simply referred the reader to it. These comments have been re-arranged so that the first appearance of a word in Sf I or II will now usually have the developed commentary and reference to it will normally be made at subsequent occurrences of the same expression. I have combined the grammatical analysis of the inscriptions, but the general lines of the analysis have remained the same. A glossary has been added, and also a reproduction of the facsimiles of the original publication prepared by Fr. J. Starcky. The text of this book should, therefore, make it possible for students of the Sefîre inscriptions to find the essentials of the research on them within the compass of one volume.

There only remains the pleasant task of thanking the many persons who have assisted me in the production of this volume. In particular, my thanks are due to the Catholic Biblical Association of

America which has generously assisted in defraying part of the expenses of the publication of this commentary. They are also due to the editors of the *Catholic Biblical Quarterly* and the *Journal of the American Oriental Society* for their permission to present the original articles in this revised form. My indebtedness to the original editors of these inscriptions, M. le Professeur André Dupont-Sommer and M. l'abbé Jean Starcky, will appear on almost every page of this book; it is my pleasure to acknowledge that indebtedness here in a formal way. In particular, I must express my thanks to M. Starcky for his kind permission to reproduce in this volume his facsimiles of the steles on pls. I-XIII and his photo of stele II on pl. XVI. Thanks are likewise due to l'Emir Maurice Chéhab, Conservateur général des Antiquités in Lebanon, for the permission to reproduce the photo of stele III on pl. XVII, and to M. le Conservateur A. Moufti, Director General of Antiquities and Museums in Syria, for the permission to reproduce the photos of stele I on pls. XIV-XV. I am also grateful to V. Rev. R. A. F. MacKenzie, S.J., Rector of the Pontifical Biblical Institute, and to Rev. Stanislas Lyonnet, S.J., editor, for accepting this work into the series " Biblica et Orientalia. " My special gratitude must be expressed to Rev. James Swetnam, S.J., the managing editor of the series, for all his time and trouble in guiding this book through its actual production. Lastly, my thanks are due to Rev. J. D. Shenkel, S.J., for his help in reading proofs.

Joseph A. Fitzmyer, S.J.
Woodstock College
Woodstock, Maryland, 21663

LIST OF ABBREVIATIONS

A. . . . . Aḥiqar (= *AP* pp. 204-48)

AA . . . . G. Garbini, " L'Aramaico antico " (see bibliography)

AANL Rendic . . *Atti della Accademia Nazionale dei Lincei, Rendiconti*

AC . . . . J. J. Koopmans, *Aramäische Chrestomathie* (2 vols.; Leiden: Nederlands Instituut voor het Nabije Oosten, 1962)

AD . . . . G. R. Driver, *Aramaic Documents of the Fifth Century B.C.* (2nd ed.; Oxford : Clarendon, 1957)

AfO . . . . *Archiv für Orientforschung*

AION . . . . . . *Annali dell'Istituto Orientale di Napoli*

AJSL . . . . . . *American Journal of Semitic Languages and Literatures*

AnArchSyr . . . . *Les annales archéologiques de Syrie*

ANET . . . . . J. B. Pritchard, *Ancient Near Eastern Texts Relating to the Old Testament* (2nd ed.; Princeton : University Press, 1955)

ANHW . . . . . G. Dalman, *Aramäisch-Neuhebräisches Handwörterbuch zu Targum, Talmud und Midrasch* (Göttingen : Pfeiffer, 1938)

AP . . . . A. Cowley, *Aramaic Papyri of the Fifth Century B. C.* (Oxford : Clarendon, 1923)

ARAB . . . . D. D. Luckenbill, *Ancient Records of Assyria and Babylonia* (2 vols.; Chicago : University Press, 1926-27)

ARM . . . . . . A. Parrot and G. Dossin (ed.), *Archives royales de Mari : Transcriptions et traductions* (Paris : Imprimerie Nationale, 1950-)

ArOr. . . . . . . *Archiv Orientální*

AšOstr . . . . . . Asshur Ostracon (M. Lidzbarski, *Altaramäische Urkunden aus Assur* [Leipzig : Hinrichs, 1921], pp. 5-15)

BA . . . . *Biblical Archaeologist*

BAG. . . . . . . C. Bezold and A. Goetze, *Babylonisch-Assyrisches Glossar* (Heidelberg : C. Winter, 1926)

BASOR . . . . . *Bulletin of the American Schools of Oriental Research*

BeO . . . . *Bibbia e Oriente*

Bibl . . . . *Biblica*

BLA. . . . . . . H. Bauer and P. Leander, *Grammatik des Biblisch-Aramäischen* (Halle a. d. S.: M. Niemeyer, 1927)

B-M . . . . . Bauer-Meissner Papyrus (=*Sitzungsberichte der preussischen Akademie der Wissenschaften* 72 [1936] 414-24)

BMAP. . . . . . E. G. Kraeling, *The Brooklyn Museum Aramaic Papyri* (New Haven : Yale University Press, 1953)

BMB . . . . . .   *Bulletin du Musée de Beyrouth*
BO . . . .   *Bibliotheca orientalis*
CAD. . . . . . .   I. Gelb, L. Oppenheim, et al., *The Assyrian Dictionary
                     of the Oriental Institute of the University of Chicago*
                     (Chicago : University Press, 1956-   )
CBQ . . . . . .   *Catholic Biblical Quarterly*
CD . . . .   Damascus Document of the Cairo Geniza
CH . . . .   Code of Hammurabi
CIS. . . . . . .   *Corpus inscriptionum semiticarum*
CML . . . . . .   G. R. Driver, *Canaanite Myths and Legends* (Old Testa-
                     ment Studies 3 ; Edinburgh : T. and T. Clark, 1956)
CRAIBL . . . .   *Comptes rendus de l'Académie des inscriptions et belles-
                     lettres*
CT . . . .   *Cuneiform Texts from Babylonian Tablets, etc., in the Bri-
                     tish Museum* (London : British Museum, 1896-   )
DBS. . . . . . .   *Dictionnaire de la Bible, Supplément* (Paris : Letouzey et
                     Ané, 1928-   )
DISO . . . . . .   C.-F. Jean and J. Hoftijzer, *Dictionnaire des inscriptions
                     sémitiques de l'ouest* (Leiden : Brill, 1965)
EA . . . .   J. A. Knudtzon, *Die El-Amarna Tafeln* (Vorderasiatische
                     Bibliothek 2 ; reprinted, Aalen : O. Zeller, 1964)
EHO. . . . . . .   F. M. Cross, Jr. and D. N. Freedman, *Early Hebrew Ortho-
                     graphy : A Study of the Epigraphic Evidence* (see
                     bibliography)
GB . . . .   W. Gesenius and F. Buhl, *Hebräisches und aramäisches
                     Handwörterbuch über das Alte Testament* (17th ed. ;
                     Berlin : Springer-Verlag, 1949)
GPL . . . . . .   Z. S. Harris, *Grammar of the Phoenician Language* (Amer-
                     ican Oriental Series 8 ; New Haven : American Orien-
                     tal Society, 1936)
Grundr . . . . .   C. Brockelmann, *Grundriss der vergleichenden Grammatik
                     der semitischen Sprachen* (2 vols.; Berlin : Reuther und
                     Reichard, 1908-13)
HTS. . . . . . .   *Harvard Theological Studies*
HUCA . . . . .   *Hebrew Union College Annual*
JAOS . . . . . .   *Journal of the American Oriental Society*
JBL . . . . . .   *Journal of Biblical Literature*
JCS. . . . . . .   *Journal of Cuneiform Studies*
JEOL . . . . . .   *Jaarbericht ' Ex oriente lux '*
JNES . . . . . .   *Journal of Near Eastern Studies*
JPOS . . . . . .   *Journal of the Palestine Oriental Society*
JRAS . . . . . .   *Journal of the Royal Asiatic Society*
JSS . . . .   *Journal of Semitic Studies*
KAI. . . . . . .   H. Donner and W. Röllig, *Kanaanäische und aramäische
                     Inschriften* (3 vols.; Wiesbaden : Harrassowitz, 1962,
                     1964)
KB . . . .   L. Koehler and W. Baumgartner, *Lexicon in veteris Testa-
                     menti libros* (Leiden : Brill, 1958)

LFLAA . . . . . P. Leander, *Laut- und Formenlehre des Ägyptisch-Aramäi-schen* (Göteborg : Elander, 1928 [= *Göteborgs Högsko-las Årsskrift* 34/4])

MAOG. . . . . . *Mitteilungen der altorientalischen Gesellschaft* (Leipzig : J.C. Hinrichs, 1925-)

MPAIBL . . . . *Mémoires présentés à l'académie des inscriptions et belles-lettres*

MUSJ . . . . . *Mélanges de l'université Saint-Joseph*

MVAG. . . . . . *Mitteilungen der vorderasiatisch-aegyptischen Gesellschaft* (Berlin : Staatliche Museen, 1896-)

NSI . . . . G. A. Cooke, *A Text-Book of North Semitic Inscriptions* (Oxford : Clarendon, 1903)

OLZ . . . . . . *Orientalistische Literaturzeitung*

OudtestStud . . . *Oudtestamentische Studiën*

Pad . . . . . . Padua Aramaic Papyrus Letters (*RSO* 35 [1960] 11-24)

PPG. . . . . . . J. Friedrich, *Phönizisch-Punische Grammatik* (Analecta Orientalia 32 ; Rome : Pontificium Institutum Bibli-cum, 1951)

PRU . . . . . . Cl. F.-A. Schaeffer, *Le Palais royal d'Ugarit* (Paris : Impri-merie nationale, 1955-)

PS . . . . *Palestinskii sbornik*

RA . . . . *Revue d'assyriologie et d'archéologie orientale*

RB . . . . *Revue biblique*

RE . . . . *Paulys Real-Encyclopädie der classischen Altertumswissen-schaft* (ed. G. Wissowa, et al.; Stuttgart : J. B. Metz-ler — A. Druckenmueller)

RES . . . . . . *Répertoire d'épigraphie sémitique*

RevArchéol . . . . *Revue archéologique*

RHR . . . . . . *Revue de l'histoire des religions*

RivBibl . . . . . *Rivista biblica*

RSO . . . . . . *Rivista degli studi orientali*

UT . . . . C. H. Gordon, *Ugaritic Textbook* (Analecta Orientalia 38; Rome : Pontifical Biblical Institute, 1965)

VAB . . . . . . *Vorderasiatische Bibliothek* (Leipzig : J. C. Hinrichs, 1907-1916)

VD . . . . *Verbum Domini*

VT . . . . *Vetus Testamentum*

VTS. . . . . . . *Vetus Testamentum, Supplements*

WZKM . . . . . *Wiener Zeitschrift für die Kunde des Morgenlandes*

ZA . . . . *Zeitschrift für Assyriologie*

ZAW . . . . . . *Zeitschrift für die alttestamentliche Wissenschaft*

ZDMG. . . . . . *Zeitschrift der deutschen morgenländischen Gesellschaft*

ZDPV . . . . . . *Zeitschrift des deutschen Palästina-Vereins*

1QapGn . . . . . The Genesis Apocryphon from Qumran Cave I

4QHen . . . . . Enoch fragments from Qumran Cave IV

1QIa . . . . . Isaiah Scroll A from Qumram Cave I

INTRODUCTION

In 1931 Sébastien Ronzevalle, S.J. first published the text of the so-called Sūjîn stele. (¹) Subsequently scholars pointed out the need of a fresh study of this inscription, based on the stele itself and on new and adequate photographs. This need was met by the splendid publication of André Dupont-Sommer and Jean Starcky, " Les inscriptions araméennes de Sfiré (Stèles I et II)." (²) This publication is obviously the fruit of many long hours of concentration on the stone itself and must now be considered the *editio princeps* of the inscription. It consists of an important introduction about the finding of the steles, a transcription, translation, commentary, glossary and, what is most important of all, twenty-nine plates of hand-copies and excellent photographs.

Since there is very good reason to believe that Ronzevalle was misled by the natives concerning the place where the steles were found and his own efforts at excavating Sūjîn in 1930 brought to light nothing new in the way of additional fragments, the new editors have abandoned the title " Sūjîn stele " for the apparently more accurate designation, Sefîre stele I. In addition to the fresh study of this Sefîre stele I their article contains the first publication of another very fragmentary inscription from the same place; this is Sefîre stele II. Both of these inscriptions were acquired by the Damascus Museum in 1948. A third stele from the same place was acquired by the Beirut Museum in 1956 and was published by Dupont-Sommer with the collaboration of Starcky in 1958. (³) All three inscriptions are related

(¹) " Fragments d'inscriptions araméennes des environs d'Alep," *MUSJ* 15 (1930-31) 237-60. Dupont-Sommer and Starcky say of this publication : " Cette édition n'est pas sans mérite, mais elle a été faite dans des conditions peu favorables : bien des lectures y apparaissent extremêment incertaines, et les photographies publiées sont généralement insuffisantes."

(²) *MPAIBL* 15 (1960, appeared in 1958) 197-351, plus 29 plates (hereafter : " Les inscriptions ").

(³) " Une inscription araméenne inédite de Sfiré," *BMB* 13 (1956, appeared early in 1958) 23-41. We shall refer to the three steles of Sefîre as Sf I, Sf II, Sf III.

not only, by their provenience but also by their contents, script, and language; and a comparative study of them is imperative. As far as can be ascertained today, almost fifty years later than the time of the first discovery, they were found at Sefîre, a small village about 15 miles southeast of Aleppo in Syria. (⁴) The village of Sūjîn is about a half mile northeast of Sefîre.

The reader is referred to the articles of Dupont-Sommer and Starcky for the details about the acquisition of the inscriptions, their physical description, the discussion of their script, etc. It is sufficient to note here that the editors are of the opinion that the same stone-cutter engraved not only both sides of stele I (against the suggestion of Ronzevalle), (⁵) but also steles II and III. The type of writing points to a date " vers le milieu du VIIIe siècle avant J.-C., après celles de Kilamou, du Zakir et de Panamou et avant celles de Bar-Rekoub et d'Azitawadda," (⁶) the same date as that given by Ronzevalle. Starcky has contributed a very useful discussion of the comparative epigraphic material in Appendix II, " Remarques épigraphiques." (⁷)

The three steles preserve texts of treaties made by a north Syrian ruler. In the first two of them he is named as Matî'el, the son of 'Attarsamak, the king of Arpad; apparently in the position of a vassal, he concluded pacts with Bir-Ga'yah, the king of KTK, a powerful Mesopotamian overlord. It is not easy to determine the relation of the three steles to each other or to establish their relative dating or sequence. Even the form of them is puzzling, for the first two, engraved on several sides of the stone employed, suggest a shape that was roughly a truncated pyramid, whereas the last one was simply a flat slab.

The *terminus ante quem* for the three inscriptions is certainly 740 B.C., the year in which the Assyrian king Tiglathpileser III conquered Arpad and made it part of the Assyrian Empire. The Sefîre inscriptions presuppose the autonomy and political independence of Arpad. Matî'el was already the king of Arpad in 754 B.C., for in the spring of 754-53 B.C. he concluded a treaty with Aššurnirāri V (appearing in the Akkadian text as Mati'ilu). It is not possible to say how long Matî'el was king before this time nor whether the

---

(⁴) R. Dussaud (*Syria* 9 [1928] 171) identified Sefîre with Šipri, mentioned in the treaty of Šupiluliumma and Mattiwaza (14th Cent. B.C.) ; but this identification is quite questionable.

(⁵) *Op. cit.*, p. 240.

(⁶) " Les inscriptions," p. 202.

(⁷) *Ibid.*, pp. 329-34.

treaty with Bir-Ga'yah recorded in Sf I and II preceded or followed
that with Aššurnirāri.   M. Noth [8] is of the opinion that Sf I B is
an early form of a treaty between Matî'el and Bir-Ga'yah, possibly
before 754 B.C., and that Sf I A represents a newly-composed renewal
of Sf I B sometime after 754 B.C., being occasioned precisely by the
new relationship with Aššurnirāri V.   On the other hand, Donner -
Röllig are inclined to date Sf I in the period before 754, and Sf II
and III after 754. [9]

This question of the relative date of the Sefîre inscriptions is
partly involved in the relationship of the three inscriptions, one to
the other.   Matî'el and Bir-Ga'yah are clearly indicated as the contracting parties in Sf I A 1, B 1; Sf II A 3, B [2], [5], C 14.   But
Matî'el's name does not appear in the fragmentary Sf III, although the
name of Arpad does (lines 1, 3, 16, 27); the name of Bir-Ga'yah is
hesitantly restored in Sf III 25.   M. Noth [10] has pointed out that
certain features in Sf III seem to presuppose a different historical
situation, so that it is possible that Sf III represents a treaty of
Bir-Ga'yah with some other (later?) ruler of Arpad.   And yet the
external similarity of the three steles is such that it would be hard to
separate even Sf III from Matî'el.   But the data are so meager
that no definite judgment can be made in this issue.

The several treaties from Sefîre, as well as the treaty of Matî'el
with Aššurnirāri V (in 754 B.C.) and the alliance of Matî'el with
Sardur III of Urartu, which Tiglathpileser III eventually brought to
an end, give us an inkling of the complicated political relations which
existed in northern Syria in the middle of the eighth century B.C.
But all such ententes must have ended when Tiglathpileser III began
his reign with a series of campaigns and defeated the Aramaeans in
Mesopotamia, Sardur III in Urartu, and Matî'el in Arpad.   The Neo-
Assyrian might was reasserted.   All these details provide an interesting historical background to the reigns of Jeroboam II (786-747 B.C.)
in Israel and Uzziah (783-742 B.C.) in Judah, as well as to the career
of the prophet Amos, in whose prophecies Asshur significantly does
not appear.

Sf I had been well worked over by many scholars on the basis
of Ronzevalle's publication; and a number of more recent discussions
have followed the publication of Dupont-Sommer. [11]

[8] *ZDPV* 77 (1961) 122-23.
[9] *KAI* 2. 274.
[10] *ZDPV* 77 (1961) 128-38.
[11] See the bibliography below, pp. 5-8.

   Despite the excellent work of Dupont-Sommer and Starcky there
are many parts of these inscriptions which are still obscure ; this is
mainly due to the fact that they are so badly preserved.   My own
study has not solved all these problems either ; however, it is hoped
that some of these observations will contribute to the understanding
of the important inscriptions of Sefîre.

BIBLIOGRAPHY

A. Sefîre I. Older Discussions

Ronzevalle, S., " Fragments d'inscriptions araméennes des environs d'Alep,"
MUSJ 15 (1930-31) 237-60.

Cantineau, J., " Remarques sur la stèle araméenne de Sefiré-Soudjin," *RA* 28
(1931) 167-78.

Dussaud, R., " Séance du 20 juin," *CRAIBL* 1930, pp. 155-58, esp. 155-56.

——, " Nouvelles inscriptions araméennes de Séfiré, près Alep," *CRAIBL* 1931,
pp. 312-21.

——, " Inscriptions araméennes de Sefiré (Soudjin)," *Syria* 13 (1932) 401-2.

Hempel, J. and Bauer, H., Review of Ronzevalle's article, *ZAW* 50 (1932)
178-83.

Bauer, H., " Ein aramäischer Staatsvertrag aus dem 8. Jahrhundert v. Chr.
Die Inschrift der Stele von Sudschīn," *AfO* 8 (1932-33) 1-16 ; cf. *Revue
archéologique syrienne* 2 (1932) 100-07.

Weidner, E. F., " Der Staatsvertrag Aššurnirâris VI [= V] von Assyrien mit
Mati'ilu von Bît-Agusi," *AfO* 8 (1932-33) 17-34.

Driver, G. R., " Notes on the Aramaic Inscription from Soudschin," *AfO* 8
(1932-33) 203-06.

Langdon, S., " Note on the Aramaic Treaty of Bar-ga'ya and Mati'el," *JRAS*
1933, pp. 23-24.

Montgomery, J. A., " Notes on Early Aramaic Inscriptions," *JAOS* 54 (1934)
421-225 [pp. 424-25 : The Sujîn Inscription].

Littmann, E., Review of S. Ronzevalle, " Notes et études d'archéologie orientale," *OLZ* 38 (1935) 166-68.

Friedrich, J. and Landsberger, B., " Zu der altaramäischen Stele von Sudschin," *ZA* NF 7 (1933) 313-18.

Alt, A., " Die syrische Staatenwelt vor dem Einbruch der Assyrer," *ZDMG*
13 (1934) 233-58 ; = *Kleine Schriften* 3 (1959) 214-32.

Friedrich, J. " Kein König *plmh* in der Stele von Sudschin," *ZA* NF 9 (1936)
327-28.

Euler, K. F., " Die Bedeutung von *spr* in der Sudschin-Inschrift im Lichte
des ATlichen Gebrauchs von *sepaer*," *ZAW* 55 (1937) 281-91.

Epstein, J. N., " Notes on the Sujin Pact," *Kedem* I (1942) 37-43 [Modern
Hebrew].

Dossin, G., " BRG'YH, roi de KTK," *Muséon* 57 (1944) 147-55.

Landsberger, B., *Sam'al* (Ankara : Türkische historische Gesellschaft, 1948),
p. 59, n. 147.

Dupont-Sommer, A., *Les Araméens* (L'Orient ancien illustré ; Paris : A. Maisonneuve, 1949), pp. 55-60, 70-71.

Rosenthal, F., " The Treaty Between KTK and Arpad," *ANET* 503b-504b.
Cross, F. M., Jr. and Freedman, D. N., *Early Hebrew Orthography : a Study of the Epigraphic Evidence* (American Oriental Series 36 ; New Haven : American Oriental Society, 1952), pp. 27-29.
Mendenhall, G. E., " Covenant Forms in Israelite Tradition," *BA* 17 (1954) 50-76.
Garbini, G., " L'Aramaico antico," *Atti della Accademia Nazionale dei Lincei, Memorie,* Classe di Scienze morali, storiche e filologiche, serie VIII, volume VII, fascicolo 5 (Roma : Accademia Nazionale dei Lincei, 1956) pp. 235-83, esp. 264-70.
Contenau, G., " La cryptographie chez les Mésopotamiens," *Mélanges bibliques rédigés en l'honneur de A. Robert* (Travaux de l'Institut Catholique de Paris 4 ; Paris : Bloud et Gay, 1957) 17-21.

B. Sefîre I. More Recent Discussions

Dupont-Sommer, A. (avec la collaboration de M. l'abbé Jean Starcky), " Les inscriptions araméennes de Sfiré (stèles I et II)," *MPAIBL* 15 (1960, appeared in 1958) 197-351 [+ pls. I-XXIX].
Donner, H., " Zur Inschrift von Sūdschīn Aa 9," *AfO* 18 (1957-58) 390-92.
Dupont-Sommer, A., " Un traité araméen du VIIIe siècle av. J.-C.," *CRAIBL* 1958, pp. 177-82.
Thomas D. W., Review of Dupont-Sommer and Starcky, *JSS* 5 (1960) 281-84.
Tsevat, M., " A Chapter on Old West Semitic Orthography," *The Joshua Bloch Memorial Volume : Studies in Booklore and History* (N. Y.: N. Y. Public Library, 1960), 82-91.
Dupont-Sommer, A., " Trois stèles araméennes provenant de Sfiré : un traité de vassalité du VIIIe siècle avant J.-C.," *AnArchSyr* 10 (1960) 21-54, [+ pls. I-X].
Koopmans, J. J., Review of Dupont-Sommer and Starcky, *BO* 17 (1960) 51-52.
Fitzmyer, J. A., " The Aramaic Inscriptions of Sefîre I and II," *JAOS* 81 (1961, appeared March 1962) 178-222.
Noth, M., " Der historische Hintergrund der Inschriften von sefîre," *ZDPV* 77 (1961) 118-72.
Garbini, G., " Sefîre I A, 28," *RSO* 36 (1961) 9-11.
Sacchi, P., " Osservazioni storiche alla prima iscrizione aramaica di Sfire," *Atti dell'Accademia Nazionale dei Lincei, Rendiconti,* ser. 8, 16/5-6 (1961) 175-91.
Picard, C., " Le rite magique des εἴδωλα de cire brûlés, attesté sur trois stèles araméennes de Sfiré (vers le milieu du VIIIe s. av. notre ère)," *RevArchéol* 1961, II, 85-88.
Soden, W. von, " Azitawadda = Mattî von Atunna ; KTK und Kasku," *OLZ* 56 (1961) 576-79, esp. 578-79.
Fensham, F. C., " Salt as Curse in the Old Testament and the Ancient Near East," *BA* 25 (1962) 48-50.
Mazar, B., " The Aramean Empire and its Relations with Israel," *BA* 25 (1962) 98-120.

Fensham, F. C., " Malediction and Benediction in Ancient Near Eastern Vassal-Treaties and the Old Testament," *ZAW* 74 (1962) 1-9.

——, " Clauses of Protection in Hittite Vassal-Treaties and the Old Testament," *VT* 13 (1963) 133-43, esp. 137-38.

——, " Common Trends in Curses of the Near Eastern Treaties and *Kudurru*-Inscriptions Compared with Maledictions of Amos and Isaiah," *ZAW* 75 (1963) 155-75.

Moran, W. L., " A Note on the Treaty Terminology of the Sefîre Stelas," *JNES* 22 (1963) 173-76.

Fensham, F. C., " The Wild Ass in the Aramean Treaty between Bar-Ga'ayah and Mati'el," *JNES* 22 (1963) 185-86.

Brekelmans, C., " Sefire I A 29-30," *VT* 13 (1963) 225-28.

McCarthy, D. J., *Treaty and Covenant : A Study in Form in the Ancient Oriental Documents and in the Old Testament* (Anal. Bibl. 21 ; Rome : Pontifical Biblical Institute, 1963), pp. 189-94.

Priest, J. F., " '*Orkia* in the *Iliad* and Consideration of Recent Theory," *JNES* 23 (1964) 48-56.

Fensham, F. C., " The Treaty Between Israel and the Gibeonites," *BA* 27 (1964) 96-100.

Hillers, D. R., *Treaty-Curses and the Old Testament Prophets* (Biblica et Orientalia 16 ; Rome : Pontifical Biblical Institute, 1964).

Segert, S., " Zur Schrift und Orthographie der altaramäischen Stelen von Sfire," *ArOr* 32 (1964) 110-26.

Hillers, D. R., " A Note on Some Treaty Terminology in the Old Testament," *BASOR* 176 (1964) 46-47.

Frankena, R., " The Vassal-Treaties of Esarhaddon and the Dating of Deuteronomy," *OudtestStud* 14 (1965) 122-54.

Thompson, J. A., " Expansions of the '*d* Root," *JSS* 10 (1965) 222-40.

Greenfield, J. C., " *bḥynwt lšwnywt bktwbt spyrh*," *Lešonenu* 27-28 (1964) 303-13.

——, " Studies in West Semitic Inscriptions, I : Stylistic Aspects of the Sefîre Treaty Inscriptions," *Acta orientalia* 29 (1965) 1-18.

——, " Three Notes on the Sefire Inscription," *JSS* 11 (1966) 98-105.

C. Sefîre II.

Dupont-Sommer, A. (avec la collaboration de M. l'abbé Jean Starcky), *Les inscriptions araméennes de Sfiré* (*stèles I et II*) (= *MPAIBL* 15 [1960, appeared in 1958] 197-351 [+ pls. I-XXIX]).

Fitzmyer, J. A., " The Aramaic Inscriptions of Sefîre I and II," *JAOS* 81 (1961, appeared March 1962) 178-222, esp. pp. 208-15.

Donner, H., " Zu Gen 28,22," *ZAW* 74 (1962) 68-70.

Veenhof, K. R., " An Aramaic Curse with a Sumero-Akkadian Prototype," *BO* 20 (1963) 142-44.

D. Sefîre III.

Dupont-Sommer, A. (avec la collaboration de l'abbé J. Starcky), " Une inscription araméenne inédite de Sfiré," *BMB* 13 (1956, appeared 1958) 23-41 (+ pls. I-VI).

——, " Une stèle araméenne inédite de Sfiré (Syrie) du VIIIᵉ siècle avant J.-C.," *CRAIBL* 1957, pp. 245-48.

Vogt, E., " Nova inscriptio aramaica," *Bibl* 39 (1958) 269-74.

Rabinowitz, J. J., " Ad inscriptionem aramaicam," *Bibl* 39 (1958) 401.

Fitzmyer, J. A., " The Aramaic Suzerainty Treaty from Sefîre in the Museum of Beirut," *CBQ* 20 (1958) 444-76.

Dupont-Sommer, A., " Une stèle araméenne inédite de Sfiré (Syrie), du VIIIᵉ siècle avant J.-C.," *Akten des vierundzwanzigsten internationalen Orientalisten-Kongress*, 1957 (ed. H. Franke ; Wiesbaden : DMG, 1959), 238-41.

Mouterde, P., Notice of Dupont-Sommer's art. and mine, *MUSJ* 35 (1958) 242-45.

Nober, P., " Ad inscriptionem aramaicam Arpadensem (adnotationes criticae)," *VD* 37 (1959) 171-75.

Garbini, G., " Nuovo materiale per la grammatica dell'aramaico antico," *RSO* 34 (1959) 41-54.

Rosenthal, F., " Notes on the Third Inscription from Sefîre-Sûjîn," *BASOR* 158 (1960) 28-31.

Noth, M. (see B above).

Vattioni, F., " La III iscrizione di Sfiré A 2 e Proverbi 1,23," *AION* ns (1963) 279-86.

——, " La prima menzione aramaica di ' figlio dell'uomo,' " *Biblos-Press* 6/1 (Rome : S. Maxia, 1965) 6-7.

Greenfield, J. C., " bḥynwt lšwnywt bktwbt spyrh," *Lešonenu* 27-28 (1964) 303-13.

——, " Studies in West Semitic Inscriptions, I : Stylistic Aspects of the Sefire Treaty Inscriptions," *Acta orientalia* 29 (1965) 1-18.

STELE I

Three preliminary remarks are necessary for the proper under-standing of the text of Sf I.   First of all, Dupont-Sommer has pointed out a feature of the stele in its present state of preservation which was missed by Ronzevalle and all subsequent scholars who had studied it.   The left side of the stele, which is not engraved and quite un-finished, is the result of a cutting of the basalt subsequent to its engraving.   This cut accounts for the exaggerated slant and dissym-metrical appearance of the stele on the left side, and for the loss of several letters at the end of each line of face A (recto) and the beginning of each line of face B (verso).   Earlier studies of the in-scription have generally neglected this constant loss of letters.   The end of the inscription was engraved on the right side of the stele, face C.   It is quite likely that the left side was also engraved, but is now entirely lost.   Secondly, the stele as reconstructed stands about 51.5 inches high and reveals that three lines have completely dis-appeared between the sixteenth on the upper part of Face A and the twenty-third on its lower part; face A therefore had originally 42 lines.   Similarly on face B the reconstruction permits one to arrive at a total of forty-five lines.   Instead of using, then, the fairly com-mon method of referring to the upper and lower parts of the faces of the steles by a, b (thus Aa, Ab, Ba, Bb, Ca, Cb), which was first employed by H. Bauer, [12] Dupont-Sommer has simplified the system, numbering all the lines on each face consecutively.   Thirdly, it should be remembered that there are no word-dividers in this script; the

[12] *AfO* 8 (1932-33) 1-16. For the convenience of the reader who may desire a table comparing the two modes of reference the following is supplied:

Old System	New System
Aa 1-16	A 1-16
Ab 1-23	A 20-42
Ba 1-15	B 1-15
Bb 1-25	B 21-45
Ca 1-9	C 1-9
Cb 1-12	C 14-25

words follow one another without any greater breaks between them
than between the individual letters. This feature provides for a difference of opinion at times as to the separation of words.

The following transcription differs slightly from that of Dupont-
Sommer and Starcky; the commentary will offer the justification of
details which differ. The *editio princeps* should be consulted for the
indication of doubtful letters.

TEXT : Sf I

Face A

1 עדי בר גאיה מלך כתך עם מתעאל בר עתרסמך מלך [ארפד וע]

2 די בני בר גאיה עם בני מתעאל ועדי בני בר גא[יה בר ועקר]

3 ה עם עקר מתעאל בר עתרסמך מלך ארפד ועדי כתך עם [עדי]

4 ארפד ועדי בעלי כתך עם עדי בעלי ארפד ועדי חב[ור....]

5 ו עם ארם כלה ועם מצר ועם בנוה זי יסקן באשר[ונה] ועם מלכ[י]

6 כל עלי ארם ותחתה ועם כל עלל בית מלך ונצבא עם ספרא ז[ה]

7 נה שם ועדיא אלן ועדיא אלן זי גזר בר גא[נ]יה קדם [......]

8 ומלש וקדם מרדך וזרפנת וקדם נבא ותנשמת וקדם אר ונש[ך]

9 ך וקדם נרגל ולץ וקדם שמש ונר וקדם ס[נ] ונכל וק[ן]

10 דם נכר וכדאה וקדם כל אלהי רחבה ואדם ו[...] וקדם הדד ח[ל]

11 לב וקדם סבת וקדם אל ועלין וקדם שמי[ן] וארק וקדם מצ[ן]

12 לה ומעינן וקדם יום ולילה שהדן כל אולהי כתך ואלהי אר[פד]

13 [פד] פקחו עיניכם לחזיה עדי בר גאיה [עם מתעאל מלך]

14 [ארפד] והן ישקר מתעאל בר עתרסמך מל[ך] ארפד לבר גא[י]

15 [ה מלך כתך וה]ן ישקר עקר מתעאל [לעקר בר גאיה...]

TRANSLATION [13]

Face A

I. *The Title, Introducing the Contracting Parties*

[1]The treaty of Bir-Ga'yah, king of KTK, with Matî'el, the son of 'Attarsamak, the king [of Arpad; and the trea]ty [2]of the sons of Bir-Ga'yah with the sons of Matî'el; and the treaty of the grandsons of Bir-Ga'[yah and] his [offspring] [3]with the offspring of Matî'el, the son of 'Attarsamak, the king of Arpad; and the treaty of KTK with [the treaty of] [4]Arpad; and the treaty of the lords of KTK with the treaty of the lords of Arpad; and the treaty of the un[ion of ....]W [5]with all Aram and with <the king of> Muṣr and with his sons who will come after [him], and [with the kings of] [6]all Upper-Aram and Lower-Aram and with all who enter the royal palace.

II. *The Gods Who are Witnesses to This Treaty*

And the st[ele with t]his [inscription] [7]he has set up, as well as this treaty. Now (it is) this treaty which Bir-Ga'[yah] has concluded [in the presence of ......] [8]and *Mullesh*, in the presence of Marduk and Zarpanit, in the presence of Nabu and T[ashmet, in the presence of 'Ir and Nus]k, [9]in the presence of Nergal and Laṣ, in the presence of Shamash and Nur, in the presence of S[in and Nikkal, in the pre]sence [10]of Nikkar and *Kadi'ah*, in the presence of all the gods of Raḥbah and *'Adam* [... in the presence of Hadad of A]leppo, [11]in the presence of Sibitti, in the presence of 'El and 'Elyan, in the presence of Hea[ven and Earth, in the presence of (the) A]byss [12]and (the) Springs, and in the presence of Day and Night — all the god[s of KTK and the gods of Ar]pad (are) witnesses (to it). [13]Open your eyes (O gods!), to gaze upon the treaty of Bir-Ga'yah [with Matî'el, the king of [14]Arpad].

III. *Curses against Matî'el, if he Violates the Treaty*

Now if Matî'el, the son of 'Attarsamak, the kin[g of Arpad] should be false [to Bir-Ga'yah, the [15]king of KTK, and i]f the offspring of Matî'el should be false [to the offspring of Bir-Ga'yah ...]

([13]) Italics indicate uncertain renderings. Words enclosed in parentheses have been inserted for the sake of the English idiom. Square brackets [ ] indicate editorial restorations of lacunae; angular brackets < > indicate editorial additions to the text.

16 [.............ן.. גש כ.ן. בני .והן ישקרן]

17 [ ]

18 [ ]

19 [ ]

20 [ ].........ן. [מן ימ]

21 [ן ו.] שדיהן ימשחןנק.מהיןזנ ושבע ותהרי שאת ואל [.............]

22 [ושבע ושנבע ישן ואל על יהינקן סיה ושבע ישבע ואל עלים יהינקן]

23 [יש ואל ו.אמר יהינקן שאן ושבע ישבע ואל עגל יהינקן שורה]

24 [ול ונאל ישקר מתע והן יהרגן ואל לחם בשט יהכן בכתה ושבע בע]

25 אשר מזי ימלך חל מלכת כמלכתה מלכתה תהוי ולעקרה ברה

[ה ויסך]

26 [ב ואבני על ארפד ויסך עמל מה וכל ובשמין בארק לחיה מה כל דד]

27 [יס ושן ושבע תולעה תאכל שן ושבע ארבה יאכל שן ושבע רד]

28 [ולינתחזה.] ירק ולינתחזה חצר יפק ואל ארקה אפי על תוי ק

29 [צע והמון המל.מרק ובעמה בארפד כנר קל יתשמע ואל אחוה]

30 [פ ויאכל.ובעמה בארפד אכל מה כל מן אלהן וישלחן ולילה קה]

31 [יהוו.. ואן. וקמל וסס נמרה.ופם דבהה ופם עקרב ופם חוה ם]

32 [ו צי ל.רבק תל ארפד ותהוי אחוה ליש מן.תחטןויש ו בתן קק עלה]

33 [ו הא קרןיתא תאמר ועקה.ואל וצדה.. ושרן וארנב ושעל צבי]

34 [ואן ....ו וביןן וביתאל ותואם. ושרן ומבלה ומזה ומרבה מדרא]

35 [ר ובנתה ארפד תקד כן באש זא שעותא תקד זי איך ואדם וחזז רנה]

36 [זא ונבשא וזנה גנבא תאמר ואל ושחלין מלח הדד בהן ויזרע בת]

37 [באן מנתעאל יקד כן באש זא שעותא תקד זי איכה הא ונבשה מתעאל]

38 [מתעאל וקשת. והדד אנרת ישבר כן אלן וחציא קשתא תשבר זי ואיך ש]

39 [ז ואיך מתעא.ל כן שעותא גבר יער זי ואיך רבוה וקשת]

40 [תע זי ואיך. רבוה ויגזרן מתעאל יגזר כן זנה עגלא יגזר י.ן]

41 [ז ואיך ר.בוה ונשי עקרה ונשי מתעאל נשי יערן כן [זנניה].רר]

[16][... and if the Benê-]Gush should be false ....] [20][   ]
from YM[........] [21][..... and should seven rams cover] a ewe, may she
not conceive; and should seven nurses] anoint [*their breasts* and]
[22]nurse a young boy, may he not have his fill; and should seven mares
suckle a colt, may it not be sa[ted; and should seven] [23]cows give
suck to a calf, may it not have its fill; and should seven ewes suckle
a lamb, [may it not be sa]ted; [24]and should seven *hens* go looking for
food, may they not *kill* (anything)! And if Matî[ʿel] should be false
<to Bir-Gaʾyah> [and to] [25]his son and to his offspring, may his king-
dom become like a kingdom of sand, a kingdom of sand, as long as
Asshur rules! (And) [may Ha]dad [pour (over it)] [26]every sort of
evil (which exists) on earth and in heaven and every sort of trouble;
and may he shower upon Arpad [ha]il-[stones]! [27]For seven years
may the locust devour (Arpad), and for seven years may the worm
eat, and for seven [years may] [28]TWY come up upon the face of its
land! May the grass not come forth so that no green may be seen;
and may its [29]vegetation not be [seen]! Nor may the sound of the
lyre be heard in Arpad; but among its people (let there rather be)
the din of *affliction* and *the noi[se of cry]ing* [30]and lamentation! May
the gods send every sort of devourer against Arpad and against its
people! [May the mo]uth [31]of a snake [eat], the mouth of a scorpion,
the mouth of *a bear*, the mouth of a panther! And may a moth and
a louse and a [. . . become] [32]to it a serpent's throat! May its
vegetation be destroyed unto desolation! And may Arpad become
a mound to [house the desert animal]: the [33]gazelle and the fox and
the hare and the wild-cat and the owl and the [   ] and the
magpie! May [this] ci[ty] not be mentioned (any more), [nor] [34]MDRʾ
nor MRBH nor MZH nor MBLH nor Sharun nor Tuʾim nor Bethel
nor BYNN nor [.... nor ʾAr]neh [35]nor Ḥazaz nor ʾAdam!

IV. *Curses with Accompanying Rites*

Just as this wax is burned by fire, so may Arpad be burned and
[her *gr*]*eat* [daughter-cities]! [36]May Hadad sow in them salt and
weeds, and may it not be mentioned (again)! This GNBʾ and [
          ] [37](are) Matîʿel; it is his person. Just as this wax is burned
by fire, so may Matî[ʿel] be burned by fi]re! [38]Just as (this) bow
and these arrows are broken, so may ʾInurta and Hadad break [the
bow of Matîʿel], [39]and the bow of his nobles! And just as a man
of wax is blinded, so may Matî[ʿel] be blinded! [Just as] [40]this calf
is cut in two, so may Matîʿel be cut in two, and may his nobles be
cut in two! [And just as] [41]a [ha]r[lot is stripped naked], so may
the wives of Matîʿel be stripped naked, and the wives of his offspring

42 ‏[י תקח גברת שעותא זא] וימחא על אפיה כן יקחן [נשי מתעאל ו]

Face B

1 ‏[רסמך מלך אר]פד ועדי בני בר גאיה עם בני מתעאל ועדי [וב]

2 ‏[ני בני בר] גאיה עם עקר מתעאל ועם עקר כל מה מלך זי

3 ‏[יסק וימלך] באשרה ועם בני גש ועם בית צלל ועם אר

4 ‏[ם כלה ועד]זי כתך עם עדי ארפד ועדי בעלי כתך עם ע

5 ‏[די בעלי א]רפד ועם עמה ועדי אלהי כתך עם עדי א

6 ‏[להי ארפד ו]עדי אלהן הם זי שמו אלהן טבי מלך

7 ‏[בר גאיה לעל]מן מלך רב ומע[ו]דיא אל[ן ...]ושמין ועדיא

8 ‏[אלן כל אלהיא] יצרן ואל תשתק חדה מן מלי ספרא ז[ן]

9 ‏[ה ויתשמען מן] ערקו ועד יאדני ו[בז מן לבנן ועד יב]

10 ‏[רדו ומן דמש]ק ועד ערו ומ..ו [ומ]ן בקעת ועד כתך

11 ‏[..........] ב[י]ת גש ועמה עם אשרתהם עדיא אל

12 ‏[ן ....]יתה השכ.הוא.. במצר ומרבה]

13 ‏[..........].. דש ......תם למתעאל בר

14 ‏[עתרסמך ....].ו.....למ.. ירב[נ.]

15 ‏[........].ע.ש..[.................]

16 ‏[   ]

17 ‏[   ]

18 ‏[   ]

19 ‏[   ]

20 ‏[   ]

21 ‏[......] לביתכם ולישמע מתעאל [ולישמען בנוה ולישמע עם]

22 ‏[ה ולישמע]ן כל מלכיא זי ימלכן בארפד ל.[...........]

23 ‏[.....]..למנין שקרתם לכל אלהי עדיא ז[י בספרא זנה והן]

24 ‏[ותשמען ותש]למן עדיא אלן ותאמר גבר עדן הא [ואנה לאכהל לא]

25 ‏[שלח יד] בך וליכהל ברי [ולי]שלח יד [בברוך] ועקרי בעקו[רך והן מ]

26 ‏[לה ימלל] עלי חד מלכן או חד שנאי ל[וכל] מה מלך מה ת[ו]עבד ויש[

and the wives of [his] no[bles! And just as ⁴²this wax woman is taken] and one strikes her on the face, so may the [wives of Matî'el] be taken [and ....

Face B

V. *The Sacred Character of the Treaty*

[The treaty of Bir-Ga'yah, king of KTK, with Matî'el, son of 'Attarsamak, ¹the king of Ar]pad; and the treaty of the son of Bir-Ga'yah with the sons of Matî'el; and the treaty of the [grandsons of ²Bir]-Ga'yah with the offspring of Matî'el and with the offspring of any king who ³[will come up and rule] in his place, and with the Benê-Gush and with Bêt-ŞLL and with ⁴[all] Ar[am; and the trea]ty of KTK with the treaty of Arpad; and the treaty of the lords of KTK with the trea[ty ⁵of the lords of Ar]pad and with its people; and the treaty of the gods of KTK with the treaty of the g[ods ⁶of Arpad; for] this is the treaty of gods, which gods have concluded. *Happy* forever *be the reign of* ⁷[Bir-Ga'yah], a great king, and *from* this treaty [   ] and heaven. ⁸[All the gods] will guard [this] treaty. Let not one of the words of thi[s] inscription be silent, ⁹[but let them be heard from] 'Arqu to Ya'd[i and] BZ, from Lebanon to Yabrud, ¹⁰from Damascu]s to *'Aru* and M..W, [and fr]om the Valley to KTK ¹¹[.......... in Bê]t-Gush and its people with their *sanctuary* this treaty ¹²[..........]YTH HŠK.HW'.. in Muṣr and MRBH ¹³[...............] DŠ .....TM to Matî'el, son [of 'Attarsamak ....]

(A few letters are legible on lines 14-15; lines 16-20 are missing.)

VI. *The Stipulations of the Treaty*

²¹[.......] to your house. And (if) Matî'el will not obey [and (if) his sons will not obey, and (if) his people will not obey, ²²and (if)] all the kings who will rule over Arpad [will not obey] the .[.......... .....] ²³[.....]..LMNYN, you will have been false to all the gods of the treaty whi[ch is in this inscription. But if ²⁴you obey and ful]-fill this treaty and say, " [*I*] am an ally," [I shall not be able to ²⁵raise a hand] against you; nor will my son be able to raise a hand against [your] son, nor my offspring against [your] offspr[ing. And if] ²⁶one of (the) kings [should speak a word] against me or one of my enemies (should so speak) and you say to any king, " What are you [going to do? " and he ²⁷should raise a hand against] my son

27 ‏[לח יד ב]ברי ויקתלנה וישלח ידה ויקח מן ארקי או מן מקני ש[ק]

28 ‏[נרת בעד]יא זי בספרא זנה והן יאתה חד מלכן ויסבנ<י> יאתה ח[נילך]

29 ‏[ואלי עם] כל [בעל] חציא וכל מה פ..ך ותקף יקפי ותנתע לי ה[....]

30 ‏[.....]. ופגר ארבא מעל פגר בארנפ]ד ... מן חד מלך לאין ומות

31 ‏[.....]ם והן ביום זי אלהן ..... מרחיא לתאתה בחילך וא

32 ‏[ותם לתא]תון בחילכם לשגב בני[ו]תי [והן עק]רונ[ך ל]יאתה לשגב אית עקר

33 ‏זי שקרת ל]אלהי עדיא זי בספרא זנה וחב... יעפן עמי ואכהל מי

34 ‏[ביר .. ..]ל וביורא [וה]א כל זי יסב ליכ]והל ל[פרק ולמשלח יד במי בי

35 ‏[ורא ומלכ]וא זי יעל וילקח לבכה או ח..... זי ילקח ... בעה .

36 ‏[....] ל]אבדת אנגדה ..מלהם ..כד בקרית אימאם והן להן שק

37 ‏[ורת ....] ז]נה והן ..ק. לי ..]לאכ.ל... להמי ..י.נשא תשלח..א.

38 ‏[.....]ם והן לתהב לחמי ...ו.]שא לי לחם ולתסך שקרת בעדיא אלן

39 ‏[ואת לתכ]הל לתשא לחם אנה כאים יקם לך ותבעה נבשך ותאזל..

40 ‏[.....]תך ולביתך ינ.. זר א.. לנבשי [ולכ]ל נבש ביתי ולט.

41 ‏[.....]בה ברך וליגזורן מ]לה מלכי אורפד] מנהם זי עדן חי

42 ‏[ן הם .....]ה .....]ה .... טלל הא וסח הא ובל הא נתרחם לנבשך אמ.

43 ‏[.........]..........כע.. עמך כן תגזר אפלא והן ......

44 ‏[.........]..[נק... יעזז קלבת ביתי על ...ח..אי אקל

45 ‏[...........][..על] ברי או על חד סרסי ויקרק חדהם ויאתה [...]

Face C

1 ‏כה אמרן]וכה כ]תבן מה

2 ‏כתבת אנה מתע]אל לזכ

3 ‏רן לברי]ולברן ברי ז

4 ‏י יסקן ב]ואשר]זי לטבת

5 ‏[א] יעבד]ו תחת] שמשא

6 ‏[ולב]זית מ]לכי ז]י כל לח

7 ‏[יה לתתעבד על] בית מ

8 ‏תעאל וברה ובר] ברה ע[ד]

and kill him and raise his hand to take some of my land or some of my possessions, you will have been fa[lse to ^{28}the trea]ty which is in this inscription. If one of (the) kings comes and surrounds m<e>, [your] ar[my] must come ^{29}[to me with] every arch[er] and every sort [of weapon], and you must *surround those who surround me* and you must *draw* for me [..... ^{30}.....] and *I shall pile* corpse upon corpse in Ar[pad] ... some king L'WYN WMWT ^{31}[.....] and if on a day when (the) gods [.....] MRḤY', you (sg.) do not come with your army and (if) ^{32}[you (pl.) do not] come with your (pl.) armies to strengthen my ho[u]se and [if your] off[spring does not] come to strengthen [my] offspring, ^{33}[you will have been false to] the gods of the treaty which is in this inscription. And (when) [...] Y'PN with me, I shall be able [to drink] water ^{34}[of the well of....]L; whoever *lives around* that well will not be able to *destroy* (it) or raise a hand against the water of[the] wel[l.] ^{35}[And the king] who will enter and take LBKH or Ḥ ......, who will take .... B'H. ^{36}[..... to] destroy 'NGD' .. MLHM .. M .. KD in the town of 'YM'M. And if (you do) not (do) so, you will have been fal[se] ^{37}[to the treaty] <which is in> this <inscription>. And if ..Q. LY ...L'K.L...LHMY.Y.NŠ', you shall send ..'. ^{38}[......]M, and if you do not give (me) my provisions, [or] deduct provisions from me, and do not deliver (them), you will have been false to this treaty. ^{39}[... You] can[not] deduct provisions 'NḤ K'YM YQM LK, and you yourself will seek and will go ^{40}[..... .....]TK and to your house YN.. ZR'.. for myself [and for eve]ry person of my household and for Ṭ. ^{41}[........] *in it your son*; and the kings of Ar[pad] will not cu[t any]thing off from them because *it is a living pact.* ^{42}[........] H .... ṬLL H' WSḤ H' WBL H' NTRḤM for yourself 'M. ^{43}[........].......... K'.. with you; so you will cut the 'PL'. And if...... ^{44}[........] NQ .... he will strengthen the QLBT of my house against ... L.Ḥ.'Y 'QL.... ^{45}[........].. [against] my son or against one of my courtiers; and (if) one of them flees and com[es....]

Face C

VII. *Reminder for the Future*

^{1}Thus have we spoken [and thus have we writ]ten. What ^{2}I, [Matî']el, have written (is to act) as a reminder ^{3}for my son [and] my [grand]son who ^{4}will come a[fter] me. May they ^{5}make good relations [beneath] the sun ^{6}[for (the sake of) my] ro[yal hou]se that no ev[il may ^{7}be done against] the house of Mat[î'el ^{8}and his son and] his [grand]son for[ever].

9 [ו··] · ו· [······· עלם]

10 [ ]

11 [ ]

12 [ ]

13 [ ]

14 [·········] מ···

15 יצרו אלהן מן יו

16 מה ומן ביתה ומן

17 ליצר מלי ספרא זי בנצבא זנה

18 ויאמר אהלד מן מלו

19 ה או אהפך טבתא ואשם

20 [ל]לחית ביום זי יעב

21 [ד] כן יהפכו אלהן אש

22 [א ה]א וביתה וכל זי [וב]

23 ה וישמו תחתיתה [ל]

24 [ע]ליתה ואל ירת שר

25 [ש]ה אשם

VIII. *Blessings*

... ... [15]may (the) gods keep [all evils] away from his day [16]and from his house.

IX. *Curses*

Whoever [17]will not observe the words of the inscription which is on this stele [18]or will say, " I shall efface some of his (its) words," [19]or " I shall upset the good relations and turn (them) [20][to] evil," on any day on which he will d[o] [21]so, may the gods overturn [22]th[at m]an and his house and all that (is) in [23]it; and may they make its lower part [24]its upper part! May his scio[n] *inherit* no [25]name!

COMMENTARY

Face A

1. '*dy* : Cst. pl. of a noun, used only in the plural, meaning "treaty-stipulations," or simply "treaty, pact." Only the emph. pl. of this noun is found in Sf III; but here we have the cst., the emph. (also in Sf II), and even the abs. (Sf I B 24, 41). The meaning of this word is certain, for it is somehow related to the Akkadian word *adē*, which is always used in the plural in the same sense. D. J. Wiseman recently published *The Vassal-Treaties of Esarhaddon* (London : British School of Archaeology in Iraq, 1958; a reprint from *Iraq* 20 [1958], Part I). In these treaties we find *adē* (always plural) used in the sense of "treaty-terms" or "vassal-treaty stipulations" (p. 3), which were imposed by the king on his vassals to insure their loyalty to his heirs, Aššurbanipal of Assyria and Šamaššumukin of Babylonia. Wiseman defines the word thus : "Although the general term 'treaty' has been used here for convenience (see p. 3), the more exact meaning is of a law or commandment solemnly imposed in the presence of divine witnesses by a suzerain upon an individual or people who have no option but acceptance of the terms. It implies a 'solemn charge or undertaking on an oath' (according to the view of the suzerain or vassal)" (p. 81). Both in Sf I and III treaty-stipulations are preserved; but '*dy*' in Aramaic is scarcely to be restricted to them. It seems to have a wider meaning, "treaty," as can be seen in the expression '*lhy* '*dy*' *zy bspr*' *znh*.

J. Cantineau (*op. cit.*, 168) related it to the Hebrew '*ēdût* and '*ēd*, Arabic *wa'ada*, "to promise," Akkadian *wadū*, *adū*, pl. *adē*, "decision, agreement, oath." The form *adē* is also found in the cuneiform text of the treaty between Aššurnirāri V and Mati'ilu (1.13; 4.17-18). Cf. the similar beginning of the very fragmentary treaty of Esarhaddon with Ba'al of Tyre (*AfO* 8 [1932-33] 31), and his vassal treaties (11. 1-6). According to W. von Soden, *Akkadisches Handwörterbuch* (Wiesbaden : Harrassowitz, 1959, p. 14), *adē* occurs in middle and new Assyrian, middle and late Babylonian. According to R. Frankena ("The Vassal Treaties of Esarhaddon and the Dating of Deuteronomy," *OudtestStud* 14 [1965] 122-54, esp. 134-36) *adē* is the specific Akkadian term for a vassal treaty. If he is correct, then this will affect the decision one must make about the character of these treaty-texts; cf. M. Noth. *ZDPV* 77 (1961) 139. See also *CAD* A, pp. 131-34; K. Deller, *WZKM* 57 (1961) 31-33; I. Gelb, *BO* 19 (1962) 159-62, esp. 160-61. Gelb's conclusion, " From the above examples, and many others ..., it is clear that *adê* (in plural) or *adû* (in singular) is a pact or agreement *imposed* by one party upon another and sworn to by the obligated party *only*. It is not a pact between equals."

The use of *adē* apparently involves the same semantic shift which is found in the Greek expression, *'orkia temnein*, " to make a covenant," frequently used in Homer (*Il.*, 2.124; *Od.*, 24.483); note the plural. These considerations must prevail in relating the Aramaic *'dy'* to the Akkadian *adē*, even over the consideration that we would normally expect the *a*-vowel to shift in Akkadian to *e* because of the *'ayin* — a shift which does not appear to be universal (cf. Akkadian *adi* and Hebrew-Aramaic *'ad*). A greater difficulty comes from the fact that *adē* is apparently from a *tertiae infirmae* root in Akkadian, whereas *'dn, 'dy, 'dy'* in Aramaic apparently do not reflect such a root.

Hempel-Bauer (*ZAW* 50 [1932] 178) related *adē* to *gl'd* of Gn 31 : 48 and (hesitatingly) to *'d* of Ex 22 : 12. In Is 33 : 8 one should probably read *'dym* (instead of *'rym*) in the sense of " treaty," as in this inscription; cf. 1QIs[a].

br g'yh : " Son of Majesty," cf. Hebrew *g'wh* and Syriac *ga'yūtā* (as explained by J. Cantineau, *op. cit.*, p. 178). H. Bauer (*AfO* 8 [1932-33] 3) compared the name to those of the type, Benjamin and Bar-Ṣur. The name should preferably be vocalized *Bir-Ga'yah*, since Aramaean names of the Assyrian period with the *br* element are transcribed thus in Akkadian documents : e.g., *Bir-Atar, Bir-Ḫanu, Bir-Ram(m)ān, Bir-Šamaš* (see W. F. Albright, " The Name of Bildad the Shuhite," *AJSL* 44 [1927] 33). On the use of the patronymic alone without a personal name, see A. Alt, " Menschen ohne Namen," *ArOr* 18 (1950) 9-24. Bir-Ga'yah is otherwise unknown. According to Dupont-Sommer, it is a symbolic name for Sardur III of Urartu, who formed a coalition against Assyria. Since no name of his father is indicated and the symbolic name may be an indication of a throne-name, Bir-Ga'yah may have been a usurper. See M. Noth, *ZDPV* 77 (1961) 145. But if so, then he would scarcely be the partner of Sf III who speaks of his father and his father's house (line 24). Yet until the contrary is proved, *Br-G'yh* must be assumed to be his real name, not just a *Deckname*. It is a genuine Aramaean name; so he is probably an Aramaean ruler more powerful than Matî'el and king of some city-state in upper Mesopotamia.

ktk : The name of Bir-Ga'yah's land has not yet been successfully identified; for various proposals, see below, pp. 127-35. In Sf I A 4, B 4 the phrase *b'ly ktk* suggests that *ktk* is a city like Arpad.

mt"l : The vassal is Matî'el, ([14]) the king of Arpad, who is to be identified with the Mati'ilu (written *ma-ti-'-AN*) of the treaty of Aššurnirāri V (754-745 B.C.) of Assyria (see E. F. Weidner, *AfO* 8 [1932-33] 17-34; D. D. Luckenbill, *ARAB*, 1.§750-60; M. Noth, *ZDPV* 77 [1961] 127). In this treaty Mati'ilu lacks a title; the campaign of the Assyrian king against him is usually judged to have taken place " im Regierungsantrittsjahre," i. e. 754 B.C. He there appears to have been a princeling in Syria between the Euphrates and the Mediterranean, north of Aleppo, in the area called by the Assyrians Bit-Agūsi (after the founder of the dynasty; see S. Schiffer, *Die Aramäer* [Leipzig: J. C. Hinrichs, 1911], p. 90, n. 6; p. 137, n. 9). His capital was Arpad (see E. F. Weidner, *AfO* 15 [1945-51] 101), but he must have exercised control over a considerable number of lesser towns, as appears from this Aramaic treaty. E. F. Weidner suggested that Mati'ilu must have soon forgotten his treaty with Aššurnirāri and perhaps under threats from Sardur of Urartu joined the latter against Assyria. Tiglathpileser III put an end to this alliance, when Arpad finally fell to him after a four year siege. Mati'ilu is mentioned several times in the *Annals* of Tiglathpileser III (see D. D. Luckenbill, *ARAB*, 1.§769, 785, 813; cf. P. Rost, *Die Keilschrifttexte Tiglat-Pilesers III.* [Leipzig: E. Pfeiffer, 1893], *Annals*, line 60: *Ma-t-'-ilu mār a-gu-us-si*).

The name *Mt"l* has been found belonging to a Dedanite king of the sixth century B.C. (see W. F. Albright, " Dedan," *Geschichte und Altes Testament* [Beiträge zur historischen Theologie 16; Tübingen: Mohr, 1953], p. 6). H. Bauer noted that in South Arabic the root *mt'* occurs in the meaning, " to save, protect," and explained the name as meaning " Gott behütet." But the name occurs in a Nabataean inscription published by J. T. Milik (*Syria* 35 [1958] 238) in the form *Mty"l*, which together with the Assyrian evidence would suggest the vocalization *Matî"el* or *Matî"il*, " protected by 'El " (*q"tîl* type; pass. ptc.); cf. *brwk Yhwh* (Gen 24 : 31; 14 : 20); see D. N. Freedman, *VT* 4 (1954) 192.

([14]) Strictly speaking, one should transcribe the name *Matî"el*, or possibly *Matî"ēl* (if one could show that the final *e*-vowel was long in such a form in the Aramaic of this period). However, for the sake of convenience we have decided to transcribe it more simply as *Matî'el*; those who realize that the name is a compound of an *'el*-theophoric element will easily supply the *aleph* omitted in the transcription.

'*trsmk* : Matî'el's father's name is a compound of the theophoric element '*tr* (assimilated form of '*Athtar*, = Akkadian *Ištar*, Hebrew '*Aštōret*, Ugaritic '*ṯtrt*) and *smk* : " 'Athtar has lent support." Cf. the names of similar formation, '*aḥîsāmāk* (Ex 31 : 6 ; 35 : 34 ; 38 : 23), *S*e*mākyāhû* (1 Chr 26 : 7), *Yismakyāhû* (2 Chr 31 : 13), *smky* (*AP* 49, 1) ; *Atar-idri, Atar-bi'di, Attar-nuri, Attar-ramat* ; '*tr*'*zr* (*CIS* 2.52). '*Attarsamak* is otherwise unknown. On '*Athtar*, see M. J. Dahood, " Ancient Semitic Deities in Syria and Palestine," in S. Moscati (ed.), *Le antiche divinità semitiche* (Studi semitici I ; Roma : Università di Roma, 1958), pp. 85-90 ; G. Garbini, " 'Atar dio aramaico ? " *RSO* 35 (1960) 25-28 ; A. Caquot, *Syria* 35 (1958) 45-60 ; J. A. Fitzmyer, *JAOS* 86 (1966) 287-88.

['*rpd w*']*dy* : Dupont-Sommer has convincingly shown that six letters have been lost at the end of this line due to the shaving off of the left side of the stele. The restoration of '*rpd* is certain ; see Sf I A 3 ; B 1.

Arpad, over which Matî'el reigned, was the capital of a small Aramaean kingdom or city-state in northern Syria. In Assyrian texts of the ninth and eighth centuries B.C. the kingdom was called Bīt Agūsi or Bīt Gūsi in the land of Yaḫan (see the note on Sf I A 16 ; also E. F. Weidner, *AfO* 8 [1932-33] 17-26). The same title, apparently a designation of the ruling dynasty, appears in Aramaic form in the fragmentary passages of Sf II B 10 and I B [11], as *byt gš*. The inhabitants of the area are referred to as *bny gš* (Sf I B 3 ; I A [16]). A predecessor of Matî'el is cryptically referred to as *br gš* among the kings allied with Bir-Hadad, the son of Haza'el, who leagued together against Zakir, the king of Hamath and Lu'ash (Zakir a 5). The title in the latter place is scarcely the name of the king who gave his name to the dynasty, because the Zakir stele dates from roughly 780 B.C., whereas we know that Bīt Agūsi was already in existence in the preceding century.

The capital of this Aramaean state is '*Arpad*, the town which is mentioned as such in the Old Testament (2 Kgs 18 : 34 ; 19 : 13 ; Is 10 : 9 ; 36 : 19 ; 37 : 13 ; Jer 49 : 23). It is the town *Arpaddu* of Assyrian texts, and was apparently first mentioned in 806 B.C. as the goal of a campaign of Adadnirāri III ; after that it is often mentioned (see O. A. Toffteen, *AJSL* 21 (1904-5) 86 ; E. Honigmann, " Arpad," *RLA* 1.153). Situated about 19 miles N of Aleppo, it is to be identified with modern Tell Refâd (see P. K. Hitti, *History of Syria* [London : Macmillan, 1951], p. 140, n. 4 ; R. Dussaud, *Topographie historique de la Syrie antique* [Paris : Geuthner, 1927], p. 468 ; Donner - Röllig, *KAI*, 2. 243).

Being the capital of a small kingdom, it was often the victim of

subjugation by powerful neighbors. During the ninth century B.C.
Arpad was dominated by Assyria, but in the early part of the eighth
century, as Assyria's power declined, Arpad seems to have achieved
some independence. We know little of its history in this period, not
even whether 'Attarsamak, the father of Matî'el, was actually king
before him. Some earlier king, as mentioned above, was indeed the
ally of Bir-Hadad *ca.* 780 B.C. Probably in the year 754-53 B.C.
Matî'el had to conclude a pact with Adadnirāri V, who made a feeble
attempt to assert Assyrian domination in the west. Matî'el swore
his loyalty to the Assyrian overlord in a pact, the stipulations of
which were not very demanding (see E. F. Weidner, *op. cit.*). But at
some time during the first part of the eighth century other influence
was exerted on Arpad. From about 900 B.C. Urartu had been grad-
ually growing into a powerful kingdom, centered about Lake Van;
it profited from the weakness of Assyria at the beginning of the
eighth century. About 750 B.C. the king of Urartu, Sardur III, son
of Argišti I, subjected many city-states to the west of the Euphrates,
from Gurgum, Melidh (Melitene), and Kummuḫ (Commagene) to
northern Syria. In the latter area he subjugated Ḫalpa (Aleppo), a
town to the south of Arpad; cf. Van Stele, E, lines 40ff; A. Goetze,
Kleinasien (Handbuch der Altertumswissenschaft, III/1: 3.3,1; Munich: C. H. Beck, 1957), p. 192. Sardur III thus managed to cut off
Assyrian power from Asia Minor and the Mediterranean coastlands.
Matî'el, the king of Arpad, apparently broke his pact with Assyria
and joined a coalition with Sardur III *ca.* 743 B.C. For Tiglathpileser III records in his third regnal year: " Sardur of Urartu revolted
against me and joined Mati'ilu " (*Annals*, line 59; ed. P. Rost, p. 12,
cf. D. D. Luckenbill, *ARAB*, 1 § 769, 785, 813).

But Tiglathpileser III, who had come to the Assyrian throne
after a revolt in Kalaḫ *ca.* 745 B.C., strove to restore the Assyrian
power. After some activity in the area of Babylonia he turned to
Urartu and Syria. He records the defeat of Sardur at Kishtan and
Ḫalpi in Kummuḫ (Commagene) on the west bank of the Euphrates.
This was the year 743 B.C. and Sardur fled to Urartu. Tiglathpileser III turned to Syria, subjugating Arpad, 'Umq, and Ya'di.
The Eponym List (Cb I) for the year 743 B.C. records: " In the city
of Arpad: the army of Urartu defeated." Apparently the ultimate
defeat of Arpad came only in 740 B.C., and its devastation must have
impressed the Syrian and Palestinian world. For a few decades later
the prophet Isaiah could use it as an example to warn the king of
Jerusalem: " the gods of the nations " did not deliver Hamath and
Arpad from the hand of the king of Assyria (Is 36 : 18-19). " Where
is the king of Hamath, the king of Arpad ..." ('*ayyēh ... melek 'Arpād*,

37 : 13).   See H. Schmökel, *Kulturgeschichte des alten Orient* (Stuttgart :
A. Kröner, 1961), pp. 611-15 ; G. Goossens, " Asie occidentale ancien-
ne," *Encyclopédie de la Pléiade : Histoire universelle* (ed. R. Grousset
et E. G. Léonard ; Paris : Gallimard), I (1956) 397-401 ; P. Naster,
*L'Asie Mineure et l'Assyrie aux VIIIe et VIIe siècles av. J.-C. d'après
les annales des rois assyriens* (Bibliothèque du Muséon 8 ; Louvain :
Le Muséon, 1938), pp. 11-27.

2. *bny bny :* " The grandsons of ...."   The occurrence of this formula
here seems to confirm the interpretation given below of the same
phrase in Sf III 21, where Dupont-Sommer preferred to take the first
bny as a form of the preposition *bên.*

   [*w'qr*]*h :* The restoration is suggested by the following phrase
'*m 'qr :* " and his offspring."   Literally, '*qr* denotes the " offshoot of
a root."   The figurative meaning of this word is now certain, not
only from its use in this context, but also from the use of it in Sf
I A 3, 15, 25, 41 ; B 2, 25, 32 ; II B 6 ; II C 15 ; III 1, 3, 11, 12,
15, 16, 21, 22, 25, 26.   A similar use of the Hebrew cognate occurs
in Lv 25 : 47, '*qr mšpḥt gr,* " a descendant of the stranger's family " ;
see H. Torczyner (Ṭur Ṣinai), *Lachish Letters* (London : Oxford University Press, 1938) 60.   J. Cantineau (*RA* 28 [1931] 169) compares
the sense of the Latin *stirps* ; cf. Dan 4 : 12, 20, 23 ; later Aram. '*iq-
qārā.*

3. *w'dy ktk 'm* ['*dy*] '*rpd :* " And the treaty of *KTK* with [the
treaty of] Arpad."   Peculiar though this restoration seems, it must
be regarded as certain, as Sf I B 4 indicates.   Does it mean that a
similar " treaty " was set up in the territory of Bir Ga'yah?

4. *b'ly :* " The lords of ...."   We originally understood this word to
mean " citizens " or " inhabitants," a meaning that is found for the
word in the Elephantine texts (cf. *b'ly yb,* " the inhabitants of Yeb,"
AP 30.22 ; 31.22 ; *b'l qryh, AP* 5.9 ; 13.10 ; 20.10 ; 46.6), that is paralleled in Hebrew *ba'ᵃlê yᵉrîḥō,* Jos 24 : 11 (a passage whose dependence
on a vassal treaty for its style and literary structure has been pointed
out by G. Mendenhall), and that may still be correct in Sf III 23,
26.   See further Jdg 9 : 2-3 ; 1 Sm 23 : 11-12 ; 2 Sm 21 : 12.   Since,
however, the *b'ly* seem to be different here from the '*m* (Sf I A 29,
30 ; I B 5, 11 ; II B 3, C 16), we should probably look on the former
word as a designation of aristocracy in the city of Arpad.   Could it
denote the remnant of the earlier Mesopotamian *maryannu*?   Cf. P.
Sacchi, *AANL Rendic.* ser. 8, 16/5-6 (1961) 186 ; M. Noth, *ZDPV* 77
(1961) 130.

ḥb[*r*] : " Union," or " federation." The restoration of this word is quite likely. After it Dupont-Sommer suggests reading '*rrṭ*]*w*, which combination he translates, " l'Eta[t d'Urart]u." At first sight the *waw* at the beginning of line 5 looks like a conjunction, " and," parallel to *w'm* further on in the line; but Dupont-Sommer suggests that it is the last letter of the proper name of a place, which is allied to " all Aram." See Sf I B 9-10 for place-names ending in -*w*. That it is a place-name is a plausible suggestion; that it is Urartu stands or falls with his thesis that Bir-Ga'yah is Sardur III. We prefer to leave the lacuna blank. The word *ḥbr* is probably the Aramaic equivalent of Akkadian and Ugaritic *ḥubûru*, " company, community, assembly," a word which W. F. Albright (" The Role of the Canaanites in the History of Civilization," in *Studies in the History of Culture* [Leland Volume; Menasha, Wisc.: G. Banta, 1942], p. 36; cf. *The Bible and the Ancient Near East* [Garden City: Doubleday, 1961], p. 359) has shown to have been used in the Phoenician world to mean a " trading company." Hence, it could easily mean here a " union," or something similar, perhaps " federation;" but scarcely anything so specific as Dupont-Sommer's " état." See M. Noth, *ZDPV* 77 (1961) 146. — Cf. *CD* 12,8 (*ḥbwr Yśr'l*), referred to by Dupont-Sommer; also 13,15 and Dn 11:6, where the root is used in a context of a treaty. Recall also its use on Hasmonaean coins; cf. A. Reifenberg, *Ancient Jewish Coins* (3rd ed.; Jerusalem, Israel: R. Mass, 1963), pp. 13, 40.

5. *'m 'rm klh* : Not only the capital city Arpad, but all Aram and *Muṣr* are included in the treaty; this expresses the extent of the coalition or union which Bir-Ga'yah has set up. While '*rm* sometimes designates merely a tribal group (see W. F. Albright, *JPOS* 15 [1935] 187), it would appear from l. 6 that '*rm* is to be understood here in a geographical sense. In the Zakir stele (a 4) Bir-Hadad (II), son of Hazael, is mentioned as the king of Aram (*ca.* 775 B.C.). — For a parallel to the suffixal use of *kl*, see *A* 12 (*'twr klh*), 55; Panammū 17 (*'šwr klh*), 19 (*byth klh*). For the possible influence of '*rm klh* on the later *Koilē Syria*, see B. Mazar, *BA* 25 (1962) 119-20.

Mṣr : If correctly read, this name would seem to be a place-name. As such it might refer to one of three different regions: (1) Egypt (which is out of question here); (2) an area east of Assyria in the Zagros mountains, northeast of Nineveh about Jebel Maqlûb (for cuneiform references and literature on this area, see P. Garelli, " *Muṣur* (mât Muṣri)," *DBS* 5, 1469-70; B. Landsberger and Th. Bauer, *ZA* 37 [1927] 76); this area is not impossible, but unlikely in the present context; (3) a region of the Taurus mountains between Cilicia and Arpad. The only evidence for the existence of this region outside of this Aramaic inscription seems to be in the *Monolith Inscription of Šalmaneser III* (see III Rawlinson 8, 92; D. D. Luckenbill, *ARAB*, 1. §611; *ANET*, pp. 278-79). This Assyrian inscription apparently contains the oldest account of the sixth regnal year of the king and mentions the coalition which was formed against him and was defeated at Qarqar (853 B.C.): Hadadezer of Damascus, Irḥuleni of Hamath, Ahab of Israel, soldiers of Que, soldiers of Muṣru, soldiers of Irqanata, Matinuba'lu of Arvad, soldiers of Usanata, Adunuba'lu of Si'an, camel-riders of Gindibu', camel-riders of Arabia, Ba'sa son of Ruḥubi from Ammon — " (all together) these were twelve kings." However, other copies of the annals of Šalmaneser III's sixth regnal year merely mention Hadadezer of Damascus, Irḥuleni of Hamath, " together with twelve kings of the sea-coast " (see E. Michel, " Ein neuentdeckter Annalen-Text Salmanassars III.," *Die Welt des Orients* 1/6 (1952) 464-465, Vs. col. II, 27-28: *a-di* 12 *šarrāni*^{meš.ni} *ša pān tam-di*; G. G. Cameron, " The Annals of Shalmaneser III, King of Assyria," *Sumer* 6 (1950) 13: *a-di* 12 *šarrāni* (*LUGAL.MEŠ-ni*) *ša pān tam-di* (Obv., col. II, l. 28); J. Laessøe, " A Statue of Shalmaneser III, from Nimrud," *Iraq* 21 (1959) 151:]*ù a-ḫat tam-ti ana A-MEŠ.*[(Reading corrected by W. G. Lambert according to the Obelisk inscription); Obelisk inscription [*ANET*, p. 279]; Bull inscription [*ANET*, p. 279]). (¹⁵) All of these copies, which omit the *explicit* mention of Muṣr, suggest, nevertheless, the location of it somewhere in the coastal area. It was apparently one of the twelve kingdoms of " the sea-coast." See further A. Alt, " Die syrische Staatenwelt vor dem Einbruch der Assyrer," *ZDMG* 88 (1934) 233-58, esp. p. 255. (¹⁶)

A difficulty, however, arises in taking *Mṣr* as a place-name because of the following phrase, *w'm bnwh zy ysqn b'šrh*, which suggests rather

(¹⁵) I am indebted to Prof. W. G. Lambert for pointing out to me several of these references. I alone am responsible, however, for the conclusion drawn from them.

(¹⁶) J. A. Montgomery (" Notes on Early Aramaic Inscriptions," *JAOS* 54 [1934] 424) suggested that Mṣr be read in 1 Kgs 10:28 instead of *mṣrym*, aligned with *Qwḥ* (Cilicia); P. Garelli (*op. cit.*, 1470-71) and Dupont-Sommer (*Les Araméens* [L'Orient ancien illustré; Paris; A. Maisonneuve, 1949], p. 71) have proposed the same reading for 2 Kgs 7:6. But this is far from certain. In the first case *mmṣrym* has probably gotten into the text by a vertical dittography; the sense is that the horses came from Cilicia and the chariots from Egypt. See R. de Vaux, " Les livres des Rois," *La sainte Bible* (de *Jérusalem*) (2nd ed.; Paris: Cerf, 1958), pp. 74,156; W. F. Albright, *Archeology and the Religion of Israel* (Baltimore: Johns Hopkins Press, 1953), p. 135.

that the name is personal. To get around this difficulty, we follow
Dupont-Sommer in adding to the text the phrase "<with the king
of> Muṣr," which is a better solution than Rosenthal's reference of
the suffix on *bnwh* to Matî'el himself (*ANET*, p. 504).

bnwh : " His sons." The orthography of this suffix is certain,
since it occurs elsewhere in this inscription (Sf I A 39, [41]; C 18);
see also Sf III 2, 8, 12, 14, 15, 16, 17; Nêrab 2.2. It may also persist
in later Aramaic in *BMAP* 3.4 (*'grwh*); [6.9] — unless we should
rather regard these examples as mere scribal misspellings.

Cross and Freedman (*EHO*, p. 29) have compared this form with
the Syriac -*awhī* and Biblical Aramaic -*ôhi*. " It differs, however, as
to the manner in which the secondary suffix has been added: **ayhū*
> **ayū* > *aw*, plus the secondary suffix produces **-awh* or **-aweh*.
The form can hardly be vocalized **awhī*, because the final *ī* is regularly indicated by the vowel letter in these texts." As far as I can
see, the preferable vocalization would be -*awh*, with consonantal *he*.

zy ysqn b'šrh : Lit. " who will come up in his place." But *b'šr*
is related to the later form *b'tr*, which has developed the meaning
" after." This phrase is used in these inscriptions (Sf I C 4; I B 3)
to designate the successor on a royal throne. Cf. Dn 2 : 39; 7 : 6;
Dt 29 : 21; Ex 29 : 30 and Akkadian *mannu šarru ša i-la-a arkiya* (*CT*
13,42-i-20). — *ysqn* is 3 pl. masc. impf. Peal of *slq*, " go up, ascend."
See *BLA* § 43.

w['m mlky] kl 'ly 'rm wtḥth : " And with the kings of all Upper-
Aram and Lower-Aram." The restoration is plausible. After the
mention of *'rm klh* in line 5, this expression, which is not found elsewhere, must be intended for greater precision. H. Bauer (*op. cit.*,
p. 4) suggested that it refers to the Euphrates River, and Dupont-
Sommer follows him in identifying Upper Aram with the Syrian Aram,
and Lower Aram with the Mesopotamian. But A. Alt (*op. cit.*, p. 254,
n. 2) has disagreed on the grounds that what was usually referred to
as Mesopotamian Aram was at this period already in the control of
Assyria. He preferred, therefore, to locate both Upper and Lower
Aram in Syria: " Oberland " about Damascus, " Unterland " about
Arpad. This seems preferable. M. Noth (*ZDPV* 77 [1961] 131)
suggests the possibility that " Lower-Aram " might have meant the
area toward the Mediterranean Sea, and " Upper-Aram " what was
more inland. It should be noted that *'ly* and *tḥt* are sometimes used
in Aramaic in the sense of " north " and " south " (respectively); see
the similar use of *'lyh* and *tḥtyh* in the Elephantine texts (*AP* 13,13-
14; 25,5-7; *BMAP* 3,7-10; 4,9-11) and especially the note in E. G.
Kraeling, *BMAP*, pp. 77-79.

6. *kl 'll byt mlk :* Ronzevalle's method of breaking up the words is preferable to that of Dupont-Sommer, who reads *kl 'l lbyt mlk.* Dn 6 : 11 (*'l lbyth*) might seem to support the latter reading with the preposition *l.* But the ptc. of the double-'ayin root is *'ālil;* see Dn 4 : 4 ; 5 : 8, where the *k*^e*tīb* has preserved the older form (*'llyn*). There is no evidence of a ptc. *'l* at this period, similar to the later Aramaic form or even the Syriac form (like *bā'ez,* built on an analogy with hollow verbs). This division of words is preferred also by J. Koopmans (*BO* 17 [1960] 52), who compares Gn 23 : 10 (*b'y š'r*) and Akkadian *ērib biti.* Moreover, it should be recalled that there are several instances where verbs expressing motion toward a place are followed by objects without a preposition : Sf III 5 [*wyhkn ḥlb*] ; Padua papyrus I v 5 [*kzy t'twn Mṣryn*], I r 3 [*bzy l' 'yty hmw Mnpy*]. J. Friedrich and B. Landsberger (*ZA* 7 [1933] 314) suggested that the expression referred to nomads who as subjects would appear from time to time before their prince in his palace. M. Noth (*ZDPV* 77 [1961] 132) suggests that the phrase may designate representatives of subordinate rulers and groups obliged to appear with more or less regularity before the king. D. J. McCarthy's explanation (*op. cit.,* p. 189), " i.e. take over the rulership," is scarcely correct. On *byt mlk* see note on Sf I C 6.

wn[*ṣb'*] : Restored by Dupont-Sommer on the basis of Sf I C 17. *nṣb* is related to the Hebrew *n*^e*ṣîb* " pillar, column " (see Gn 19 : 26) and should be vocalized *naṣība',* as the later Aram. from *nṣyb* (Nabataean, *RES* 1088, 1) indicates. It is a *qatīl* type, not *qatl,* as P. Joüon maintained (*MUSJ* 5 [1911-12] 414). Cf. Bir Hadad 1 ; Zakir a 1 ; Hadad 1 ; Panammū 1.

7. *śm :* This verb is used with *'dy* in Sf I B 6 ; cf. Panammū 1, 20 ; Ps 81 : 6 (*'ēdût biyhôsep śāmō,* " He (God) made a pact with Joseph." Cf. J. C. Greenfield, *Acta orientalia* 29 (1965) 9.

w'dy' 'ln w'dy' 'ln : There is no need to suspect dittography here ; the first instance is an additional direct object of *śm,* while the second is the subject of a nominal sentence of which *zy* (comp. rel.) is the predicate.

gzr : Lit. " to cut in two, divide," as in Sf I A 40. It is here used figuratively, " to conclude a pact or treaty." Perhaps the rite alluded to in line 40 is the source of the expression. Dupont-Sommer compares the similar Hebrew and Greek expressions, *krt bryt* and *'orkia temnein.* To this we may add the Akkadian *TAR be-ri-ti,* discussed by W. F. Albright, " The Hebrew Expression for ' Making a Covenant ' in Pre-Israelite Documents," *BASOR* 121 (1951) 21-22 ;

cf. O. Loretz, *VT* 16 (1966) 239-41; D. J. McCarthy, *op. cit.*, pp. 53-54. See also Virgil, *Aeneid* 12, 161-215; Livy 1,24.8; 9,5.3; E. Bickerman, " Couper une alliance," *Archives d'histoire du droit oriental* 5 (1950) 133ff.; J. Henninger, " Was bedeutet die rituelle Teilung eines Tieres in zwei Hälften?" *Bibl* 34 (1953) 344-53. Cf. Job 22 : 28; Gn 15 : 17; Dn 4 : 14, 21; Neh 10 : 1 (*krt 'mnh*).

At the end of this line *qdm* is certainly to be restored, as in the following context; the name of some deity should also be read there, the consort or partner of *mlš* in the next line. Dupont-Sommer suggests *qdm Ḥld rb'*, " in the presence of Haldi the great," the chief god of Urartu. This again depends on his identification of Bir-Ga'yah as Sardur III.

The solemn character of the treaty is indicated by the listing of gods who are witnesses to it. Such a list is common to vassal treaties of this type. The vassal treaties of Esarhaddon have a list of gods which follows the introductory paragraph (and the seal impressions); D. Wiseman, *op. cit.*, p. 22. Such a list is also found in the treaty of Aššurnirāri V with Mati'ilu, in which many of the same pairs of gods are mentioned as here, but there the list follows the stipulations of the treaty (Rev. VI, 6-27); see D. J. McCarthy, *op. cit.*, pp. 196-97. For oaths sworn " in the presence of " the gods, see Esarhaddon's Vassal Treaties, 11. 41-42.

8. *mlš :* " Mullesh." An otherwise unknown deity, most likely the second of a pair, as in the following series of divine names. One would expect the first two deities mentioned to be the principal gods of KTK. Friedrich and Landsberger (*ZA* 7 [1933] 315) suggested a connection between *mlš* and the theophoric element in the name Ardi-[il] *Mullēšu*, " servant of Mullēšu," a proper name known from the Persian period (see H. V. Hilprecht and A. T. Clay, *Babylonian Expedition*, vol. 9 [Philadelphia : University of Pennsylvania, 1898], pp. 50, 77). M. Noth (*ZDPV* 77 [1961] 165) would read *'ngt* before *mlš*, a corrected form of *'nht* (see, however, comment on Sf I A 38).

The first group of gods must be those venerated by Bir-Ga'yah; the second group, beginning with Hadad of Aleppo, must be the gods of Matî'el.

mrdk wzrpnt : " Marduk and Zarpanit." In the following list of names of paired gods, the majority is Babylonian, but a few are Canaanite. Is this an attempt to represent the main areas and peoples covered by the treaty? The first pair is Marduk and Zarpanit, the Babylonian god and his consort, who are also found in the treaty of Aššurnirāri V (Rev. VI, 10). In Esarhaddon's Vassal Treaties (1.433) Marduk's epithet is " the eldest son "; from earliest times he

appears as the son of Enki and as the local god of the city of Babylon, worshipped in the temple of Esagila. His consort here is
Zrpnt, which in Akkadian is normally spelled *Ṣarpānītu*. Her name
has been explained as meaning " shining like silver," but according
to B. Meissner, *Babylonien und Assyrien* (Kulturgeschichtliche Bibliothek 4; Heidelberg: C. Winter, 1925), 2.16, the Assyrians explained
it by popular etymology as *Zer-banītu*, " she who creates posterity."
In fact, her epithet in Esarhaddon's Vassal Treaties is " who gives
name and seed " (l. 435). This may account for the initial *zayin* in
the Aramaic form of the name.

nb' wt[šmt] : " Nabu and Tashmet." The second pair is likewise
Babylonian and the name of the consort can be restored with certainty,
since Nabu and Tashmet often follow Marduk in lists of gods; see
the Nabonidus stele (*ANET* 310b); Aššurnirāri V (Rev. VI, 10). The
name *Nabū* is often said to mean " the brilliant one ", but this is
not certain. This god was associated with the town of Borsippa,
where he had his principal temple, Ezida. Dupont-Sommer regards
the Aramaic spelling *nb'* here as curious and suggests the vocalization
Nebâ, comparing the Hebrew *Nᵉbô*. In the Aramaic ostracon (Clermont-Ganneau §277) published by him (*RHR* 128 [1944] 29) we find
the god's name written *nbw* in the first half of the sixth century B.C.
in Egypt. However, both the form on the ostracon and the Sefîre
form can be explained as an attempt to write a final long *u*, *Nabū*.
Cf. the writing *h'* for the 3rd pers. pron. masc. in Sf III 8, 13, 22.
Note that the similar name of the Transjordanian territory in the
Meša‘ inscription is spelled *nbh* (line 14). — The names of the first
four gods (*Nabū, Tašmetum, Marduk, Ṣarpanītum*) are found together
on a late Assyrian cylinder seal discovered at Samaria; see J. W.
Crowfoot, G. M. Crowfoot, K. M. Kenyon, *The Objects from Samaria*
(London: Palestine Exploration Fund, 1957), p. 87, § 18 (+ pl. XV).

['r wnš]k : " 'Ir and Nusk." Bauer suggested the restoration of
these names on the basis of their occurrence in the treaty of Aššurnirāri V (Rev. VI, 15). If correct, we do not have here a god and
his consort, as in the foregoing pairs, but a pair of Babylonian gods.
Irra was in very early times the god of pestilence, called the " lord
of the storm and destruction," who devastated the earth by war, fire
and pestilence; his consort was Ninmug and he had a temple in La-
gash. But he was often identified with Nergal, especially in Kutha.
Here he is associated with Nusk, the god of fire, who drives away
darkness and founds cities. His consort was Sa-dar-nunna; both were
regarded as the children of Sin and Ningal. Nusk is known as a
deity venerated in Aramaean territory from the Nerab inscriptions,
1, 9; 2, 9.

9. *nrgl wlṣ :* " Nergal and Laṣ." This pair is the well-known Babylonian god of the underworld and his consort; they too figure in the treaty of Aššurnirāri V (Rev. VI, 12), but precede Irra and Nusk. Nergal was originally a manifestation of Šamaš, the sun-god, but in time became god of the underworld. In the latter capacity his consort was normally Ereškigal; but in the temple of Kutha Laṣ was venerated as his consort; likewise in the temple of Tarbiṣ, built by Sennacherib in honor of Nergal.

šmš wnr : " Shamash and Nur." In the treaty of Aššurnirāri V (Rev. VI, 9) we find Šamaš, the Babylonian sun-god, and his consort Aya. Instead of the consort *nr* occurs here. Former commentators, unwilling to accept Ronzevalle's reading, changed it to *Wer* (cf. Zakir a 1). But the reading is certain and Dupont-Sommer suggests that it is the name of a god *Ner*, otherwise found only in the personal names Ner (1 Sm 14 : 50), Abner (1 Sm 14 : 51), Abiner (1 Sm 14 : 50). However, H. Donner (" Zur Inschrift von Sūdschīn Aa9," *AfO* 18 [1957-58] 390-92) has brought together cuneiform evidence to show that *nūru*, an epithet of various gods connected with light (Aya, Nusk), could also be treated itself as a god. If he is correct, then we should return to Ronzevalle's original suggestion of " Šamaš et Nûr." However, it should be noted that in Ugaritic *nyr* occurs as an epithet of the moon-god; see C. H. Gordon, *Ugaritic Textbook* [Rome: Pontifical Biblical Institute, 1965], p. 443. Šamaš was also venerated in Aramaean territory, as is clear from Nêrab 1, 9; Zakir b 24; Hadad 2, 11; Panammū 22. In Esarhaddon's Vassal Treaties (l. 422) he bears the epithet, " the light of the heavens and earth " (*nūr šamamē u qaqqari*).

s[n wnkl] : " Sin and Nikkal." Ronzevalle's restoration is still the most likely here. In the treaty of Aššurnirāri V (Rev. VI, 8) Sin and Ningal precede Šamaš and Aya. Sin was the Babylonian moon-god, worshipped above all at Ur, whence his cult spread to Harran. His name occurs in the personal name of the priest of *Śhr* in Nêrab 1, 1, *Śnzrbn*. In Esarhaddon's Vassal Treaties (l. 419) he bears the epithet, " the brightness of heaven and earth." Sin's consort was Ningal, later pronounced as Nikkal, as in Nêrab 1, 9; 2, 9, and as such should be restored here. See A. F. Key, *JBL* 84 (1965) 20-26.

10. *nkr wkd'h :* " Nikkar and Kadi'ah." This pair of deities is quite difficult to identify. R. Dussaud (*CRAIBL* 1931, p. 315) suggested that these gods were mentioned in a hymn to Tammuz under the names *Nakar* and *Kadi* (IV R 29 : 1). This identification, however, has been rejected by Friedrich and Landsberger (*ZA* N.F. 7 [1933] 315) with good reason, because KA.DI is an ideogram; cf. E. Weid-

ner, *AfO* 9 (1933-34) 98-99.   J. Cantineau (*RA* 28 [1931] 170) proposed
Nikkar and *Kadi'a*, referring to M. Jastrow, *Die Religion Babyloniens
und Assyriens* (Giessen: J. Ricker, 1905), I. 162, 185.   F. Rosenthal
gives " Nikkar and *Kada'ah* " (*ANET*, p. 504).   But no attempt to
identify them has really succeeded.

  kl 'lhy rḥbh w'dm[... : Rosenthal (*ANET*, p. 504) translated this
expression thus: " all the Gods of Commons and Land (?)."   He
obviously related *rḥbh* to the root *rḥb* (" be wide open ") and *'dm* to
'dmh (" ground, land ") in Hebrew.   H. Bauer (*op. cit.*, p. 5) had
suggested this as a possibility, but also mentioned *Ruḥba* as the name
of a place southeast of Damascus.   R. Dussaud (*op. cit.*, p. 321) suggested rather a place called *Raḥeba* or *Raḥbā* on the Euphrates, the
modern Meyadin, in whose neighborhood an ancient fortress still
preserves the old name; we follow Dupont-Sommer in accepting this
identification.   Such a phrase, " all the gods of X (place-name)," is
found in vassal treaties, for instance in those of Esarhaddon (ll. 31ff.:
" by all the gods of Asshur, by all the gods of Nineveh, by all the
gods of Calah," etc.).   See also the treaty of Esarhaddon with Ba'al
of Tyre (Rev. II, 8-9; *AfO* 8 [1932-33] 32-33).   In such case' *dm*[
must also be a place-name, perhaps some name like *'Adāmāh* (Jos
19 : 36) or *'Admāh* (like Gn 10 : 19; 14 : 2,8), or simply *'Adam* (which
seems to appear below in Sf I A 35 as the last of a list of place-
names).   In Jos 3 : 16 *'dm* should probably be read as *'Adāmāh*; see
1 Kgs 7 : 46; 2 Chr 4 : 17; cf. N. Glueck, *BASOR* 90 (1943) 5-6
(= Tell ed-Dâmieh); W. F. Albright, *JPOS* 5 (1925) 33, n. 37.   Of
course, it is possible that the name *'dm* here is related to the Hebrew
'Edōm, or to the Ugaritic *udm* (Keret 277) or Akkadian *Udūmu*.
The phrase, " the gods of KTK," and probably also the " gods of
Arpad," is found in Sf I B 5-6.   Donner - Röllig prefer the translation,
" Götter der Wüste und des Fruchtlandes " (*KAI* 2.239).

  [*wqdm hdd ḥ*]*lb* : " In the presence of Hadad of Aleppo."   This
phrase was restored by H. Bauer (*op. cit.*, p. 5), since Hadad of Aleppo is mentioned in the treaty of Aššurnirāri V (Rev. VI, 18), followed
by Palil and the Seven-godhead.   Šalmaneser III mentions having
offered sacrifices before Adad of Aleppo (Monolith inscription, *ANET*,
p. 278-79).   On a famous temple of Hadad in Aleppo, see M. J. Dahood, " Ancient Semitic Deities in Syria and Palestine," p. 77.   The
town *ḥlb* is mentioned in Sf III 5.   Hadad is the West-Semitic (Amorite?) name of the storm-god; he is known as Adad in Babylon from
the time of the Amorite dynasty.

11.   *wqdm sbt* : " In the presence of Sibitti," the Seven-godhead, who
is also mentioned in the treaty of Aššurnirāri V (Rev. VI, 20), as well

as in that of Esarhaddon with Ba'al of Tyre (Rev. II, 5: *dsibitte ilāni^meš qardute*) and in his vassal treaties (l. 464). " Le chiffre sacré s'appliquait aux sept dieux des cieux ou aux sept dieux des enfers, avec l'arrière-pensée d'exprimer ainsi la totalité des dieux bienfaisants ou malfaisants. Souvent le nom de ' Sept ' terminera une énumération de divinités, comme pour englober celles qu'on a omises. Il existait à Ninive un temple des Sept " (É. Dhorme, *Les religions de Babylonie et d'Assyrie* [Les anciennes religions orientales II; Paris: Presses universitaires de France, 1949], p. 79; see also J. Bottéro, " Les divinités sémitiques anciennes en Mésopotamie," in *Le antiche divinità semitiche*, pp. 48-49). Sibitti was a Babylonian deity, here inserted in the second half of the list of gods, where the Canaanite deities appear.

wqdm 'l w'lyn : " In the presence of 'El and 'Elyan." This pair of gods is West-Semitic or Canaanite. The name 'El is well-known in the Ugaritic texts and in the OT; it also occurs in Hadad 2 (b^is), 11,18; Panammū 22. In the Canaanite pantheon he was regarded as the lord of the gods; see R. Dussaud, *Les religions des Hittites et des Hourrites, des Phéniciens et des Syriens* (Les anciennes religions orientales II; Paris: Presses universitaires de France, 1949), p. 360; M. Pope, *El in the Ugaritic Pantheon* (VTS 2; Leiden: Brill, 1955); W. F. Albright, *Archaeology and the Religion of Israel* (Baltimore: Johns Hopkins Press, 1953), pp. 72-73. *'Elyôn* is a name familiar in the OT, as an epithet of *'El* (Gn 14:18-22; Ps 78:35), of Yahweh (Ps 7:18; 47:3), of Elohim (Ps 57:3; 78:56); it is also used in parallelism with 'El (Num 24:16; Ps 73:11; 107:11), with Yahweh (Dt 32:8-9; 2 Sm 22:14 [= Ps 18:14]; Ps 91:9), with 'Elohim (Ps 46:5; 50:14), with Shaddai (Num 24:16; Ps 91:1). It is also used alone in Ps 9:3; 77:11; 82:6; Is 14:14.

In these cases, of course, *'lywn* designates the monotheistic God of Israel. Here in Sf I it appears as one of a pair with 'El. In the preceding pairs it was always a question of distinct deities, which suggests that 'El and 'Elyān are distinct Canaanite gods here too. The relation of the Aramaic *'El wa-'Elyān* to the Hebrew *'El 'Elyôn* is complicated by the fact that in Ugaritic we have divine names sometimes used alone and sometimes connected by *w-*, which apparently denote one god. Contrast *Qdš wAmrr* (C. H. Gordon, *Ugaritic Textbook*, Text 51: IV, lines 8, 13) with *Qdš yuḥdm šb'r / Amrr kkbkb lpnm* (lines 16-17) and *Qdš Amrr* (*'Anat* 6:11); similarly *aḫr mgy Kṭr wḤss* (Text 51: V, line 106), where the double name *Kṭr wḤss* is used with a singular verb. See further *Kṭr wḤss* in Text 68:7-8 (with singular verb); 2 Aqht V:17-18 (contrast lines 10,11); *Nkl wIb* (Text 77:1, to be contrasted with 77:17,18). Recall also the strange *'ir w'qaddīš* of Dn 4:10,20. Cf. G. Levi della Vida, " El Elyon in

Genesis 14 : 18-20," *JBL* 63 (1944) 1-9 ; M. Pope, *op. cit.*, pp. 55-58 (with the literature cited there). — In 1QapGn (12,17 ; 20,12.16 ; 21, 2.20 ; 22,15.16[bis].21) '*lyn* appears constantly as '*lywn*, which form should probably be regarded as a Hebraism ; it does not necessarily point to an original '*Elyawn* (*pace* F. Rosenthal, *ANET*, p. 504), which would appear in this period with a *waw*. Hence the vocalization '*Elyān*, which in our opinion is preferable to '*Elyūn*, suggested by S. Segert, *ArOr* 32 (1964) 125.

wqdm šmy[*n w'rq*] : Calling upon heaven and earth as witnesses to a treaty is also found in Hittite pacts (*ANET*, p. 206). A certain numinous character was attributed to these natural phenomena, and they were probably objects of worship. A similar usage is found in the OT ; see Dt 4 : 26 (*ha'îdôtî bākem hayyôm 'et-haššāmayim w'et-hā'āreṣ*) ; 30 : 19 ; 31 : 28. For an interpretation of this usage see H. B. Huffmon, *JBL* 78 (1959) 291, n. 23 ; also W. L. Moran, *Bibl* 43 (1962) 317-20. Cf. Zakir b 25-26. — See M. Delcor, " Les attaches littéraires, l'origine et la signification de l'expression biblique ' prendre à témoin le ciel et la terre '," *VT* 16 (1966) 8-25.

[*wqdm mṣ*]*lh wm'ynn* : " In the presence of the Abyss and the Springs." *ṣwlh* has been restored by Dupont-Sommer, as in Is 44 : 27 (*ṣûlāh*) ; but then an instance of a medial long *u* fully written would be introduced, which, while not without some parallels in the Aramaic of this period (see *y'wrn*, Sf II B 4 ; *šwr'*, Zakir a 17 ; *rwḥ*, Sf III 2 ; *ymwt*, Sf III 16), is quite rare. For that reason it would be better to restore the alternate suggestion of Dupont-Sommer, *mṣlh* (like Zech 1 : 8). *m'ynn* is probably to be vocalized *ma'yānīn*, like the later Aramaic *ma'yānā* and the Hebrew *ma'yān*, and not like the Syriac *m^e'înā*. For parallels in Hittite and Greek writers, see H. Bauer (*op. cit.*, p. 5).

12. *wqdm ywm wlylh* : " In the presence of Day and Night." For parallels to this formula, see W. L. Moran, *Bibl* 43 (1962) 319. The *plena scriptio* of *ywm* here agrees with the normal practice for un-contracted diphthongs in the Aramaic of this period. A propos of *lylh* Dupont-Sommer remarks, " A lire soit *laylāh*, comme en hébreu, soit plutôt *lêlêh*, ce qui est la forme proprement araméenne (état emph. *lêl^eyâ*)." Throughout the various phases of Aramaic the form of the noun is seen to be either a reduplicated stem **laylay* or else **layil*. The reduplicated stem could scarcely yield the Hebrew form *laylāh*. Since there is no reason to regard *lylh* here as emphatic (being parallel to the abs. *ywm*), it should be vocalized as *laylêh*. A dissimilation of the diphthongs has produced the contraction in the last syllable ; which contraction is indicated by *he*. The same form occurs in 1QapGn 19,14; it is the same phenomenon which appears in *swsh* (*sūsê*[*h*] < *sūsay*) *ḥd qlyl*, " a swift horse " (*A* 38 [emph.: *sūsyā*]), and probably also in *ybʻh* (< *yibʻay) in Sf III 2. For this reason the explanation of *lylh*, given by F. M. Cross and D. N. Freedman (*EHO*, p. 27), as *laylā* is unacceptable; likewise for that of G. Garbini (*AA*, p. 260); S. Segert (*ArOr* 32 [1964] 123). We simply have to admit a dissimilated contracted diphthong here in the second syllable; how otherwise explain the *yodh* in the first syllable and the *he* in the second?

śhdn : Dupont-Sommer takes this word as a noun in apposition to the preceding names, understanding the following *kl* '[*lhy ktk w'lhy 'r*]*pd* as a vocative with the subsequent imperative, " (O vous), tous les d[ieux de KTK et dieux d'Ar]pad, ouvrez vos yeux ... " For the restoration of the lacuna, see Sf I B 5-6. That the gods are addressed seems clear; but it is preferable to take *śhdn* '[*lhy ktk w'lhy 'r*]*pd* as a nominal declarative sentence, resuming the foregoing, " All the god[s of KTK and the gods of Ar]pad (are) witnesses (to it)." Donner-Röllig also prefer the nominal sentence with *śhdn* as predicate (*KAI*, 2.246). Dupont-Sommer calls attention to the rôle of the gods as witnesses in the Hittite treaty of Šuppiluliuma with Mattiwaza (see *ANET*, p. 205), " We have called the gods to be assembled and the gods of the contracting parties to be present, to listen, and to serve as witnesses." See also the end of the list of gods in the treaty between Mursilis and Duppi-Tessub of Amurru (*ANET*, p. 205), " Let these be witnesses to this treaty and to the oath." Or the treaty of Mursilis II with Talmišarruma of Aleppo (rev. 9-10), " May the gods of the land of Ḫatti and the gods of the land of Aleppo be witnesses to these words." To this Hittite evidence we may add that of the Old Testament: Gn 31:47-50, where Jacob and Laban have erected the cairn which Jacob called in Hebrew *galʻēd*, but Laban in Aramaic *yᵉgar śāhᵃdūtā*, " a cairn of witness (or testimony)." Laban concludes, " Remember that God is witness between you and me " (*r*ᵉʻ*ēh* 'lôhîm ʻēd bênî ûbênêkā, v. 50). Cf. Jb 16:19; Panammū 22 (*wkl 'lhy y'dy*), 2 ('*lh y'dy*).

13. *pqḥw* : " Open," the Peal impv. pl. of *pqḥ*, " open the eyes." Vocalize probably *paqaḥū*. The word *'ynykm* probably contains two uncontracted diphthongs, *'aynaykum*. For similar notions, cf. Dn 9:18 (*p*ᵉ*qaḥ*[*h*] ʻ*ênêkā ûr*ᵉʻ*ēh*, " open your eyes and see," in a prayer adressed to God); also 2 Kgs 6:20; 19:16; Is 37:17. Cf. the Hittite treaty of Tudḫaliyas IV with Ulmi-Tessub of Dattasa, obv. 50-51: " Let the gods see and be witnesses " (cf. D. J. McCarthy, *op. cit.*, p. 184).

lḥzyh : " To gaze upon (the treaty)." Dupont-Sommer remarks, " Noter cet infinitif sans *m*- et avec désinence fm. *âh*; cf. III 6 *rqh* (inf. de la racine *rqq* > *r'*')." Cf. G. Garbini (*RSO* 34 [1959] 49, 51), who hesitatingly goes along with Dupont-Sommer's view. There is considerable evidence for the Peal inf. without preformative *mem* in early Aramaic; see note on *rqh trqm*, Sf III 6 *ad fin*. But the question remains whether *ḥzyh* is Peal and whether it has a fem. ending. There is no evidence elsewhere in Aramaic for a Peal inf. with a fem. ending. Moreover, the parallel cited *rqh* is not derived from *rqq*, but from a *tertiae infirmae* root *rqw/y* (with which F. Rosenthal agrees; see *BASOR* 158 [1960] 29). Consequently, it is better to regard *ḥzyh* as a Pael inf. with the normal ending expected of infinitives of derived conjugations in Aramaic: *ḥazzāyāh*. A difficulty with this explanation is that *ḥz'* is not otherwise attested in Pael; but the example in Nêrab 2 : 5 (= *KAI*, 226.5) is usually overlooked: *wb'yny mḥzh 'nh bny rb' bkwny whwm 'thmw*. This does not mean " and with my eyes, what do I see? " (so F. Rosenthal, *ANET*, p. 505), as if *mḥzh* = *mh ḥzh*. Rather *mḥzh* is the Pael ptc. and the phrase should be translated, " and with my eyes I gazed upon my children to the fourth generation."

14. *whn* : The normal Aramaic conditional conjunction; see Jean - Hoftijzer, *DISO*, 66. It is also found occasionally in the Hebrew texts of the OT; see Jer 3 : 1 ; Is 54 : 15 ; etc.

yšqr : " Should be false." In Sf III this verb always occurs in the perfect and in the apodosis of a condition expressing a stipulation (likewise in Sf I B 23,27-28,36-37,38 ; II B 9,14,17-18). Here it occurs in the imperfect (as also in Sf I A 15,24 ; II A 3), where there is no question of treaty stipulations. See note on Sf III 4. Cf. the treaty of Aššurnirāri V (Obv. I, 15): *šummu* [I]*Ma-ti-'-ilu ina a-di-e ta-mi-ti ilāni*[ᵐᵉˢ *i-ḫa-ṭu*] . . . ; Esarhaddon's Vassal Treaties (l. 513).

16. [*bny*] *Gš* : So restored on the basis of Sf I B 3 ; *byt gš* is also possible (see Sf I B 11 ; II B 10). It is the designation of the people of *Bīt-Agūsi*, another name for Arpad ; or more probably the designation of the ruling dynasty in Arpad. The Assyrians under Aššur-nāsirpal II (883-59) know of the ruler of Gusi in the land of Yaḫan (cf. D. D. Luckenbill, *ARAB*, 1. §477). In the time of Šalmaneser III (858-24 B.C.) the people are called *Aramē mār Gusi* (*ARAB*, 1. §614), *Guzi* (*ARAB*, 1. §600, 610), *Agusi* (*ARAB*, 1. §582, 601). In the campaign of Adadnirari III of 805 B.C. Arpaddu is referred to as *Bīt-(A)gūsi*. See S. Schiffer, *Die Aramäer : historisch-geographische Untersuchungen* (Leipzig : J. C. Hinrichs, 1911), p. 90, n. 6 ; p. 137, n. 9 ;

M. F. Unger, *Israel and the Aramaeans of Damascus: a Study in Archaeological Illumination of Bible History* (London: J. Clarke, 1957), p. 166; R. P. Boudou, *Liste des noms géographiques* (Orientalia 36-38; Rome: Pontifical Biblical Institute, 1929), p. 7. Cf. M. Liverani, " Bar-Guš e Bar-Rakib," *RSO* 36 (1961) 185-87. In the Zakir stele (a 5) *br Gš* denotes the king of Arpad. Before [*bny*] *Gš* one can restore confidently *whn yšqrn*; so Dupont-Sommer, Donner - Röllig.

21. After the break in which lines 17-20 have disappeared we find ourselves in the midst of curses, parallels of which have been found in many Assyrian and Hittite treaties. Cf. the treaty of Šamši-adad V with Marduk-zākir-šumi I (*AfO* 8 [1932-33] 27-29), of Esarhaddon with Ba'al of Tyre (*ibid.*, pp. 29-34); Annals of Aššurbanipal, Cylinder B, ix [*ANET*, p. 300]. See also Hos 9: 11,14; Lam 4: 3-4; and the extensive study of this subject in D. R. Hillers, *Treaty-Curses and the Old Testament Prophets* (Biblica et Orientalia, 16; Rome: Pontifical Biblical Institute, 1964).

š't: " Ewe." This is apparently the abs. sg. fem. with the old ending *-at* (another case of it would be *bq't* [Sf I B 10], and possibly Sf I C 20, if Dupont-Sommer is correct in interpreting *lḥyt* as singular; but the plural is not impossible there). The abs. pl. *š'n* is found in l. 23. Dupont-Sommer is probably correct in relating it to the Hebr. *śeh*, Ugar. and Phoen. *š*, Accad. *šu'u* and Arab. *šā*, even though there appears to be a relation between it and later Aramaic *t't'* (E. Sachau, *Aramäische Papyrus und Ostraka aus einer jüdischen Militär-Kolonie zu Elephantine* [Leipzig: J. C. Hinrichs, 1911], pl. 63, §1 i 12; also on an unpublished ostracon [§170] of the Clermont-Ganneau collection mentioned by Dupont-Sommer) and Ugar. *ṭat* (C. H. Gordon, *UT*, 49: II: 7,29). In such case we would have to write *š't*. Is this the same word as Panammū 6,9 (*š'h*)? — Cf. W. F. Albright, *HTS* 22 (1966) 44; S. Segert, *ArOr* 32 (1964) 119.

'l: " Not." See note on Sf III 7; here the adv. is used in a negative wish (= a curse in a treaty).

thry: " May she not conceive." The vocalization of the form *thry* is problematical: should it be *tihray* or *tihrê*? Though no impfs. of *tertiae infirmae* verbs occur with a final *yodh* in Sf III (cf. impr. *hwy* in Sf III 22), there are several cases of this ending in the other two inscriptions (*thwy*, Sf I A 25,32; II A [4],6; [*y*]*tnšy* II A 4). These forms with final *yodh* must be compared with those in final *he* (*ytḥzh* Sf I A 28; *y'th* I B 28; Sf III 11; *t'th* I B 31; Sf III 11; especially with *yhwh* Sf II A 4; *yb'h* II B 8; Sf III 2; *tb'h* Sf II B 17; *yhwnh* II B 16; *tršh* Sf III 9; *trqh* III 18; *tkh* III 13). This evidence seems to point to the fact that the final *ay* diphthong was undergoing contraction at this time, or perhaps had already undergone it in pronunciation, at least in the case of *tertiae infirmae* roots.   For a less likely explanation, see S. Segert, *ArOr* 32 (1964) 124.

We persist in regarding the last syllable of the imperfect of *tertiae infirmae* verbs as vocalized with an original *a*-vowel, for otherwise it would be impossible to explain such a form as *tpnw* (Sf III 7). In later vocalization this form would be *tipnô* (compare the Biblical Aramaic form *yibnôn*, Ezr 6 : 7).   This must be derived from *tipnaw, and should be so vocalized in these inscriptions.   This would point to a thematic *a*-vowel throughout the imperfect; and this *a*-vowel conveniently explains the forms in final *he* and final *yodh* (= contract-ed and uncontracted diphthongs in a period of transition).   There is no valid reason to import from Hebrew the explanation that some forms are built on the active *galay and others on the stative *galiy. This may be adequate for Hebrew, but what is the evidence for it in Aramaic, and especially in the imperfect?

The same explanation (an *a*-vowel) likewise suits the noun forms: *lylh* (I A 12), *'rbh* (I A 27), *ṣdh* (I A 33), *gdh* (II A 2), *'ryh* (II A 9), *ṣby* (I A 33). — H. Bauer (*op. cit.*, p. 7) regarded the root *hry* as " *sonst nicht aramäisch.*"   Though it is found in 1QapGn 2, 1 (*hry'nt'* [Kutscher's reading]), 15 (*hrywn'*), we may still ask whether it is a genuine Aramaic form.

wšb' [*mhy*]*nqn* :   Abs. pl. fem. Haph. ptc. of *ynq*, " nurses," re-stored on the basis of the words in the following lines.

ymsḫ[...: Dupont-Sommer restores [*n šdyhn w*], and translates, " que sept nourrices oigne[nt leurs mamelles et] allaitent un enfant." He explains, " en frottant leurs mamelles d'huile ordinaire ou aroma-tisée, les femmes pensaient sans doute obtenir un lait plus abondant." However, he gives no evidence of such a belief in antiquity.   D. R. Hillers (*op. cit.*, p. 61, n. 52) suggests that the explanation may be more prosaic, since it is a common practice of nursing mothers to prevent soreness, cracking, etc.   The curse of dry breasts is paralleled in Hos 9 : 14; Lam 4 : 3-4.

22.   *'lym* :   " A lad or young boy."   The word is found in 1QapGn 2, 2 (*'wlym*') for a baby boy.   It is the diminutive *qutayl* form; hence *'ulaym*.

ssyh :   Abs. sg. fem., " mare," here used in a collective sense. In later Aramaic (Imperial and Biblical) the noun used with cardinal numbers is usually in the plural; this we find also in line 23 (*š'n*), 21 (*mhynqn*).   But the verb is plural, *yuhayniqān*.   Vocalize : *sūsyāh*.

'l :   " A colt."   Vocalize : *'īl*, as in later Aramaic and Syriac.

23. *šwrh* : Abs. sg. fem., " cow," again in the collective sense. Possibly this is the same word as *š'h wšwrh* (*Panammū* 6,9). Vocalize: *šawrāh*.

š'n : Abs. pl. fem. of *š't* (line 21).

'mr : " A lamb." Cf. *'imm ᵉrā* in later Aramaic; see Ezr 6 : 9, 17; 7 : 17. Accad. *immeru*. Vocalize: *'immar*.

24. *bkth* : The reading is certain, but the interpretation of this line is difficult. The word *bkth* is explained by Dupont-Sommer as related to later Aramaic *'abbakā* and Syriac *bakkā*, " a cock," having, however, a double fem. ending, *-t*, *-āh*, and meaning " hen." The parallels which he offers for the double fem. ending are all derived from *plural* nouns in *Hebrew*. If he assumes that *bkth* is plural, why should it be emphatic when used with a cardinal (all the other examples are absolute)? It seems that we have an abs. sg. fem. But what is the root and the meaning? The idea of hens killing is also puzzling. The context seems to demand the mention of some small animal after the mares, cows, and ewes. Even though Dupont-Sommer's interpretation of this line encounters difficulties, we prefer it to that of J. N. Epstein (" Notes on the Sujin Pact," [Mod. Hebr.] *Kedem* 1 [1942] 39), who translated this line *ylkw lpšwṭ* (*lmtwḥ*) *ḥwt ḥ'rb wl' ybynw* (*wl' yṣlyḥw bml'ktm*), " (seven weaving women) will go to stretch out weaving yarn and shall not understand (and shall not succeed in their work)." He related *bkth* to Syriac *bkt*, " to weave "; explained *bšṭ* as = *pšṭ*, an inf., and *lḥm* as = Arab. *luḥmatuⁿ*, " woof, weft," and related *hrg* to Syr. *hrg*, " to ponder over." These suggestions are interesting, but hardly fit the context after the animals mentioned. Moreover, we would expect a *lamedh* before the inf. *bšṭ* (cf. Sf I A 13; I B 34). *hrg* in the sense of " succeed " is farfetched.

D. R. Hillers (*op. cit.*, pp. 71-74) has offered another interpretation which is very attractive and suits the context as a curse involving the loss of men to satisfy the desires of prostitutes. He would read *wšb' bnth bšṭ lḥm w'l yhrgn* and would translate, " And may his seven daughters go looking for food, but not seduce (anyone)." The reading of *bnth* instead of *bkth* does eliminate grammatical difficulties; and the explanation of *yhrgn* as a Haphel form of *rgg* is attractive (in Syriac the Peal form is found with the meaning " desire, covet, lust "; cf. 2 *Aqht* 6 : 34-35). Thus translated, the curse would seem to be parallel to the Tell Halaf malediction : " Whoever erases (my) name and puts (his) name, may he burn his seven sons before Adad, may he release his seven daughters as prostitutes for Ishtar " (see B. Meissner, *AfO Beiheft* 1 [Berlin, 1933], pp. 72-73; W. F. Albright, *Anatolian Studies* 6 [1956] 75-85). However, this maledication really says just the opposite of the lack of men for prostitutes seeking business and food; in the Tell Halaf malediction the curse is prostitution itself, in Sefîre I it would be the lack of men to be seduced by the "daughters" turned prostitutes. The parallel of Is 4:1 is closer, and that of Dt 28:68 even more so. Attractive as Hillers' suggestion is, it should be noted that H. Bauer (*op. cit.*, p. 7) years ago made a similar one in an attempt to improve on Ronzevalle's reading; he translated the line, "und seine sieben Töchter mögen in Herumschweifen nach Brot gehen, und sie sollen nicht ...." His comment was: "ist doch wohl 'Hurerei' gemeint." It was, accordingly, in the light of Bauer's suggestion that Dupont-Sommer scrutinized the stone anew and insisted on the certainty of the reading of *bkth*: "La lecture de ces 4 lettres est tout à fait sure." The photographs seem to confirm his insistence. Hillers, however, remarks, perhaps too confidently, "If this is so, the error was that of the original stonecutter, who confused *k* and *n*, which in this period are roughly similar in form." In the light of all this we prefer to remain with the tentative understanding of the line proposed by Dupont-Sommer — until something better is proposed.([17])

yhkn : See note on Sf III 5.

bsṭ lḥm : "Looking for food," lit. "in search of food." *šṭ* is to be understood as an inf. (Peal, without preformative *mem*) of *šwṭ*, "rove about" (see Job 1:7; 2:2). Hillers cites the interesting parallel of Nm 11:8.

w'l yhrgn : "May they not kill (anything)." The curse seems to say that the animals will not kill anything. The word *hrg* is used in Hebr. of an animal (Jb 20:16); it is found in Aramaic in Hadad 26,33,34; Panammū 3,5,7, and in Moabite (Mešaʿ 11). See the note above for further discussion.

whn yšqr mtî['l wl]brh : "And if Matî['el] should be false < to Bir-Gaʾyah > [and to] his son." At the end of the line there is room for only four letters, two of which must be the end of Matî'el's name, i.e. -'l, and the other two must be *wl*-, required by the syntax. Something has, therefore, been omitted, to which the suffix on *lbrh* refers, and this can only be the name of Bir-Gaʾyah, which is supplied

---

([17]) Hillers also mentions a chronological difficulty connected with this interpretation: "The domestic fowl was not introduced in large numbers to the Near East and Europe until the Persian period, and even if hens were sporadically imported before that time — they had long been raised in India — they would not have been present in sufficient quantity to figure in an 8th century curse ...." (p. 72). How do we know? His footnote about the earliest certain artistic representation of a cock (on the well-known seal of Jaazaniah from Tell en-Nasbeh [*ca.* 600 B.C.]) cites an example before the Persian period.

in the translation.   Moreover, this addition is confirmed by the fragmentary text of Sf II A 3, where Bir-Ga'yah's name is certain and
the context is quite similar to this line.

25.   *kmlkt ḥl mlkt ḥl mzy ... :*   " May his kingdom become like a kingdom of sand, a kingdom of sand, as long as ...." The problem here
is one of the division of words. We prefer this reading, which is
basically that of H. Bauer (*op. cit.*, pp. 7-8), to that of Dupont-Sommer, *kmlkt ḥlm lkt ḥlm zy ymlk*, which he translates, " que son royaume soit comme un royaume de songe $<$ $>$, sur lequel régnera Assur ! " He appeals to Ps 73 : 20 ; Jb 20 : 8 for a similar use of
" dream," and considers the letters *lkt ḥlm* as dittographical.   Donner-
Röllig (*KAI*, 1.41 ; 2.239) prefer to read *kmlkt ḥl mlkt ḥlm zy* ..., and
translate, " dann soll sein Königreich wie ein Sandkönigreich, ein
Traumkönigreich werden, das Assur beherrscht." They appeal to the
same biblical loci.   This is better than Dupont-Sommer's explanation,
but it encounters the difficulty that one would expect the retrospective
pronoun on *b* or *'l* to follow the relative *zy*. Dupont-Sommer sensed
this difficulty and referred to Joüon, *Grammaire de l'Hébreu biblique*,
§158i.   But can the prep. be omitted with *mlk*? It still seems possible
to explain the expression *mlkt ḥl* as dittographical, since it occurs
before in the line ; a " kingdom of sand " is, moreover, no more
forced than the " dream-kingdom." The sense of Bir-Ga'yah's curse
is that if Matiʿel is unfaithful to the treaty, then may the might of
the great threat of Assyria fall upon his kingdom rendering it one of
sand.   He hopes that it will be a worthless kingdom as long as
Asshur is powerfully ruling.

   mzy ymlk 'šr :   " As long as Asshur rules." Dupont-Sommer admits that the reading of the final *reš* is not certain. If it is correct,
then we have the defective writing of Aššur, which otherwise turns
up *plene scriptum* ; see Bir-RKB 9 ; Panammū 7,11,12(bis),13,15,16,17.
The *plena scriptio* persisted in later Aramaic : *'šwr* (1QapGn 17,8) ;
'twr (*A* 3,4,5,8, etc.). The only other places where it occurs defectively are Kilamuwa 8 and 1 Chr 5 : 6 (both not Aramaic). It is admittedly not impossible here, though unusual. We interpret *mzy* as
$=$ *mn zy*, a temporal conjunction ; cf. Dn 4 : 23. The sense seems to
be that Bir-Ga'yah is wishing misfortune to Matiʿel's kingdom at the
hands of Asshur, if he is not faithful to the treaty. But who is
'šr? If the god, should we not expect him to be mentioned in the
list of deities? More likely it refers to the country ; but then would
Bir-Ga'yah be wishing that Assyria be so strong as to reduce Arpad?
What sort of relations between Bir-Ga'yah and Assyria are implied
here?

[*ysk h*]*dd* : " May Hadad pour (over it)." The first word is
supplied as in the following line. For the restoration of Hadad, see
lines 36,38. The mention of the name of a god is usual in such
treaty-curses; cf. the treaty of Aššurnirāri V (Rev. IV, 4.8; V, 5); of
Šamši-adad V with Marduk-zākir-šumi I (*passim*); of Esarhaddon with
Ba'al of Tyre (Rev. II, 1-19) and his Vassal Treaties (11. 414-93).

26. *kl mh* : The interpretation of this word is now certain; it has
nothing to do with *k*ᵉ*limmā*, " disgrace " (so G. R. Driver, *AfO* 8
[1932-33] 204; Cross and Freedman, *EHO*, p. 28), or with a king's
name (see note on Sf I B 2), but means simply " every sort of."
It occurs in Sf I A 30; I B 2; III 16,28,29. See also the Tariff of
Palmyra (Cooke, *NSI* §147) i, 12 (*klm' gns klh*). In Bir-RKB 15 it is
written *kl.mh* (with a word-divider between the pronouns).
    lhyh : Abs. sg. fem., " evil." See note on Sf III 2.
    b'rq wbšmym : " (Which exists) on earth and in heaven." Cf.
the treaty of Aššurnirāri V (Rev. IV, 8); 2 Sm 22 : 8.
    [*'bny b*]*rd* : Restored by Dupont-Sommer, comparing Jos 10 : 11;
Is 30 : 30.

27. *wšb' šnn* : " For seven years." *šnn* is the abs. pl. of the fem.
šnh, used adverbially.
    'rbh : " The locust." G. Garbini (*AA*, p. 247) has analyzed this
form as an emphatic. But this is impossible, since the cognates in
Hebrew (*'arbēh*), Ugaritic (*irby*) and Akkadian (*arbū, erbū, erebū*) show
that the final consonant is weak, probably *-y*. Hence, the *he* probably
represents a contraction from *-ay* (Cross and Freedman, *EHO*, p. 28,
prefer an original *-iy*). Cf. Esarhaddon's Vassal Treaties (1. 442-43):
" May the locust who diminishes the land devour your harvest."
Note the similar sequence of hail and devouring locusts in Ex 10 : 5;
Ps 105 : 32-34. See too S. Segert, *ArOr* 32 [1964] 124.
    twl'h : " The worm." Cf. the later Aramaic *tôla'tā*, Syr. *tawla'tā*
Hebr. *tôlē'āh*; vocalize : *tawla'āh*. Cf. Dt 28 : 39; Jon 4 : 7.
    [*ys*]*q* : " Come up." See Sf I A 5; also possible would be [*yp*]*q*,
from *npq* (see line 28).

28. *twy* : An unknown word. Is it perhaps related to Ugar. *thw*,
Arab *tyh*, and Hebr. *tôhû*, which Koehler - Baumgartner translate as
" waterless, impassable desert "? It must refer to some sort of blight,
since it follows the attack of locusts and worms and precedes the
mention of the lack of vegetation. J. Koopmans (*BO* 17 [1960] 52)
wonders whether it might not be related to Hebrew *t'y, t'w* (Dt 14 :5;
Is 51 : 20), which seems to mean " Wildschaf, Wildstier." Does this

really fit the context though? — For the sequence *twy*, *twlʿh*, *'rbh* (in reverse order), cf. Dt 28 : 38-42 and see M. Weinfeld, *Bibl* 46 (1965) 424, n. 2.

'rqh : "Its land," a fem. suffixal form, and not an emphatic (*pace* G. Garbini, *AA*, p. 247). Vocalize: *'arqah*.

ḥṣr : "Grass." Cf. the later Aram. *ḥaṣīrā*, Hebr. *ḥāṣīr*; and the treaty of Aššurnirāri V (Rev. IV. 20): *urqit ṣēri lū lā uṣṣā*, "may the green of the field not come forth" (cf. D. J. McCarthy, *op. cit.*, p. 196), Dt 29 : 22 (*wᵉlô yaʿᵃleh bāh kol-ʿēśeb*).

wlytḥzh : Dupont-Sommer divided the words thus, *wlyt ḥzh*, equating the first word with the later Aram. *lyt* (< *lᵉ 'yty*), which he translated, "qu'on n'y voie plus de verdure." He is followed by J. Koopmans (*AC*, p. 51). His translation is correct, but he has not explained the form *ḥzh* resulting from such a division. Since the prefixed negative *lā-* is abundantly attested (see Appendix, Morphology, IV. 2), we prefer to read it here together with an Ithpeʿel form: *wa-lā-yitḥazêh*. But rather than understand it as a negative wish (which would demand rather *'l* with impf.), we prefer to regard it as a sort of result clause, "so that there may not be seen ...." The same is true of the restored form at the end of the line. The Ithpeʿel forms occur in line 29 (*ytšmʿ*), line 32 (*yštḥṭ*). See G. Garbini, "Sefire I A, 28," *RSO* 36 (1961) 9-11, who compares Bir RKB 16 and Lv 10 : 9.

29. *'ḥwh* : "Its vegetation"; the same word occurs in line 32. Dupont-Sommer relates it to Hebr. *'āḥû*, "grass" (Gn 41 : 2,18; Job 8 : 11) and Ugar. *'aḫ*, "meadow." T. O. Lambdin ("Egyptian Loan Words in the Old Testament," *JAOS* 73 [1953] 146) regards it as derived from Egyptian; so too J. Vergote, who translates it "fourré de papyrus" (*Joseph en Égypte* [Louvain: Publications universitaires, 1959], pp. 57-66). But see the remarks of B. Couroyer, *RB* 66 (1959) 588; J. M. A. Janssen, *JEOL* 14 (1955-56) 68. The final *he* is to be taken as a fem. suffix, referring to Arpad; vocalize *'aḥwah*.

ytšmʿ : Note the lack of metathesis here in contrast to *yštḥṭ* (line 32).

ql knr : "The sound of the lyre." Dupont-Sommer refers to Ez 26 : 13, "And the sound of your harps shall be heard no more," and to the treaty of Aššurnirāri V (Rev. IV, 19), "then may the farmer in his field not strike up a song." Cf. Apoc 18 : 22. Vocalize *kinnār*.

wbʿmh : "Among its people." Is the reading certain here? If it is then we have an expression parallel to that of line 30. In both cases the suffix is fem., referring to Arpad (fem. in l. 35).

hml mrq : "(Let there rather be) the din of affliction." In

interpreting this phrase, we originally followed Dupont-Sommer, even
though his solution was not completely satisfactory.   It is necessary
to supply an adversative conjunction here in the translation, which
will contrast this and following nouns with *ql knr*.   Dupont-Sommer
relates *hml* to Hebr. *hᵃmullāh*, " din," Jer 11 : 16 ; Ez 1 : 24.   The
word *mrq* is better understood as a noun, " affliction," derived from
the root *mrḍ*, related to Hebrew *mrṣ* (" be sick "), Akkadian *marāṣu*,
Arabic *mariḍa*, and later Aramaic *mᵉraʿ*.   This plausible interpretation has been proposed by C. Brekelmans, " Sefire I A 29-30," *VT*
13 (1963) 225-28.

   whm[*wn ṣʿ*]*qh* : " And the noise of crying."   This reading has
been proposed by C. Brekelmans (*ibid.*) and it is certainly preferable
to Dupont-Sommer's *whm*[*wn l*]*qḥ*, which he translated, " et le tumulte
du conquérant."   H. Bauer (*op. cit.*, p. 8) read the beginning of l. 30
as *qh*, and the photograph (pl. VI) shows that this is preferable to
Dupont-Sommer's reading of *qḥ*.   The difficulty of the *plena scriptio*
of *hmwn* still remains.

30. *wyllh* : " Lamentation," cf. later Aram. *yᵉlaltā*, Hebr. *yᵉlālāh*
(Is 15 : 8).   Note its similar parallelism to *ṣᵉʿāqāh* in Zeph 1 : 10.   Cf.
Dt 28 : 47-57.

   mn kl mh ʾkl : " Every sort of devourer."   The use of *mn* here
is peculiar ; Dupont-Sommer regards it as the preposition *min* and
takes it as " probablement partitif," translating, " des dévoreurs de
toute espèce.   This is probably correct ; but could it possibly be the
interrogative-indefinite pronoun *man* ?   Cf. the piling up of indefinite
particles in Syriac (a feature which is admittedly rare, however, at
this period).   *ʾākil* is the ptc.   For the curse of devouring animals,
see D. R. Hillers, *op. cit.*, pp. 54-56.   Cf. Lv 26 : 22 ; Dt 32 : 24.

   [*p*]*m* : " Mouth," to be vocalized *pum* (< **pumm*).   Cf. the
repetitious use of *ina pi*, in an entirely different context, however, in
Esarhaddon's Vassal Treaties, ll. 111ff.

   ḥwh : " Serpent," as in later Aram. *ḥiwyā*, pl. *ḥiwwīn*.   The form
here is probably abs. sg. fem., as are most of the other animals which
are mentioned.   Vocalize : *ḥiwwāh*.   Cf. Jer 8 : 17.

31. *ʿqrb* : " Scorpion," as in later Aram. *ʿaqrabbā*, Hebr. *ʿaqrāb*,
Arab. *ʿaqrabⁿ*, Akkad. *aqrabu*.   The expression, " the mouth of a
scorpion," is strange because the scorpion attacks with its tail ; cf.
Apoc 9 : 10.

   dbhh : " A bear."   Dupont-Sommer says that the reading *dbhh*
is certain, but he prefers to correct it to *dbrh*, comparing the later
Aram. *dabbᵉrītā*, *dibborītā*, Syr. *debbārtā*, " bee, wasp."   We prefer to

interpret *dbhh* as a fem. form of the later Aram. *dubbā*, Hebr. *dōb*, for the bear fits better into the context, and the *ursus syriacus* was well known in that part of the world. Cf. 1 Sm 17 : 34 ; Hos 13 : 8. The form *dbhh* is peculiar ; it should be related perhaps to *khsy*, " my throne " (perhaps *kuhsī* for *kussī*) in Sf III 17, even though the *he* follows.

    nmrh : " Panther," the female, since the word is abs. sg. fem. Cf. later Aram. *nimrā*, Syr. *nemrā*, Hebr. *nāmēr*, Akkad. *nimru*, Arab. *nimrun*. Cf. Jer 5 : 6 ; Hos 13 : 7 ; Hab 1 : 8.

    ss : " Moth," related to later Aram. and Syr. *sāsā*, Hebr. *sās*, Akkad. *sāsu*. Cf. *A* 184, 186 ; Hos 5 : 12 ; Is 51 : 8 ; *Gilgamesh Epic*, 12 : 93-94.

    qml : " Louse, " agreeing with the Arab. *qamlu*[n], against the later metathesized form in Aram. *qalm*[e]*tā* and Syr. *qalmā*.

    w' [..yhww] 'lh qq btn : This part of the sentence is most difficult. Dupont-Sommer reads *w' [p ypln] 'lh qqbtn*, which he translates, " et, en ou [tre, que s'abbattent] sur elle des perdrix (?) ! " He understands *'lh* as a form of the prep. *'l* (*'alêha*). If he is correct, then we have a case of the defective writing of the contracted medial diphthong *ay* ; compare *'pyh* (Sf I A 42) ; *'ly[h]* (Sf III 9). We have no better solution for this word. However, it seems better to begin a new sentence with *wss wqml* because they are not preceded by *pm* like the foregoing words. Further, Dupont-Sommer relates *qqbtn* to Syr. *qaqbānā*, " partridge," and Akkadian *qaqabānu*. But what about the *t* preceding the *nun* ? It can scarcely be a fem. form. It is more likely that we have two words here, as J. Cantineau (*RA* 28 [1931] 172) once suggested. We relate *btn* to Ugar. *btn*, " serpent," *bašmu* in Akkadian (cf. W. von Soden, *Akkadisches Handwörterbuch*, p. 112), but *pitnā* in later Aram., *patnā* in Syr., and *peten* in Hebr. This would mean that Proto-Semitic *tha* is here represented by *t*, as in *yrt* (Sf I C 24). We have *b* instead of *p*, as in *nbš* for *npš* [Sf III 5-6 ; I B 40,42 ; II B 5 ; Hadad 17,21,22 ; Panammū 18], and possibly in *'lb* for *'lp* [Hadad 34]. Cf. G. Garbini, " Considerazioni sulla parola ebraica *peten*," *RivBibl* 6 (1958) 263-65. *qq* is, furthermore, not the word for " pelican," but the early form of *qō'ā*, " throat, neck," found in the Talmud. An interesting parallel is found in *Berakot* 49a (Goldschmidt 1, 175) : *zqpyh Rb Ššt lqw'yh 'ly khwwy'*, " da reckte R. Šešeth seinen Hals gegen mich wie eine Schlange." We have, then, the expression " toward it the throat of a serpent." It seems likely in this curse that a wish is being expressed that even the small insects may become something far more voracious toward Arpad than was ordinary. Hence, we restore *yhww* (= *yihwaw*). — Cf. P. Nober, *VD* 39 (1961) 112 ; W. F. Albright, *The Protosinaitic Inscriptions and their Decipherment* (HTS 22 ; Cambridge : Harvard, 1966), p. 39.

32. [yš]tḥṭ : "May it be destroyed." Dupont-Sommer has most likely restored this verb correctly, explaining it is an alternate form of šḥṭ and noting the confusion of the two roots in Syriac. It is probably an Ithpaʿal jussive with metathesis. Cf. The Treaty of Aššurnirāri V (Rev. V, 5-6).

lyšmn : "Unto desolation." Lit. "for a desert;" cf. Hebr. yᵉšîmôn. Vocalize : yašîmān (qatīl-ān type). Cf. Dt 32 : 10 ; Ps 68 : 8.

tl : "A mound," i.e. a tell ; cf. Hebrew tēl, Aramaic tillā, Arabic telluⁿ, Akkadian tillu.

l[rbq ṣy] Restoration of Dupont-Sommer, who compares Hebr. rbṣ and later Aram. rbʿ, "lie down," often used of animals. The restored form would be a noun, the nomen regens of an extended construct chain. ṣy is restored by Dupont-Sommer on the basis of Is 13 : 21 ; see also 34 : 11-15 ; Zeph 2 : 13-15.

33. ṣby : "Gazelle" ; cf. Hebr. ṣᵉbî, Akkad. ṣabītu, Arab. ẓabyuⁿ, later Aram. ṭabyā. The latter would point to a form like ṣabêy here. See the note above on thry (line 21).

wšʿl : "Fox" ; cf. Hebr. šûʿāl, later Aram. taʿᵃlû, Arab. ṯuʿâluⁿ. Cf. Ez 13 : 4 ; Lam 5 : 18.

ʾrnb : "Hare" ; cf. Hebr. ʾarnebet, Syr. ʾarnᵉbā, Arabic ʾarnabuⁿ, Akkad. annabu. The reš is probably a secondary substitute for the doubled n ; compare Darmeśeq and Dammeśeq ; korsᵉyā and kussu.

šrn : "The wild-cat," well-known as a devourer of fowl and a general pest. Dupont-Sommer relates the word to Akkadian šurānu. However, F. C. Fensham ("The Wild Ass in the Aramean Treaty between Bar-Gaʾayah and Matiʿel," JNES 22 [1963] 185-86) maintains that the final n is not clear and could be read as m. Hence it would be possible to understand šrm as the equivalent of Akkadian sirrimu, "wild ass," an animal which plays a part in ancient Near Eastern maledictions. Cf. J. Nougayrol, "Sirrimu (non *purîmu) ʿane sauvage,' " JCS 2 (1948) 203-8 ; D. J. Wiseman, Vassal Treaties of Esarhaddon, pp. 59-60 (kima sirrimme). Cf. Is 32 : 14. But what about Akkadian s and Aramaic š? Or should one write ś? J. C. Greenfield ("Three Notes on the Sefire Inscription," JSS 11 [1966] 98-105, esp. 98-100) has adequately disposed of Fensham's suggestion and brought together additional data to support Dupont-Sommer's interpretation.

ṣdh : Probably the "owl" ; cf. Arab. ṣadâ, later Aram. ṣadᵉyā or ṣadyā. The latter word, however, can mean in Aramaic either some "unclean bird" or a type of "grasshopper." Either meaning could be defended here, but the owl is obviously preferable in the context. Vocalize : ṣadêh (abs. sg.).

'qh : " Magpie," so Dupont-Sommer, relating it to the Arab. 'aq'aqu^n. Perhaps to be vocalized: 'aqāh (abs. sg. fem.).

'l t'mr : 3 sg. fem. short impf. (= jussive) passive of 'mr; yuqtal type, also attested in Sf I A 36 (t'mr?), 38 (tšbr), 40 (ygzr, ygzrn), 41 (t'rrn?); 42 [tqh], yqhn); Sf II C 3 (y[r]šmn). Dupont-Sommer compares a similar use of 'mr in Hebr. (Ps 40:11; Neh 6:19) in the sense of " mention." It occurs also in Sf I A 36.

qr[yt' h'] : This restoration of Dupont-Sommer makes good sense, as it would refer to Arpad, and the following list of names connected by waw makes the suggestion all the more plausible. They are probably the " daughter-cities " of Arpad (cf. Num 21:25, 32, etc.), towns (or even regions) which were subject to Matî'el. M. Noth (ZDPV 77 [1961] 136, n. 51) observes that the words beginning with mem might seem to be appellatives rather than proper names; but since they are coordinated to obvious names, they too should undoubtedly be so regarded.

34. mdr' : Its location is unknown. The root in the name may be like that of Dūrā (Dn 3:1) or Akkad. Dūru. S. Segert (ArOr 32 [1964] 122) would consider this name to be an emphatic state of a common noun, meaning " settlement. "

mrbh : A name perhaps like the Biblical M^eríbāh (Ex 17:7; Ps 95:8; etc.). Its location is unknown.

mzh : Perhaps Mazêh. Dupont-Sommer refers to Mazî, the name of place near Tyre attested in the Talmud.

mblh : Unknown site.

šrn : " Sharun." This is probably the town of Sa-ru-na mentioned in one of the inscriptions of Tiglathpileser III as one of the alāni ša ^mat Bīt A-di-ni (see S. Schiffer, op. cit., p. 71). See also W. F. Albright, The Vocalization of the Egyptian Syllabic Orthography (American Oriental Series 5; New Haven: American Oriental Society, 1934), p. 55. It is probably to be identified with modern Sārîn, about 31 mi. NNE of Tell Refâd, on one of the tributaries of the Sājûr River. Cf. D. D. Luckenbill, ARAB, 1, §821; K. Elliger, Festschrift Otto Eissfeldt (Halle a. d. S.: M. Niemeyer, 1947), p. 93.

tw'm : " Tu'im." Dupont-Sommer compares this name with Tu'immi in the Annals of Tiglathpileser III (III. 24, 148; ed. P. Rost): Tu-'-im-mi. cf. D. D. Luckenbill, ARAB, 1 §772. If this identification is correct, then we have another instance of a medial long u written with waw.

byt'l : Though no Bethel is known in Aramaic territory, this name is probably the same as the biblical name (cf. Gn 12:8; 13:3; etc.).

bynn : Unknown site.

35. [']*rnh* : Understood by Dupont-Sommer as Arne, one of the principal towns of the kingdom of Arpad, perhaps the modern Erwin, situated *ca.* 13 mi. SW of Arpad; see R. Dussaud, *Topographie historique de la Syrie*, p. 468. M. Noth (*ZDPV* 77 [1961] 137) suggests that this may be ^{uru}*Ḥaurāni* (*Ḥa-u-ra-a-ni*) of Tiglathpileser III's list (Kleine Inschrift, 2.26); it has been identified by K. Elliger (*Festschrift O. Eissfeldt*, p. 93) with Ḥawart en-Nahr, *ca.* 9 mi. ENE of Arpad.

ḥzz : " Ḥazaz." Most likely the *Ḥazazu* of various Akkadian texts; see S. Schiffer, *op. cit.*, p. 71 ; D. D. Luckenbill, *ARAB*, 1. §821. It lay east of the upper course of the River 'Afrîn, *ca.* 8 mi. NNW of Arpad. The modern Arabic name, however, is *A'zâz*.

'*dm* : " Adam." Probably the same place as that mentioned in line 10 (see note there).

'*yk zy* : The same formula is found in lines 38, [39] ; but in line 37 we have '*ykh zy*. The latter should not be taken as evidence that the former form was pronounced '*aykā*, the difference being merely graphic. It is more likely a fuller form with the adverbial ending *ā*; cf. P. Leander, *LFLAA*, §47*b*. It is a formula used to introduce curses which are to affect Matî'el and his people; they are accompanied by some dynamistic rite, symbolizing the gravity of the oaths sworn. Cf. the passage in the treaty of Aššurnirāri V (Obv. I, 15 ff.), where Mati'ilu is compared to a ram taken from the herd at the head of which he will no longer stand. The Akkadian equivalent of '*yk zy* is *ki ša*, a formula also used in a series of similar curses in Esarhaddon Vassal Treaties (1. 530).

tqd : " Is burned." 3 sg. fem. impf. Peal of *yqd* (stative formation); vocalize : *tiqqad*.

š'wt' : " Wax." The meaning is clear, but the vocalization and orthography present a bit of a problem. In Syriac the form attested is *š*^e'*ôtā* and *š*^e'*ūtā*, whereas Jewish Aramaic preserved it as *ša'awtā*, *š*^e'*ūtā* and *ša'^awātā*. The Hebrew form is *ša'^awāh*, and the Arabic *sa'watu*ⁿ. Hence the question arises, do we have the form *ša'awta'* or *ša'ūta'*? It is hard to say for certain, but it would be better to regard the form as diphthongal, given the predominance of evidence for the *plena scriptio* of uncontracted diphthongs over against that for medial long *u*. S. Segert (*ArOr* 32 [1964] 125) prefers to regard it as a fem. in *-ût*. H. Bauer (*op. cit.*, p. 9) pointed out the similarity of these ritual formulae involving wax figurines to the Hittite military oaths (see J. Friedrich, " Der hethitische Soldateneid," *ZA* 35 [1924] 163 : I, 41-45 ; II, 1-3 [*ANET*, p. 353]). Here the figurine was roughly in the form of a town; in line 37 it would represent Matî'el (cf. line 39 " man of wax "). See also Esarhaddon's Vassal Treaties (ll. 608-10).   For references relating this practice to the larger context of magic, see J. Cantineau (*RA* 28 [1931] 174); C. Picard, " Le rite magique des εἴδωλα de cire brûlés, attesté sur trois stèles araméennes de Sfiré," *RevArchéol* 1961, 85-88.

b'š : " By fire." Dupont-Sommer calls attention to the masculine form of the noun here, whereas in later Aramaic it is usually fem.: *'šh* (AšOstr 17; *AP* 30,12; *A* 103,104,222), *'iššātā, 'eššātā* (Syr.). Cf. Akkad. *ušātu*, Ugar. *ušt*. The form of Dn 7 : 11, *'eššā* (with *aleph*, not *he*) is usually regarded as fem. sg. abs. There is no reason why it could not be the emph. sg. m., related to the form found here. — For a similar expression see Ps 68 : 3.

At the end of this line Dupont-Sommer supplies *w[bnth r]bt*, which he translates, " et [ses filles nom]breuses," referring to the daughter-cities of Arpad (see note on *qryt' h'*, line 33). The first word seems plausible, but the restoration of *[r]bt* raises certain questions, which Dupont-Sommer himself sensed. Can the abs. pl. fem. (archaic form like Sf III 2,22) modify a suffixal form? Does the adj. *rb* ever have the meaning " many " in Aramaic? Normally, it means " great," and if the restoration is correct, it must be so translated.

36. *wyzr' bhn hdd mlḥ* : " May Hadad sow salt in them." For the practice of spreading salt on a devastated town, see Jgs 9 : 45 (Abimelech treats Shechem in this fashion); Dt 29 : 22; Jer 17 : 6; Zeph 2 : 9; Jb 39 : 6. The same practice is attested in Assyrian annals; see the Cylinder Inscription of Tiglathpileser I, VI : 14; cf. E. A. W. Budge and L. W. King, *Annals of the Kings of Assyria* (London : British Museum, 1902), l. 79; E. Weidner, *AOB* 1 (1926) 116-17; *AfO* 5 (1928-29) 90-91 (line 39). Is this merely " un geste magique," as Dupont-Sommer suggests? Is it not rather a wish expressed that the god Hadad will render the area of the towns completely unproductive — an idea which is expressed by the figure of " sowing salt? "   Cf. F. C. Fensham, " Salt as Curse in the Old Testament and the Ancient Near East," *BA* 25 (1962) 48-50.

šḥlyn : "Weeds." Dupont-Sommer translates this word as "cresson" (watercress), comparing it with the Mishnaic *šiḥlayīm, šᵉḥālîm*, later Aramaic and Syr. *taḥlê* (identified by I. Löw, *Aramäische Pflanzennamen* [Leipzig : W. Engelman, 1881], p. 396, as *lepidium sativum*). The word seems to be related to the Akkad. *saḥlê*, which is used in an identical way in one of the Annals of Aššurbanipal : *nagē* ᵐᵃᵗ*Elam*ᵏⁱ *ušaḥrib ṭābta* ˢᵃᵐ*saḥlê ušappiḥa ṣiruššun*, " the districts of Elam I laid waste, salt and cress (or tares) I strewed thereon " (G. R. Driver, *AfO* 8 [1932-33] 204); see Rassam-Cylinder, VI. 78-80; D. D. Luckenbill, *ARAB* 2. §811; *VAB* 7.56-57.

The context of both the Akkad. and Aram. texts demands the name of some destructive weed. The form is problematical also. Is it *šaḥlīn* (with medial long *i* fully written) or *šaḥlayin*? Even the quality of the first consonant may be questioned; if it is related to the Mishnaic and Syriac words, it would be *š*. Cf. also the occurrence of the word in the Elephantine Ostracon (Cairo Museum, No. 35468b): *wšḥlyn ṭb ks' z'yr'* (*RES* 3.1296; *AC* 35). Cf. R. C. Thompson, *A Dictionary of Assyrian Botany* (London: British Academy, 1949) 55-61; B. Landsberger, *OLZ* 25 (1922) 343, n. 3.

w'l t'mr gnb' znh w[nbš' z'] mt''l wnbšh h' : This is the reading of Dupont-Sommer, which he translates, " et qu'on n'en parle plus! Ce bandit(?)-ci et [cette âme-ci], c'est Mati'el et son âme." In such an interpretation *t'mr* is taken as 3 sg. fem. impf. pass. (*yuqtal* type; see note on line 33 above). The identification of Matî'el with a figurine would then be the burden of the next sentence. It has in its favor a similar statement of identity found in the treaty of Aššur-nirāri V (Obv. I, 21-22): " This head is not the head of the ram; it is the head of Mati'ilu." The difficulty is the meaning of the word *gnb'*. Normally, it would mean " thief " (*gannābā*); Dupont-Sommer mentions another meaning found apparently only in Jewish Aramaic, " tail " (*gōn*ᵉ*bā* or *g*ᵉ*nūbtā*). The latter meaning does not fit the context at all; the former meaning is not too satisfactory either. But there is a further difficulty. The sentence beginning with *w'l t'mr* seems to have *gnb' znh* as its object. Could it not possibly be, " And you shall not mention this *GNB'*; the GNB' is Matî'el and it is his person," reading *w'l t'mr gnb' znh w[gnb' h']* *mt''l wnbšh h'*. For prohibitions in the treaty, cf. Sf III 9.

37. *nbšh*: If the reading is correct, this is another case of *nbš* instead of *npš*; see note on Sf I A 31 (*btn*) and Sf III 6. The following *h'* (singular) is hardly the copula for both *mt''l* and *nbšh*, as Dupont-Sommer seems to take it. Vocalize: *hī'*.

kn yqd m[t''l b']š : " So may Matî'el be burned by fire." Cf. Esarhaddon's Vassal Treaties (ll. 608-11): " Just as they burn an image (made) of wax in the fire and dissolve one of clay in water, so may your figure burn in the fire and sink in water."

38. *tšbr* : Lit. " Is broken." The form is 3 sg. fem. impf. pass. (*yuqtal* type; see note on line 33). The verb which precedes is sg., even though the subject is compound, *qšt'* (fem. sg.) and *ḥṣy'* (masc. pl.).

ḥṣy' : " Arrows," the cognate of Hebr. *ḥēṣ*, later Aram. *ḥṭ* (A 126, 128), Arab. *ḥuzwatuⁿ*, Akkad. *uṣṣu*. See below, I B 29.

'*nrt* : " Inurta," i.e., Ninurta. According to Dupont-Sommer the reading '*nht* is " practically certain," even though he does mark the *he* with a dot. Ronzevalle and Bauer had both read it as *reš*, while G. R. Driver preferred a *šin*. The latter is in my opinion definitely to be excluded as a reading, even though the reading now adopted here comes substantially to what Driver was aiming at. Dupont-Sommer interpreted the word '*nht* as the name of the goddess *Ana-hita*, the Persian goddess of fertilizing waters, who is here coupled with Hadad. He claimed that she was later identified with Ishtar and became quite popular in the Semitic world. In the Hellenistic world she was known as *Anaitis*. In favor of this identification he cited the similar " smashing of a bow " ascribed to Ishtar, " the lady of battle and war," in Esarhaddon's Vassal Treaties (see line 453); cf. D. J. McCarthy, *op. cit.*, p. 202. Even though the preceding verb (*yšbr*) is again singular (see note above on *tšbr*), the copula before Hadad's name calls for the name of some other deity preceding it. In this regard Dupont-Sommer's suggestion is plausible; but it is otherwise linked to his questionable thesis that KTK is Urartu, which he maintains was under early Median influence; and this would explain the presence of Anahita there. But, as M. Noth has pointed out (*ZDPV* 77 [1961] 165), would one expect the name of Persian goddess here, in a text coming from the middle of the eighth century? Noth rightly rejects this identification and would rather read '*ngt*, the name of an otherwise unknown deity (see his restoration of I A 7). But his suggested reading is scarcely convincing. J. C. Greenfield (*JSS* 11 [1966] 100-3) has brought together several telling arguments against the reading '*nht* and its interpretation as Anahita: (1) This name is first attested epigraphically only about three centuries later; (2) the identification of Anahita with Ishtar is also highly questionable at this period, even if it is admissible in Hellenistic syncretism; (3) the preceding verb *yšbr* (3 sg. masc.) would call for a masc. name as the first deity of the pair. Consequently, Greenfield proposes to return to the reading of Ronzevalle, '*nrt*, and to interpret it as " Inurta," i.e., Ninurta, a god of both fertility and of battle (see D. Edzard, " Ninurta," *Wörterbuch der Mythologie* [ed. H. W. Haussig; Stuttgart: E. Klett, 1961], I. 114-115). He is known particularly as a god who breaks the weapons of the enemy (*ᵈNinurta qardu ašārid ilāni ᵍⁱˢkak-kēšunu ušebbir*, " warlike Ninurta, eminent among the gods, broke their weapons "; cf. E. Ebeling, *MAOG* 12/2, p. 8, line 31). More-over, Greenfield has found Ninurta and Hadad (called Zababa and Adad) closely related in the curse formulae of the *Narû* inscriptions (cf. *CH* rev. xvii, 61-90). The spelling of the name, '*nrt*, is also found on an Aramaic (Ammonite?) stamp-seal, recently published by N.

Avigad ("Seals of Exiles," *IEJ* 15 [1965] 222-32, esp. 222-28): *ḥtm mng'nrt brk lmlkm*, "seal of Mannu-ki-Inurta, blessed by Milkom." The form *'nrt* represents the Assyrian phonetic pronunciation of the name which appears as *'nwšt* (= Inušta) in Aramaic dockets on Babylonian tablets (see A. T. Clay, "Aramaic Indorsements on the Documents of the Murašu Sons," *Old Testament and Semitic Studies in Memory of William Rainey Harper* [Chicago: University Press, 1908], I. 285-322; see esp. Nos. 27, 31, 14, 25. L. Delaporte, *Épigraphes araméens* [Paris: P. Geuthner, 1912], Nos. 51, 52, 62, 75. *Éphem* 3.63. See further H. Tadmor, "A Note on the Seal of Mannu-ki-Inurta, *IEJ* 15 [1965] 233-34).

     [*qšt mt''l*] : This restoration is demanded by the phrase at the beginning of line 39. For parallels to the breaking of weapons by a god, see the Code of Hammurabi, R 28, 3-4 (G. R. Driver and J. C. Miles, *Babylonian Laws* (Oxford: Clarendon Press, 1955], 2, 104-5); R. C. Thompson, *The Prisms of Esarhaddon and Ashurbanipal* (London, 1931), p. 12, line 75; treaty of Esarhaddon with Ba'al of Tyre (Rev. II, 18); Hos 1:5 (*w ᵉšābartî 'et-qešet yiśrā'ēl*); Jer 49:35.

39.   *rbwh* : "His nobles." For the suffix see the note on Sf I A 5.

     y'r : "Is blinded." This form is prob. 3 sg. masc. impf. pass., not of the simple stem, but of the causative stem of *'wr* (= is caused to be blind). A few Hophals are recognized in Biblical Aramaic (see *BLA* §36r,t). This form would rather be an *'Ophal*, since there is no *he* present before the *'ayin*. *'Ophal* perfects have turned up in a text from Qumran Cave 4; see J. T. Milik, "Hénoch au pays des aromates," *RB* 65 (1958) 71 (*'hzy't* 4QHenᵇ 1 i 5,8; *'hlp*[*t*] 4QHenᵈ 6,8; *''brt* 4QHenᵈ 7). Cf. the Hebr. impf. pass. Hoph. (?) *yûdaš* from the hollow root *dwš*. Vocalize: *yu'ar*. — For similar cases of the blinding of figurines, see the treaty of Aššurnirāri V (Rev. VI, 2) and the Hittite military oath (III, 2-10).

40.   *ygzr* : "Is cut in two." 3 sg. masc. impf. pass. (*yuqtal*-type). The cutting up of a calf in a rite of covenant-making resembles the scene found in Gn 15:9-18; see further Jer 34:18, where the calf is cut in two and the contracting parties pass between the bloody parts of the victim, symbolizing their readiness to suffer the same fate if they violate the pact. For a full discussion of the possible meanings of this rite, see J. Henninger, "Was bedeutet die rituelle Teilung eines Tieres in zwei Hälften?" *Bibl* 34 (1953) 344-53; A. González Nuñez, "El rito de la alianza," *Estudios bíblicos* 24 (1965) 217-38. Cf. the figurative use of *gzr* in line 7 above. In the treaty of Aššurnirāri V (Obv. I, 13-14) a ram is mentioned as being brought up explicitly to conclude the pact (*a-na a-di-e* ᵈ*Aš-šur-nirāri ... itti* ᴵ*Ma-ti-'-ilu ša-ka-ni*); the enumerated parts of the ram (head, hind leg, blood) suggest dismemberment. Cf. Esarhaddon's Vassal Treaties (ll. 551-54). These parallels make the alternate translation given by H. Bauer and F. Rosenthal, " castrate," rather unlikely.

'gl' znh : " This calf." The same animal is used in the rite of Jer 34 : 18 (*hā'ēgel*) and of Gn 15 : 9 (*'eglāh*).

rbwh : " His nobles," see note on line 39.

[*w'yk zy t'rr z*]*n*[*yh*] : " And just as a harlot is stripped naked ...." We have accepted here the suggestion of D. R. Hillers (*op. cit.*, pp. 58-60), which pressed to its logical conclusion the suggestion that Bauer had made; we had preferred to read a form of *'rr* at the end of line 40 to correspond with *y'rrn* in the following line. Dupont-Sommer reads *y'bd* and *y'bdn* and translates, " [Et de même que sert ce]lui-[ci], qu'ainsi servent les femmes ...." He admits, however, the difficulty that *'bd* does not have the meaning of "serve, be a slave," in Aramaic, even though the noun *'abdā* does occur. Only the tops of the letters *bd* are preserved and they could just as easily be read *rr*. This reading was suggested long ago by H. Bauer (*op. cit.*, p. 10) and seems to us to have more to commend it than *'bd*. It makes good sense in the context, and there are the biblical parallels in Nah 3 : 5; Jer 13 : 26-27; Ez 16 : 37-38; Hos 2 : 5 to support Hillers' contention that one should read *znyh*, " harlot," instead of the demonstrative pronoun *znh* (which otherwise lacks a noun). *t'rr* would be 3 sg. fem. impf. pass. (*yuqtal*-type) and *y'rrn* would be the 3 pl. fem. of the same form; vocalize *yu'rarān*. H. Bauer mentions the practice of Assyrian kings which parallels this curse. Hillers is undoubtedly right in suggesting that this curse is probably not accompanied by any ritual action.

42. [*tqḥ*] : 3 sg. fem. impf. pass. (*yuqtal*-type), agreeing with the restored fem. subject. See note on Sf I B 27.

wymḥ' : " One strikes." This form is preferably explained as 3 sg. masc. impf. Peal active (not passive, as Dupont-Sommer would have it, for it would have to be fem. to be treated as passive). The subject is impersonal, " and one strikes."

'pyh : " Her on the face," lit. " (strikes) against her face." The form *'pyh* is written fully (contrast *'lh* in line 32) and is probably to be vocalized as *'appayh*; for other examples cf. Sf III 9, 23.

yqḥn : 3 pl. fem. impf. pass. (*yuqtal* type) of *lqḥ*, with assimilated (?) *lamedh*; see note on Sf I B 27.

There is scarcely any connection between the end of face A and the beginning of face B. The relation of the treaty (or treaties) on the two sides of this stele is still a matter of dispute. Dupont-Sommer is inclined to think that the preamble and the beginning of the stipulations of the treaty on face B began on the left side (= face D), the side that was subsequently shaved off. M. Noth (*ZDPV* 77 [1961] 122-23), however, considers Dupont-Sommer's view to be quite improbable; he prefers to regard Sf I as the base of some sculpture or relief, on which the inscription of Sf I B really began. In his opinion, face B is more probably the beginning or the front of the monument (further reasons for the priority of face B are given by him on pp. 124, 135, 169). He is accordingly inclined to date Sf I B before 754 B.C. and Sf I A after that year, when Matî'el concluded a pact with Aššurnirāri V; the text of Sf I A would then be " eine (neugefasste) Erneuerung von I B " (p. 169, n. 161). It must be admitted, however, that either the view of Dupont-Sommer or of Noth is possible; there is nothing inherent in the text of Sf I A or B which makes it imperative to date either one before the other; we just do not know what the precise relationship of the two treaties recorded on this stone is. Of the two opinions Noth's is less well-founded for all its citing of apparent reasons. There is nothing that really rules out Dupont-Sommer's suggestion that the text began on face D.

Face B

The reverse side of the inscription, especially in its lower half, is badly preserved. Dupont-Sommer and Starcky have done an excellent job in clearing up many of the obscure points which previously existed. However, many difficulties still remain; we have not been able to solve all of them, but perhaps some of the following remarks will help in the understanding of them. The first line of face B begins in the midst of a sentence, and we are possibly dealing with a new section of the treaty, in which the contracting parties are once again listed. The beginning of the lines on this side of the stele are lost, corresponding to the loss of the end of the lines on face A. But even the loss of seven or eight letters (as calculated by Dupont-Sommer) cannot account for the whole of the beginning of this section. It must have begun on some other part of the monument, possibly on the lost left side, or face D.

1. [*rsmk mlk 'r*]*pd* : " ... 'Attarsamak, the king of Arpad." This phrase is restored by Dupont-Sommer, who argues that something like *'dy br g'yh mlk ktk 'm mt''l br 't* ... must have preceded. H. Bauer

(*op. cit.*, p. 12) was of the opinion that face B represented a renewal of the treaty by the sons of Bir-Ga'yah and Matî'el, which took place after the capture of Arpad by Tiglathpileser III in 740 B.C. However, it is certain that Matî'el is still one of the contracting parties (see B 13, 21), and since the stipulations of the treaty are entirely lacking on face A, the introduction which we have at the beginning of face B must be understood as the solemn introduction to this section. Lines 1-13 stress the sacred character of the treaty.

w'dy bny ... : Cf. Sf I A 2, and notes there.

2. [*bny bny br*] *g'yh :* " [The grandsons of Bir]-Ga'yah." Restored as in Sf I A 2, corresponding to *'qr*; note the similar telescoping of expressions for descendants there.

kl mh mlk : " Any king." The use of this indefinite pronoun in the Sefîre inscriptions (see note on Sf I A 26) is now clear. There is no question here of a king by the name of *plmh* (see J. A. Montgomery, *JAOS* 54 [1934] 425; especially J. Friedrich, " Kein König PLMH in der Stele von Sudschin," *ZA* 9 [1936] 327-28); cf. Sf III 28. This detail of dynastic succession is probably not significant; it is formulaic, and absent in Sf I A. Cf. M. Noth, *ZDPV* 77 (1961) 130.

3. [*ysq wymlk*] *b'šrh :* Dupont-Sommer reads merely [*ymlk*], appealing to Sf I B 22. But the reading of this line in his note does not agree with the reading he gives of the line itself, where we read not *kl mlky' zy ymlkn b'šrh*, but *b'rpd*. The verb usually construed with *b'šr-* is *slq* (see Sf I C 3-4; I A 5); we expect it here, but it is too short to fill out the whole lacuna. Hence we prefer to read [*ysq wymlk*] *b'šrh*. This gives a restoration of eight letters, whereas Dupont-Sommer admits that " il y a place normalement pour 7 signes."

w'm bny gš : " And with the Benê-Gush." See note on Sf I A 16. H. Bauer (*op. cit.*, p. 12) was the first to identify this expression with Bīt-Agūsi.

w'm byt ṣll: " And with Bêt-ṢLL." Though the reading is not certain here, Dupont-Sommer depends on Sf II B 10, *wbyt gš wbyt ṣll*, where it is certain and *byt gš* is coordinated with *byt ṣll*.

Dupont-Sommer would idenitfy the name as topographical, the Aramaic name of ᴷᵘʳ*A-ṣal-li* (*ARAB*, 1. §475, 480). Since, however, this district lies on the route from Calah to Carchemish, to the west of Bīt-Baḫiani, there is the problem, which Dupont-Sommer recognized, of Arpad extending its power so far to the east. M. Noth (*ZDPV* 77 [1961] 129) prefers to regard the name as dynastic, being parallel to *byt gš*. Both here and in Sf II descendants of Matî'el are mentioned in the immediately preceding context. This would suggest that *byt ṣll* is the name of a prominent family in Arpad.

wʿm ʾr[m klh] : "And with all Aram." Restored according to Sf I A 5. This seems to imply that the title of Matîʿel is really "king of Arpad and of all Aram." Cf. Bir-Hadad 3 (= *KAI* 201.3).

4. *wʿd]y ktk* : Cf. Sf I A 3.

bʿly : "The lords of (Arpad)." See note on Sf I A 4. Here they are clearly distinct from the "people" (*ʿmh*), line 5.

5. *wʿdy ʾlhy ktk ʿm ʿdy ʾ[lhy ʾrpd]* : "And the treaty of the gods of KTK with the treaty of the gods of Arpad." The sacred character of the treaty is stressed in the statement that it is not merely concluded in the presence of the gods (Sf I A 6 ff.), but is a treaty of the very gods themselves. Cf. Sf I B 23, 33 ; Sf III 4, 14, 17, 23 ; and D. J. McCarthy, *op. cit.*, p. 40.

6. *w]ʿdy ʾlhn hm zy śmw ʾlhn* : "For this (is) the treaty of the gods, which the gods have concluded." Possibly *ky* would be a better restoration before *ʿdy*, if there be room for it ; it occurs in Sf III 22. For the idiom *ʿdy* *śym*, see note on Sf I A 6-7.

ṭby mlk [br gʾyh lʿl]mn : The restoration and interpretation of the last part of this line and most of line 7 are quite conjectural. Dupont-Sommer reads *ṭb ymlk* at the end of this line, "Qu'heureusement règne [Bar-gaʾayah à jam]ais." This is not an impossible solution, but the adverbial use of *ṭb*, modifying a verb, strikes us as strange, and is otherwise unattested, as far as we know. There seems to be a wish expressed here, as Dupont-Sommer acknowledges. Another possibility is to divide the letters differently : *ṭby mlk*. In this case we would have the construct pl. *ṭūbay* (from *ṭūbā*, "goodness"), often used in wishes in the Targums, and akin to Hebrew *ʾašrê*. In such an interpretation we would expect *mlkʾ*, if the second word meant "king." However, it is possible that *mlk* means rather "reign, kingship," and is a cst. itself. Hence translate "Happy forever be the reign of B." Vocalize : *ṭūbay mulk*. See the note below on Sf I C 6.

7. *[lʿl]mn* : The more usual Aramaic expression for "forever" is *ʿd ʿlm* (Sf III 24, 25) or *lkl ʿlmyn* 1QapGn 20,12 ; 21,10.12 [here, however, with the Hebr. ending -*m*]) But in Dn 2 : 4,44 ; 3 : 9 ; 5 : 10 we find *lʿlmyn* The wish refers to the everlasting character of the pact which is sworn, especially in the presence of gods ; cf. Gn 9 : 16 (*bryt ʿwlm*) ; Ex 31 : 16 ; Lv 24 : 8 ; 2 Sm 23 : 5 ; etc.

mlk rb : " A great king." At first sight the expression, coming behind the name of a king (if correctly restored), reminds one of the common Akkadian title, *šarru rabbu*. The phrase is in the absolute state, and Dupont-Sommer interprets it as a predicate, " (en tant que) roi grand." He remarks, " S'ils étaient en apposition, il faudrait l'état emphatique : *mlk' rb'*." Donner - Röllig (*KAI*, 2.253) also sense the syntactic problem, and prefer to regard the phrase as an adverbial construction, rather than an appositive. This too is forced. It seems that much depends on the nuance to be conveyed. In fact, the absolute is often used with proper names as an appositive; see *byt'l 'tr dy 'nth ytb*, " Bethel, the place where you are dwelling " (1QapGn 21, 9); *'srwk br plṭw kmr zy ḥn[wm]* (*AP* 13,15); *'nny br 'z[ryh l]ḥn lyhw* (*BMAP* 1,2 ; see further 2,2 ; 3,3.25 ; esp. 12,20). — The expression would refer, according to M. Noth (*ZDPV* 77 [1961] 146), to Bir-Ga'yah as head of the *ḥbr*, mentioned in Sf I A 4. It is, moreover, the classic title of the suzerain in the Hittite treaties (see D. J. McCarthy, *op. cit.*, 29); cf. *ANET*, p. 203.

wm'[dy]' 'l[n ...] wšmyn : An almost unintelligible phrase due to the lacuna.

8. *yṣrn* : " And all the gods shall guard this treaty." The verb is 3 pl. masc. long impf. Peal of *nṣr*, " guard, keep." Vocalize: *yiṣṣarūn*. Cf. Sf I C 15,17. Being the long impf. with *nun*, it can hardly express a wish here. The same root occurs unassimilated in Nêrab 1,12-13 ; the old orthography (with *ṣ*, as here) is also preserved in the Adon Letter, line 8 (*Semitica* 1 [1948] 44 ; see my treatment of this expression in *Bibl* 46 [1965] 52-54), whereas the later form *nṭr* begins to appear at Elephantine (*AP* 27,1 ; *A* 98, 192, 209). — J. C. Greenfield (*Acta orientalia* 29 [1965] 9) compares the Hebrew *nṣr 'dwt* (Ps 25 : 10 ; 119 : 2).

w'l tštq ḥdh mn mly spr' zn[h] : " And let not one of the words of this inscription be silent." *tštq* : 3 sg. fem. juss. Peal; vocalize : *tištuq*. On *mly spr' znh*, see Sf I C 17 ; cf. K. F. Euler, *ZAW* 14 (1937) 281-91.

9. *[wytšm'n]* : " Let them be heard." So restored by Dupont-Sommer; if correct, it must be vocalized as 3 pl. fem. impf. Ithpe'el, *yitšama'ān*, since the subject is *mly spr' znh*. However, a short impf. is really needed here, something like *ytšm'h* ; but we hesitate, since it is apparently not otherwise attested in this period.

Donner - Röllig (*KAI*, 2.254) think that this expression reveals that the inscription was regarded " magically as a witness," for it can not only hear (cf. Jos 24 : 26-27), but also speak. That the expression is figurative is clear, but that it is intended in a magical sense is another question. But see D. J. McCarthy, *op. cit.*, p. 66, who thinks that " the text is conceived of as an active divine agent which proclaims the treaty by its own power."

[*mn*] *'rqw w'd y'd*[*y w*]*bz* : " From 'Arqu to Ya'di and BZ." We are following here the restoration of Dupont-Sommer as modified by B. Mazar (*BA* 25 [1962] 118.). *'Arqū* has been identified by the latter as 'Arqa in the vicinity of Ṣumur on the coast; cf. Gn 10 : 17 (*'rqy*). It is known from inscriptions of Tiglathpileser III (Kl. Inschrift, I, line 2 ; D. D. Luckenbill, *ARAB*, 1. §772,815,821) and is undoubtedly the city Irqata mentioned in the Amarna letters (cf. J. Knudtzon, *EA*, 75 : 26 ; 100 : 3,8). It has been identified as Tell 'Arqa not far from the basin of the Nahr el-Kabir ; it is thus a southern limit in this descriptive expanse over which the words of the treaty are to be heard. Given the space for the restored *'ayin*, the name has nothing to do with *Raqqu*. Ya'di is the kingdom known from the inscriptions of Hadad (1, 9, 21, 25) and *Panammū* (1, 2, 5, 7, 8, 12), as well as from Kilamuwa I.2 (= *KAI* 24.2). This identification has been accepted by almost all commentators on the Sefîre inscriptions. It indicates that Matî'el, as " king of all Aram," had annexed even the kingdom of Ya'di ; it is presented here as the northern boundary of his realm. The vocalization of the name *Y'dy* is still problematical. The standard vocalization, *Ya'udī*, was based on what many regard as an original false identification : *Yaudu* in Assyrian inscriptions. But this should preferably be interpreted as Judah (in the south). H. Winckler (*Altorientalische Forschungen*, I [Leipzig : E. Pfeiffer, 1897], 1-23) identified the Assyrian *Ya-u-du/i* with the northern district *Y'dy* of the Aramaic and Phoenician texts ; and this led to the vocalization of the Aramaic name as *Ya'udi*. However, it has since been shown that this identification is highly questionable ; see W. F. Albright, *BASOR* 100 (1945) 18, n. 8 ; E. R. Thiele, *JNES* 3 (1944) 156-61 (who showed that Izriyau of *Ya-u-di* in the Assyrian texts is none other than Azariah [Uzziah] of Judah) ; B. Landsbergei, *Sam'al : Studien zur Entdeckung der Ruinenstätte Karatepe* (Erste Lieferung ; Ankara : Türkische historische Gesellschaft, 1948), p. 22, n. 42 ; p. 36, n. 76 (who insists that *Y'dy* in the Kilamuwa inscription must have been pronounced *Ya'adiya* and would scarcely have been represented in Assyrian texts as *Ya-u-du* ; when the latter refer to the northern district, they call it *Sam'alla*) ; and especially H. Tadmor, " Azriyau of Yaudi," *Scripta hierosolymitana* 8 (1961) 232-71. Despite the efforts of G. Garbini (" Sul nome *Y'dy*," *RSO* 31 [1956] 31-35) to relate the name *Y'dy* to the Assyrian *Yaudu* and to derive from the latter its vocalization, it must be recognized that the con-

vincing arguments are all for the contrary view. So we prefer the vocalization *Ya'dī* in Aramaic and *Ya'diya* in Phoenician.

There is a further problem which this line raises and which calls for some comment. According to most commentators *Y'dy* has been regarded as the designation of the *land,* while *Śam'al* has been taken as the name of the capital or principal town of *Y'dy* (e.g., Donner - Röllig, *KAI*, 2. 32, 207, 216). Part of the reason for this view is the occurrence of the name *Sa-ma-al-la* with the determinative *uru*, indicating it was a town or city. In Kilamuwa I.2 the name *y'dy* also occurs in a phrase suggesting that it is a country or land (*mlk gbr 'l y'dy*). If, however, the identification of *'rqw* is correct and it is the town of 'Arqa, then one would expect that the other term of the comparison would also be the name of a town. The identification is further complicated by the fact that *mlk śm'l* occurs in Zakir a 7 as the designation for the king along with the kings of several other lands or countries (*mlk 'rm, mlk qwh, mlk 'mq, mlk grgm, mlk mlz*).

bz : The identification of this name has not yet been established. It may be a name like *Bûz* (Jer 25 : 23 ; Gn 22 : 21), though the latter spot is out of the question here for it lies in the region of Têma and Dedan and is apparently the same as the Assyrian proper name *Bāzu,* " the Arabian hinter-land of the island of Tilmun, modern Bahrein " (W. F. Albright, " Dedan," in *Geschichte und Altes Testament* [Alt-Festschrift ; Beiträge zur historischen Theologie, 16 ; Tübingen : Mohr, 1953], p. 8, n. 2). One would expect it to be the name of a spot in the north near Ya'di.

mn lbnn w'd yb[rdw] : " From Lebanon to Yab[rud]." This phrase suggests a geographical extension similar to the previous one. It probably refers to Mt. Lebanon, often used in the OT as the north border of the land of Canaan (see Dt 11 : 24 ; Jos 1 : 4). Here it would designate the northwestern border of " lower Aram." This suggestion of B. Mazar (*BA* 25 [1962] 118) seems preferable to that of M. Noth (*ZDPV* 77 [1961] 153) that it refers to the Anti-Lebanon. Vocalize : *Libnān* ; cf. Syr. *Lebnān*, Hebr. *L^ebānôn*, Accad. *Labnānu*. For *yb*[...] Dupont-Sommer suggested some name like *yb*[*nh*] or *yb-*[*l'm*]. Our original suggestion that it might be *Yabrūd,* mentioned in the Annals of Aššurbanipal (see S. Schiffer, *op. cit.*, p. 139 ; D. D. Luckenbill, *ARAB*, 2. §818) has found support in the geographical discussion of B. Mazar (*op. cit.*, p. 118). Yabrud is situated on the road from Damascus to Aleppo, near el-Nebq. In Hellenistic and Roman times it was called *ta Iabrouda* (see Ptolemy, *Geography*, 5.15). geographical discussion of B. Mazar (*op. cit.*, 118). Donner - Röllig (*KAI*, 2. 254) make no attempt to restore the lacuna.

10. [*wmn dmś*]*q w'd 'rw wm..w :* At the beginning of this line the
lacuna is one of ten letters according to the transcription of Dupont-
Sommer. The first three letters are restored as the end of the name
Yabrud (*-rdw*), the final *waw* being used in conformity with the
spelling of other names which end thus in these lines. It is not
certain, however, and could be dropped. But even if it is read (with
B. Mazar), there is still room for seven letters and therefore Mazar's
restoration of the beginning of the line is insufficient. He proposes
this: [*rdw wdmś*]*q w'r'rw wm*[*nṣ*]*wt*, " (from Lebanon to) Iab[rud,
and Damas]cus, and Aroer and Ma[ns]uate, ..." (*op. cit.*, p. 118). He
is led to this interpretation by the association of Damascus and Aroer
in Is 17:1-2. But on closer inspection there are several difficulties
which must be faced here: (a) the need for more letters to fill up
the lacuna (as already mentioned); this calls for *wmn* before the
name *dmśq*; (b) if the restoration of *wmn* is correct, then there must
be a corresponding *w'd*, as in line 9. If this is accepted, then Dupont-Sommer's otherwise very plausible reading *w'r'rw* (which he
understood as *'Arâ'iru* and related to the name for three different
cities mentioned in the OT: one in Moab [Nm 32:34, = *'r'r* of Meša'
26], another in Transjordan east of Rabbat Ammon [Jos 13:25; Jgs
11:33], a third in Judah [1 Sm 30:28, perhaps = *Araru* of the
Amarna letters, *EA*, 256.25]) is called in question. If we read the
first three letters of this complex as *w'd*, then we are left with a
name *'rw*, coordinated to a topographical name *wm..w*. Here B.
Mazar reads *wm*[*nṣ*]*wt*, and although he italicizes the final *t*, there is
no possibility of reading it. Dupont-Sommer makes no provision for
an extra letter at this point and there is no trace of a *taw* in the
photograph. Consequently, his restoration is implausible, and we
prefer to leave this lacuna blank for the time being. — As for *'rw*,
which emerges from the division of the words proposed above, is it
not possible that this is the town called *Arā* in the *Annals* of Tiglathpileser III, line 128 (see D. D. Luckenbill, *ARAB*, 1. §770). It was
the town later called Arra in Chalcidice, twenty miles south of Chalcis,
and identified with modern Ma'arrat en-No'mân, SSE of Aleppo; see
E. Ebeling, *Reallexikon fur Assyriologie*, I. 125. This would give yet
another expanse in the present context, from Damascus to 'Aru.

[*wm*]*n bq't w'd ktk :* "And from the Valley to KTK." The
fem. noun *bq't* (obviously abs. sg.) must be related to the Hebr.
biq'āh " valley." But to what valley does it refer? It must be used
here as a proper name. In the Bible, as Dupont-Sommer has noted,
the Hebrew word can designate the valley of the Jordan (Dt 34:3),
the plain of Esdrelon (Zech 12:11), " valley of the Lebanon " (Jos
11:17; 12:7; cf. Amos 1:5 *bq't 'wn*), and the plain of Shinar (Gn

11 : 2). Dupont-Sommer hesitates between the last two, but prefers the latter because he identifies KTK with Urartu. The expression would thus indicate the extent of the Urartian-Aramaean coalition against Assyria. This depends, once again, on the correctness of the identification of KTK as Urartu. The mention of Lebanon in the previous line and of *bq't* here seems to point to a region closer to what is called today the Beqa'. The words of the treaty are to be heard *from* an area near the land of Arpad; hence it seems better to look for the places introduced by *mn* in the region around Arpad. Since M. Noth (*ZDPV* 77 [1961] 154) eventually identifies KTK with Kisik in southern Mesopotamia, he understands *bq't* here to refer to a river-plain of the middle Euphrates. This is implausible; see below, pp. 131-32.

11. *b]yt gš* : See note on Sf I A 16.

'*šrthm* : "Avec leur sanctuaire (?)." So Dupont-Sommer interprets this word, which is not read with certainty. He relates it to the Akkad. *aširtu*, "sanctuary." For '*šr* meaning "a sanctuary," see Pyrgi 1 (cf. *JAOS* 86 [1966] 288-89); *CIS* 1. 3779 : 6.

12. *bmṣr wmrbh* : Possibly the two places which occur above; Sf I A 5, 34.

21. The lower half of face B seems to deal entirely with treaty-stipulations. Certain phrases show that in general they are of the same type as those in Sf III. The latter aids somewhat in the interpretation of this face.

wlyšm' : "And ... will not obey." An example of the prefixed negative *lā-*; see Appendix, Morphology, IV.2; and note on Sf III 5. The introductory conjunction, "if," does not appear here, but probably it occurred in the foregoing lacuna; it is demanded by the sense. It is however, possible, as Dupont-Sommer suggests, that the *waw* has the force of *hn*, as in Hebrew. Note the similarity of this part of the treaty with Sf II B 2-3.

23. *lmnyn* : Unintelligible in the context; perhaps one should read *lšmyn*.

šqrtm : Here probably 2 pl. masc. pf. Pael; see note on Sf III 4.

z[y bspr' znh] : "Which is in the inscription," restored as in Sf I B 28, 33. *spr'* denotes here the text of the inscription engraved on stone; there is no reason to suppose that it was written at first on some soft material. In Sf I C 17 we find *mly spr' zy bnṣb' znh*, "the words of the inscription which (is) on this stele." Such a use of the root *spr* to express an inscription engraved on stone sheds interesting light on the expression *spr hbryt* in Ex 24 : 7 ; 2 Kgs 23 : 2 ; 2 Chr 34 : 30 and especially in 2 Kgs 23 : 21, *kktwb 'l spr hbryt*. See also Jos 8 : 32 ; Is 30 : 8 ; Dt 27 : 2-8 ; Kilamuwa I. 14-15 ; Aḥiram Sarcophagus, 2.   Cf. D. R. Hillers, *op. cit.*, p. 46.

24.   [*tšm'n wtš*]*lmn* :   " You obey and fulfill."   This phrase is restored according to the sense of the context, which demands the opposite of the previous stipulation ; see also Sf II B 4 (*phn tšm'*).   *tšlmn* should probably be understood as Aphel ; vocalize : *tašlimūn*.   See F. C. Fensham, " Clauses of Protection in Hittite Vassal-Treaties and the Old Testament," *VT* 13 (1963) 133-43, esp. pp. 137-38.

   gbr 'dn h' [*'nh*] :   Dupont-Sommer takes only the first three words together, translating, " C'est un homme (avec qui j'ai conclu) des pactes."   *gbr 'dn* seems to be the Aram. equivalent of the Akkad. *bēl adê*, which is used of a vassal in Sennacherib's Annals (*Oriental Institute Prism* [H²], col. II, l. 74 ; ed. D. D. Luckenbill, p. 31 ; cf. *ANET*, p. 287).   It seems to yield better sense to take the restored *'nh* as the subject, " I am an ally."   *'dn* is apparently the abs. pl. of *'dy* and *'dy* ; see note on Sf I A 1.

   [*l'khl l'šlḥ yd*] *bk* :   " I shall not be able to raise a hand against you."   This restoration is based on Sf II B 6 (*pl'khl l'šlḥ y*[*d bk*]).   *'khl* is 1 sg. impf. Peal of *khl* ; *'šlḥ* is 1 sg. impf. Peal of *šlḥ*.   The use of a finite complement to the verb *khl* (or *ykl*), instead of a complementary infinitive (see Sf I B 34 [*l*]*prq wlmšlḥ*), is often found in later Aramaic : see *BMAP* 2, 13 (*l' 'kl 'nṣl lplṭy mn tḥt lbbk*, " I shall not be able to take Palti away from you ") ; 3,14. 17 ; 4,13. 14 ; 6,15bis ; 7,[36]. 38. 40. 41 ; etc.   For the idiom *šlḥ yd b*, cf. Zakir b 21 (*mn yslḥ b*[*h 'yt ydh*]) ; Gn 37 : 22 ; 1 Sm 24 : 11 ; Est 2 : 21 ; Dn 11 : 42. See also Esarhaddon's Vassal Treaties, ll. 66-67, 365.

25.   [*mlh ymll*] *'ly* :   " Should speak a word against me."   Dupont-Sommer restores *mllh ymll*, in which *mllh* is the Pael inf. used as an inf. abs. in Hebrew ; the latter usage is attested in Sf III 18.   There is really no need for an intensifier here, and the idiom seems to be closer to that of Sf III 1-2.   So it would be better to restore simply *mlh*, " a word."

26.   *ḥd mlkn* :   " Any king."   Note the use of the abs. pl. here ; the same expression occurs in line 28.   See note on Sf III 1 ; contrast Sf I B 8.

   mh t[*'bd*] :   " What are you going to do ? "   This conjectural restoration should be understood of some hostile suggestion made by Matî'el or his descendants to some ill-disposed third party, tempted to rebel against Bir-Ga'yah. Vocalize: *ta'bid* (the thematic vowel in later Aramaic is *i*).

27. *wyqtlnh* : " And kill him." 3 sg. masc. energic impf. Peal with suffix; vocalize: *wa-yiqtulinneh*. For energic forms of the impf. before suffixes, see Sf III 17 (*y'brnh*), 20 (? *t'šqny*). For *qtl* instead of *qṭl* (i.e., without emphatic *ṭ*), see further examples, Sf II B 9; Sf III 11, 18, 21; Panammū 8, and Arabic *qatala*.

wyqḥ : 3 sg. masc. impf. Peal of *lqḥ*, " to take." This assimilated form of the impf. also occurs in Sf III 2; but the unassimilated form is found in Sf I B 35 (*ylqḥ*). The impf. Pass. (*yuqtal*-type) was met earlier in an assimilated form in Sf I A [42], 42. Apropos of these forms appearing in the same inscription, cf. the discussion of K. Petráček and S. Segert (*ArOr* 24 [1956] 131-34, esp. p. 133 [" so zeigt es sich, dass im Altaramäischen das Verbum *lqḥ* nicht assimiliert wurde ..."]); cf. *ArOr* 32 (1964) 120. Cf. *AP* 67.18; *CIS* 2.141 : 3.

mn : " Some of (my land)." Dupont-Sommer rightly takes this word in the partitive sense, comparing Gn 8 : 20 (*wyqḥ mkl hbhmh*).

mqny : " My possessions." Related to the Hebr. *miqneh*, " possession, cattle." Vocalize: *miqnay* (pl.); cf. Ex 17 : 3. It is possibly the singular *miqnī*, used collectively.

š[qrt b'd]y' : " You will have been false to the treaty." Cf. Sf I B 23, *šqrtm* (2 pl.). For the formula, cf. the treaty of Mursilis II and Niqmepa of Ugarit (J. Nougayrol, *PRU* 4.97), IV D 2, lines 21', 28',37',40'.

28. *zy bspr' znh* : " Which is in this inscription." See note on Sf I B 23.

y'th : " Comes ;" 3 sg. masc. impf. Peal; vocalize *yi'têh* (< *yi'tay*) and see note on *thry* (Sf I A 21).

ḥd mlkn : See Sf I B 26.

wysbn<y> : " And surrounds me." Dupont-Sommer reads *wysbn* and translates, " et qu'il m'encercle." For such a translation we should expect *wysbny*, since the final *ī* is usually represented by *yodh* in these inscriptions; cf. *t'šqny* (Sf III 20). Since the next word begins with a *yodh* (*y'th*), we should probably regard the loss of the final *yodh* as a case of haplography. Vocalize: *yissubinnī*.

ḥ[ylk] : " Your army." Restored on the basis of the same word in lines 31-32.

29. This line is badly preserved. Dupont-Sommer reads it as follows : ['*ly 'm*] *kl* [..] *ḥṣy' wkl n'p..kwt qpy qpy wtnt 'lyh* [....]. He marks the *ln'* and *kw* as doubtful letters. We are not convinced that he has broken up the letters correctly toward the end of the line; since the vassal is being addressed, it is likely that *wt* goes with *qp*, yielding a 2 sg. masc. verbal form.   Our attempt to read the line — which may suggest to someone else a still better solution — is as follows: [*'ly 'm*] *kl* [*b'l*] *ḥṣy' wkl mh p..k wtqp yqpy wtnt' ly h*[....], " to me with every archer and every sort [of weapon], and you must surround those who surround me and you must draw for me [....]."   For the restoration of *b'l* cf. the Hebr. expression *ba'ªlê ḥiṣṣîm* (Gn 49:23). For *p..k* we have no suggestion, unless the uncertain *waw* is to be read as a *yodh* together with the preceding *kaph*, yielding *ky*.   Could it be *pgz*, like the later Aram. *pāgōzā*, " battering projectile " (Jastrow p. 1132)?   *tqp yqpy* might be regarded as 2 sg. masc. impf. Peal of *yqp* and the Peal ptc. plural with the 1 sg. suffix from the same verb.   *yqp* would be a byform of *nqp*, " to go around, surround " (like *yṣb* and *nṣb*, *y'b* and *n'b* [Bir-RKB 14]).   *tnt'* might be the 2 sg. masc. impf. Peal of *nt'* (attested in Syriac in the sense " to draw"; in Hebrew " to knock out " [Jb 4:10]).   The difficulty with the last suggestion is that this would be a rare case of an unassimilated Pe Nun verb; but cf. *tnṣr* (Nêrab l. 12).   *Pace* Donner - Röllig (*KAI*, 2.256), if written with an *'ayin* in early Aramaic, it can scarcely be related to Hebrew *ntṣ*.

30.   *wpgr 'rb' m'l pgr b'r*[*p*]*d* :   The final *mem* of *'rb'm*, as read by Dupont-Sommer, is not clear; it could be a *nun*.   This badly preserved clause must mean something like, " and I shall pile (lit. " multiply ") corpse upon corpse in Arpad."   Part of it is found again in Sf II B 11:   ]..*y wpgr ..k 'l pgr*[, which confirms the division of words here.   *'rb'n* could be some form of the verb *rb'* (" increase, multiply "). J. C. Greenfield (*JSS* 11 [1966] 103-5) would explain it as the 1 sg. impf. Pael with energic *nun*.   For instances of the latter he appeals to *A* 82 (*'šbqn*, where *k* is to be understood from the context).   Similar forms are found in *AP* 35.5 (*'šlmn*, " I shall pay in full," viz. " it "); *A* 119 (*tlqḥn*, " you shall take "); *AP* 8.10 (*tntnn*); see *LFLAA* §19*d-e*.   Greenfield's explanation of the verbal form in *-n* may be correct, but it is quite anomalous outside of Egyptian Aramaic, and so it gives us pause.   If the *mem* is retained, is it not possible that it is part of the following preposition, like Hebr. *m'l*?   Cf. Ps 108:5. Greenfield cites a number of parallels to the saying itself; these are quite interesting and illuminating: an Akkadian Amorite example in a Mari letter (A 1121, obv. 19-21; cf. A. Lods, " Une tablette inédite de Mari," *Studies in Old Testament Prophecy* [ed. H. H. Rowley; Edinburgh: T. and T. Clark, 1950], pp. 103-10); biblical examples

(Ps 61 : 7, *yamîm 'al-y^emê melek tôsîp* ; Is 30 : 1 ; Jer 4 : 20 ; Job 16 : 14) ; and a Phoenician example (Karatepe [= *KAI* 26], A I 6-8).

mn ḥd mlk : " Some king." The phrase *mn ḥd* is possibly the indefinite expression found seven times in Sf III 9-10 ; there it is usually followed by a *nomen rectum* which is plural, at least in sense. Perhaps *mlk* then has a collective sense here.

l'wyn : As yet unexplained. Donner - Röllig, (*KAI*, 2.256) consider the possibility of the word being related to Hebr. *'awen*, which seems unlikely in the context. Could it be a proper name?

wmwt : S. Segert (*ArOr* 32 [1964] 125) suggests that *mwt* might possibly be the infinitive and would vocalize it *mawt*. If it is the inf., would it not rather be vocalized *mūt* ; and if so, is this another case of medial long *u* being fully written? Cf. Sf III 16, *ymwt* (= *yamūt*).

31. *whn bywm zy 'lhn ... :* " And if on a day when (the) gods ...." We should perhaps expect the emph. state (*bywm'*), but the almost identical expression occurs in Sf I C 20 (*bywm zy y'b*[*d*] *kn*). Cf. also *AP* 30,28 (*mn gbr zy*).

mrḥy' : Unintelligible.

w'[*tm lt'*]*twn* : " You (pl.) do not come." Is *'tm* the form of the 2nd pl. masc. independent personal pronoun at this period? It is not otherwise attested. The forms, however, of *hm* for the 3 pl. masc. (Sf III 5-6) and *-km* (Sf III 5,7,21) for the 2 pl. masc. suffix suggest that the independent form would have had *mem* at this period. Later we find *'antūn* or *'attūn*.

32. *lśgb* : This form is related by Dupont-Sommer to the later Aram. *śgb* (Pael), " to strengthen, fortify." But the form cannot be a Pael inf. here, since it lacks the usual ending (*-ūt* or *-āh*). It must be a Peal inf. without the preformative *mem*.

'yt : This *signum accusativi* occurs elsewhere in these inscriptions : Sf II B 8 ; II C 5(bis), 14 ; Sf III 11,<13> ; see also Zakir b 5, 10, 15, 16, 27. Since it is also attested in Phoenician in the same form, the second letter must be regarded as a consonant. Instead of the vocalization *'ayat*, which we originally proposed (see *CBQ* 20 [1958] 466), we prefer to follow the suggestion of J. Friedrich (*PPG* §256) and vocalize it *'iyyāt* (changing Friedrich's short *a* to a long one in view of the later Aram. form *yāt*; cf. Syriac *l^ewāt* [to which *wth*, Hadad 28, must be related]). S. Segert (*ArOr* 32 [1964] 126) would simply vocalize it *'īt*, which is certainly problematical. The syntactical function of this particle remains a mystery in these inscriptions, since it is not always used and the reason why it is used does not clearly emerge.

33. *wḥb* : Both the *ḥ* and the *b* are marked as doubtful letters. After the foregoing phrase, one would normally expect *whn*.

w'khl my [*byr ...*] : " I shall be able [to drink] water [of the well of ...]." There seems to be question here of the use of the water of some well for Bir-Ga'yah's army. Could one restore the lacuna at the beginning of line 34 thus : [*byr byt ṣl*]*l*?

34. *ysb* : " Whoever lives around." Lit. " as for that well, whoever surrounds." 3 sg. masc. impf. Peal of *sbb*, " surround." See line 28.

[*l*]*prq wlmšlḥ yd* : " Will not be able to destroy (it) or raise a hand against ...". Apparently two infinitives are used as complements to *lyk*[*hl*], whereas a finite complement is used in lines 25 and 39. If [*l*]*prq* is correctly read, then we have a Peal inf. without pre-formative *mem* (contrast *lmšlḥ*) ; see line 32 above (*lšgb*) and note on Sf III 6 (*rqh*).

by[*r'*] : " The well." The word is related to the Hebr. *b*ᵉ*'ēr*, Moab. *br*, later Aram. *b'r* (*AP* 27,6), *br'* (*AP* 27,8), Syr. *bīrā*, Jewish Aramaic *b*ᵉ*'erā* (obviously a Hebraism). In fact, the Hebr. form is often regarded as a hypercorrection. Hence vocalize : *bīra'* (with *plena scriptio* of medial long *i*). S. Segert (*ArOr* 32 [1964] 126) would vocalize it rather as *bayr-*.

35. *lbkh 'w ḥ ....* : Perhaps proper names.

ylqḥ : Note the double occurrence of the unassimilated form of the impf. of *lqḥ*, with which should be compared *yqḥ* (Sf I B 27), *tqḥ* (Sf III 2), *yqḥn* (Sf I A 42). See note on Sf I B 27.

36. [*l*]*'bdt* : " To destroy." Inf. Pael of *'bd*. The *-ūt* ending is found both with and without a suffix (Sf III 11, 15, 16 *hmtty*, *hmtt*). Vocalize : *'abbādūt*. The same form occurs in Sf II B 7. — We can make nothing of the majority of this line, except for the three words at the end.

whn lhn : " And if (you do) not (do) so." This expression, which occurs also in Sf III 4, 9, 14, 20, seems to mean something like, " And if you do not do so," since the usual conclusion is " you will have been false to all the gods of the treaty," or " you will have been false to this treaty." It is a negative protasis, referring to the fore-going stipulation, couched either in the form of a command or of a prohibition. In Sf III 4,14 it follows a positive command ; in the other two cases, it follows a prohibition (lines 9,20). According to Dupont-Sommer the first *hn* is the usual Aramaic conditional conjunc-tion, the *l* is the negative (usually prefixed in these inscriptions ; cf. Sf I B 21), while the second *hn* is probably the 3 pl. fem. pers.

pronoun, used in a neuter sense, " this." He also suggests the possibility of considering the second *hn* as the interjection, " voici " (cf.
Gn 3 : 22 ; 4 : 14 ; 11 : 6 ; etc.). Then the meaning would be, " Et
sinon, voici...." Donner - Röllig (*KAI*, 2.256) follow Dupont-Sommer
in this explanation. But he adds that " voici " in Aramaic is generally *h'*, *hlw*, *'lw*, *'rw*, sensing the difficulty of this explanation. While
lhn occurs in later Aramaic as a subordinate conjunction, meaning
" if not " (or " except " — see *A* 107, 120, 154 ; *AP* 8 : 11, etc. ; *BMAP*
4 : 20, etc.) and also as a coordinate conjunction, meaning " but "
(*AP* 9 : 6, 7, 9, etc. ; *BMAP* 4 : 16, etc. ; Ezr 5 : 12), neither use seems
to fit here, if the preceding *hn* means " if." In favor of the first *hn*
meaning " if " in this stele we have the use of *whn*, " and if," elsewhere (Sf I A 14 ; Sf III 4,6). The second *hn* then is most likely to
be taken as an emphatic adverb, such as occurs in the Sabbath ostracon published by Dupont-Sommer (" L'ostracon araméen du Sabbat
[Clermont-Ganneau 152]," *Semitica* 2 [1949] 31), concave side, lines
3,7. A similar word is also found in *AD* 6 : 2 ; 12 : 3 (which Driver
translates " lo," and would like to change to *h'*). In these texts the
meaning of *hn* seems to be " surely ;" but in the abbreviated phrase
of these Sefîre inscriptions it must mean something like " so." Hence
whn lhn should be understood as " and if not so." Jean - Hoftijzer
(*DISO*, p. 66) also prefer this explanation.

37. There is not enough space for any of the usual formulae found
in these inscriptions involving the word *šq*[*rt*], if it is to end so soon
in [*z*]*nh*. Dupont-Sommer has restored the singular *b'd'*, which is
most unlikely, since the singular is unattested. Either some other
formula, otherwise unknown, was used here, or the engraver has
skipped part of the usual formula ; we should probably read *šq*[*rt*
b'dy' <zy bspr'> z]*nh*.

    whn : This word begins a new stipulation, but most of the line
is illegible. The stipulation must deal with the furnishing of food and
provisions for Bir-Ga'yah's army. Perhaps *lhmy* on this line should
be read as *lḥmy*, as in line 38.

38. *lthb :* " You do not give." Apparently this form is the 2 sg.
masc. impf. Peal of *yhb* with the prefixed negative. This is a rare
occurrence of the impf. of this verb which in later Aramaic is usually
replaced by the impf. of *ntn*. Vocalize : *lā-tihab* (< *tihhab*).

    ...[.]*š' ly lḥm :* " Deduct provisions from me." Dupont-Sommer
suggests restoring here *whn* [*t*]*š' ly lḥm*, " and if you take food away
from me."

wltsk : " And do not deliver." Cf. Sf III 5, 7 (*ltsk lhm lhm*) ; see note on Sf III 5).

39. *lts'* : " You cannot deduct," 2 sg. masc. impf. Peal of *ns'* ; another case of a finite complement to the verb *khl* ; see note on Sf I B 24-25 ; contrast line 34.

    'nh k'ym yqm lk : ? ?

    wtb'h nbšk : Lit. " and your soul will seek," i. e., and you yourself seek. For *nbš* instead of *npš*, see note on Sf I A 37.

40. The lacuna probably contained some words expressing the object of the verb of " going " at the end of line 39. The first two letters preserved suggest a feminine noun with the suffix -*k*, some word coordinated with *lbytk*, perhaps something like *lqrytk*. With the space at the end of line 39 and that at the beginning of line 40 we may suggest reading *wt'zl* [*nbšk lqry*]*tk wlbytk*, " and will yourself go to your town and to your house."

    [*wlk*]*l nbš byty* : " And for every person of my household." Dupont-Sommer compares *napšôt bêtô* (Gn 36 : 6).

41. *wlygz* [*rn m*]*lh mlky* '[*rpd*] : " The kings of Arpad will not cut anything off from them." This restoration is completely conjectural. However, one should note the occurrence of the phrase *mlky* '[*rpd*], the restoration of which is quite likely; cf. Sf III 1,[3],27 ; Sf II C 15. M. Noth (*ZDPV* 77 [1961] 135, n. 48) rejects this obvious restoration in favor of a hypothetical historical reconstruction which is itself " problematisch."

    zy 'dn hy[*n hm*] : Dupont-Sommer suggests the translation, " Parce que [ce sont] des pactes viv[ants] (?)." If correct, we have another example of the abs. pl. of '*dy*' ; see Sf I B 24 and the note on Sf I A 1.

42. Unintelligible except for *lnbšk*.

43. *kn tgzr* : " So you will cut the *'PL*'." The last word looks like '*p l*' at first sight, but it cannot be the conjunction and the negative, since *whn*, " and if," follows it and the negative is usually written merely *l*-. It must then be a noun, the object of *tgzr*, or its subject (if fem.). — Is '*pl*' a metathesis for '*lp*'? See note on Sf I A 40.

44. *y'zz* : Dupont-Sommer suggests that this word is a Pael impf., " he will strengthen."

45. Dupont-Sommer reads this line as follows: .....] *pdy'k'lḥbsrhy wyqḥqḥ bhm w.nt*[.]. However, a number of the letters can be read differently and we find here a sentence related to a stipulation of Sf III. Read [.......]..['*l*] *bry 'w 'l ḥd srsy wyqrq ḥdhm wy't*[*h* ...], and translate, " against my son or against one of my courtiers; and (if) one of them flees and com[es ...]." Cf. Sf III 4-5. In the case of *b* instead of *p* there seems to be a cross-bar discernible in the photograph. The *waw* of *'w* seems quite clear. The traces of the doubtful *ḥ* might just as well be the second *s* in *srsy*. There is nothing against taking the vertical shaft between the two *qoph*'s as a *reš* (*yqrq*).

Face C

The engraving of the inscription on this face of the monument is coarser and less carefully executed.

1. *kh 'mrn* : Probably the 1 pl. pf. Peal, " thus we have spoken." There is no indication that the final long *a*, found in later Aram., was written or pronounced. There is fluctuation in this regard as early as the first letter in Cowley's collection (dated 495 B.C.); cf. *yhbn* (line 2), *yhbnh* (line 5). See P. Leander, *LFLAA* §25*a*. The first plural refers to both Bir-Ga'yah and Matî'el.

[*wkh k*]*tbn* : " And thus have we written." Dupont-Sommer leaves the lacuna vacant and reads a *t* before *bn* only with some hesitation. However, the context seems to call for something like this restoration which had previously been suggested.

mh : " What." The interrogative pronoun used as an indefinite relative; it serves as the subject of the nominal sentence of which *lzkrn* is the predicate.

2. *ktbt* : " I have written," 1 sg. pf. Peal of *ktb*. Matî'el is thus named as the one who has ordered the engraving of the inscription as a reminder of the pact concluded with Bir-Ga'yah.

lzkrn : Vocalize : *la-zikrān* ; cf. Hebr. *zikkārôn*.

4. *ysqn* : Cf. Sf I A 5 ; B 3. Vocalize : *yissaqūn*.

lṭbt['] *y'bd*[*w tḥt*] *šmš'* : " May they make good relations beneath the sun." Dupont-Sommer had translated this clause, " en vue du bien qu'ils agissent devant le soleil," reading *qdm* instead of *tḥt*, which he also admitted as possible. He sensed the difficulty in the expression *qdm šmš'*, even though he could appeal to *A* 93 (*yqyr* [*qd*]*m šmš*), because *qdm* would normally suggest the presence of a deity, and the name Šamaš would scarcely be in the emphatic, if it were meant. For this reason we prefer *tḥt šmš'*, which is closer to the *taḥat haššemeš* of Qoh 1 : 3, 9, 14 ; 2 : 11 ; Tabnit 7 ; Ešmunʿazor 12, even though these occurrences are of later date.

The real problem in this clause, however, is the meaning of *ṭbt'*. Dupont-Sommer understood it as the fem. sg. emph., preceded by the prep. *l*, " pour le bien ;" similarly Donner - Röllig (*KAI*, 2.257). However, W. L. Moran (" A Note on the Treaty Terminology of the Sefîre Stelas," *JNES* 22 [1963] 173-76) has proposed for *ṭbt'* the meaning of " friendship, good relations," or more specifically " amity established by treaty." He appeals to Akkadian parallels which make this interpretation quite plausible. In Akkadian there is the expression *ṭūbtu u sulummû*, " friendship and peace " (cf. L. W. King, *Chronicles Concerning Early Babylonian Kings*, II [London : Luzac, 1907), 58 : 6 ; D. J. Wiseman, *Chronicles of Chaldaean Kings (626-556 B.C.) in the British Museum* [London : British Museum, 1956], 59 : 29 ; *CT* 34 : 29 ii 27), and *ṭābūta* (*ṭābutta*) *epēšu*, " to make (a treaty of) friendship " (Amarna letters, *EA* 136 : 8-13 ; 138 : 53 ; 11 r 22 ; cf. C. Virolleaud, *RA* 38 [1941] 2 : 9-13), and in the Mari letters the semantic parallel of *damqātum* (lit. " good things "; cf. G. Dossin, *RA* 36 [1939] 51). The same Aramaic expression occurs below in Sf I B 19-20 and Sf II B 2, where the fitness of this interpretation is perhaps more evident than here. It is also found in the Adon Letter, line 8 (*wṭbth ʿbdk nṣr*, " your servant has kept his good relations "); see *Bibl* 46 (1965) 52-54. D. R. Hillers has also pointed out that this interpretation illuminates several OT passages as well (" A Note on Some Treaty Terminology in the Old Testament," *BASOR* 176 [1964] 46-47) : Dt 23 : 7 (cf. Ezr 9 : 12) ; 2 Sm 2 : 6 (see also G. Buccellati, *BeO* 4 [1962] 233). Moran, however, attempted no translation of this line of the treaty because the text is so damaged. What we have suggested is not without its difficulties, because the form *ṭbt*['], as restored by Dupont-Sommer, is emphatic ; and we have construed the prefixed *lamedh* as the *signum accusativi* (since the phrase seems to be the equivalent of the Akkadian *ṭābūta epēšu*), even though elsewhere in these inscriptions the form of the latter is rather *'yt*. But cf. Sf I C [23].

6. [*lb*]*yt m*[*lky*] : " For the sake of my royal house." If this reconstruction of Dupont-Sommer is correct, then we must vocalize it *la-bayt mulkī*, for the latter word cannot be *malk* (" king ") and is probably the abstract noun, *mulk-*, " kingship, reign, kingdom." Possibly it also occurs in Sf I B 6. According to H. L. Ginsberg this

word occurs in the Adon Letter (*Semitica* 1 [1948] 44), line 1: *mr'*
mlkn, "lord of kingdoms," equalling the Ptolemaic title *kyrios basi-*
leiôn (see "An Aramaic Contemporary of the Lachish Letters,"
BASOR 111 [1948] 25); but see *Bibl* 46 (1965) 45-47; E. G. Kraeling,
BMAP, pp. 17-18, n. 69. At any rate, *mulku* is found in Ugar. and
Phoen. in the same sense; see *BASOR* 87 (1942) 35, n. 20; *JBL* 56
(1937) 142; *AJSL* 57 (1940) 71-74. The vocalization with *u* is found
in Arab. *mulku*[n] ("sovereignty, Herrschaft"); it is also reflected in
the Wen-Amun Report 2, 19 (*mrk.f*, "his dominion"), compared with
2,12 (*mu-r-ku*), as G. S. Glanzman has informed me.

kl lḥ[yh] : "No evil may be done." On *lḥ[yh]* (fem. sg. abs.)
see the note on Sf III 2.

15. *yṣrw* : "May they keep away"; 3 pl. masc. short impf. (= juss.)
Peal of *nṣr*; vocalize: *yiṣṣarū*. Since this verb is usually construed
with a direct object, Dupont-Sommer concludes that the two following
instances of *mn* cannot be that of the preposition, but must either
be particles (meaning "en vérité, certes") like *mt* in the Hadad and
Panammū inscriptions, or else the interrogative-indefinite pronoun *man*
used in the sense of "ceux-ci, ceux-là." He translates accordingly,
"que des dieux gardent qui ses jours et qui sa maison!" *ywmh*
and *byth* thus become the direct object of the verb *yṣrw*. As a
parallel he appeals to Kilamuwa 10-11 (*w'nk lmy kt 'b wlmy kt 'm*,
"and I was as a father to some and as a mother to others"). However, it is not impossible that the direct object of *yṣrw* has been lost
in the lacuna which precedes. In Hebrew there are a number of
cases of *nṣr* with a direct object and *mn* in the sense of "guard
from dangers, preserve" (see Ps 12 : 8 ; 32 : 7 ; 64 : 2 ; 140 : 2,5). Moreover, the distributive use of *my* in Phoenician is clear, but the parallel
is not exact; for *my ... my* is not used in apposition to a noun already
expressed, as would be the case here.

ywmh : "His day," i. e. his life-time. Dupont-Sommer interprets this form as a plural noun with a suffix (= *yômôhi*). This
cannot be correct, for all other cases of plural nouns with the 3 sg.
masc. suff. are written *plene*, thus *-wh*. The defective writing should
not be admitted until a clear, undisputed case of it is recognized.
Vocalize: *yawmeh*. — For a Hittite parallel to this blessing, cf. the
treaty of Mursilis II with Duppi-Tessub, 21** (*ANET*, p. 205).

17. *lyṣr* : "Will not observe," lit. "keep, guard." Prefixed negative; 3 sg. masc. impf. Peal of *nṣr*. The Akkad. cognate, *naṣāru*, is
used in the identical sense of "guarding the treaty" in Esarhaddon's
Vassal Treaties (line 291); cf. *Bibl* 46 (1965) 52-54.

bnṣb' : See the comment on Sf I A 6. For a similar Hittite
formula, cf. the treaty of Mursilis II and Duppi-Tessub, 20** (*ANET*,
p. 205).

18. *'hld* : " I shall efface." The reading of this word is certain and
is confirmed by Sf II C 1-2, [*wmn y*]*'mr lhldt spry' 'ln mn bty 'lhy'*,
" and whoever will give orders to efface these inscriptions from the
bethels." Two other passages must also be considered: *wyzḥl h' mn
ld spr*[*y*]*' mn bty* [*'*]*lhy'*, " should that (man) be frightened from
effacing the inscriptions from the bethels " (Sf II C 6-7); and *w*[*y*]*'mr
ld* [*sp*]*ry' 'ln mn bty* [*'*]*lhy'*, " and order (him), ' Efface these inscriptions from the bethels ' " (Sf II C 8-10). The various forms of the
verb which occur in these places suggest that we have both Haph.
and Peal forms of the same root, meaning " efface." Dupont-Sommer
suggests that the root is either *lwd* or *ldd*. I believe that *lwd* is
preferable. *'hld* is 1 sg. impf. Haph (vocalize: *'uhalīd*); *hldt* is Haph.
inf. (vocalize: *halādūt*); *ld* is Peal impv. (vocalize: *lūd*). The root
lwd is otherwise unattested in Aram. and Hebr., unless it is the
cognate of *lwz* in Prov 3 : 21; 4 : 21, as suggested by Dupont-Sommer.
S. Gevirtz (*VT* 11 [1961] 144) compares it with *lwz* of Mishnaic
Hebrew, but is this really a different root? Note that in Prov 3 : 21
it is parallel to *nṣr* (as here), and in 4 : 21 to *šmr*. If the root is
correctly analyzed as *lwd* and is related to Hebrew *lwz*, then there is
an interesting case of the early shift of $z > d$ in the writing that
is now attested here.

mn mlwh : " Some of its words." The suffix might refer either
to *spr'* or to Matî'el; our translation has favored the former. For
the partitive use of *mn*, see Sf I B 27. G. Garbini (*RSO* 34 [1959]
47) strangely reads *mlwk*, which is perhaps only a typographical
error.

19. *'hpk* : " I shall upset," the form is 1 sg. impf. Peal of *hpk*,
" overturn, upset." Cf. Dt 23 : 6, where the verb is also used in a
figurative sense; in line 21 it has a more literal force.

ṭbt' : " The good relations," i.e., treaty relations or amity. See
note on Sf I C 4 above. Moran notes (*op. cit.*, p. 176) that the contrast with the generic " evil," which plays on the etymology of *ṭbt'*,
is no real difficulty against the specific meaning he attaches to the
latter.

'śm : 1 sg. impf. Peal of *śym*, " set." Lit. " I shall set (them,
i.e., the good relations [emph. pl. fem.]) for evil things." Vocalize: *'aśīm*.

20.   [*l*]*lḥyt* : Abs. pl. fem.; see note on Sf III 2 (*lḥyt*), cf. Panammū 4 (*qyrt, ḥrbt yšbt*), 8 (*qtylt*), 13 (*mḥnt?*).

    bywm zy : See note on Sf I B 31.

21.   *'š*[*' h*]*'* : " That man." If the reading and restoration are correct, we have another very early attestation of the noun *'š*, "man," in Aramaic; cf. Zakir a 2 ; Hadad 11(?), 34. It is found in this form in both Phoen. and Moabite; the form *'yš* is abundantly attested in later Aramaic (*AP* 8, 11. 12. 16 ; 20,10. 12. 13. 14 ; etc. ; *A*, passim). Vocalize : *'īša'*. This is the first occurrence, however, of the emph. state, if the restoration is correct.

23.   *tḥtyth* [*l'*]*lyth* : " May they make its lower part its upper part," an explanation of the preceding verb *yhpkw*. Cf. E. Herzfeld, " Summa imis confundere," *Archäologische Mitteilungen aus Iran* 5 (1933) 143-48 ; the words are probably fem. forms of the gentilic adjectives *taḥtāy* and *'illāy*.

24.   *w'l yrt* : " And may he not inherit." If this form is interpreted correctly by Dupont-Sommer, we then have an early example of a Proto-Semitic *tha* appearing in Aramaic as *t*, whereas it normally is *š* in these inscriptions. See note on *btn* (Sf I A 31). Vocalize : *yirat* (< *yirrat*).

    šr[*š*]*h* : " His scion." The noun is related to the Hebr. *šōreš*, " root." But it is here used in the sense of " scion " (cf. Is 11 : 10 ; 14 : 29). *šuršu* in Akkad. can also have the meaning of " sprout, scion " (used in parallelism to *līpu*). Vocalize : *šuršeh*. For a similar idea, cf. Eshmun'azor 11 ; Is 37 : 31 (= 2 Kgs 19 : 30) ; Zakir b 28 ; Karatepe (= *KAI* 26) A I 10 ; Larnax Lapethou III.3 (cf. A. M. Honeyman, *Muséon* 51 [1938] 286).

    'šm : The word for " name " is also found elsewhere with a prothetic *aleph* in Aramaic; see Sf II B 7 ; Hadad 16,21 ; *RES* 1786, 10 (?).

STELE II

Stele II was obtained by the Damascus Museum in a very fragmentary form, consisting of a dozen bits. When put together, they yielded the middle portion of three sides of a monument which must have been similar to stele I. The left side, which is preserved in this case with its entire width, equals the width of the side of stele I (35 cm.). For further particulars about the physical state of this stele, see the remarks of Dupont-Sommer (pp. 293-94).

The names of the parties who have made the treaty which is recorded on this stele are the same as those on stele I, viz. Bir Ga'yah (II A 3, B [5]) and Matî'el (II C 14). The character of the curses on face A recalls that of the curses inscribed on Sf I A 21ff., even though there are slight differences. The utterances regarding the fulfilment or the non-fulfilment of the treaty stipulations also recall those of Sf I B 21ff. And the concluding lines of the treaty on face C resemble those of Sf I C 18ff. The differences, slight though they are, show that stele II is not simply a second copy of stele I. It must represent a revision of that treaty, or vice versa. S. Segert (*ArOr* 32 [1964] 111) calls it a " second recension ... with numerous variants." Because of the bad state of preservation of this monument it is really impossible to specify further the relation of steles I and II. They are both closely related to each other, and more so than either of them is to stele III. On this question, see further pp. 3, 94.

TEXT : Sf II

Face A

1 [יהינקן על ואל ישבע ושבע שורה יהינקן עגל ואֹ[ל ישבע ושבע

2 [שאן יהינקן אמר ואל ישבע ושבע עזן יהי֯]נקן גדה ואל יש

3 [בע ושבע בכתה יהכן בשט לחם ואל יהרגן והן יש֯]קר לבר גאיה ול

4 [ברה ולעקרה תהוי מלכתה כמלכת חל ואשמה י֯]תנשי ויהוה קב

5 [רה .... וש]בע שנן שית שב

6 [.............................. וש]בע שנן תהוי [.]

7 [..............................].֯ בכל רברבי ·

8 [.............................].֯ ואת. [.....].֯ וארקה וצע

9 [נקה .... ויאכל֯] פם אריה ופם [..].֯ ופם נמר[ה] ..

10 [ ].֯הו....פ.[.].֯ח.. מ.[...]

11 [ ].א֯ד....בדב֯.[...].....[...]

12 [ ].֯א זי בית ....[..].֯פ.נ.י

13 [ ].֯זו.ב֯ב...[...].....[...]

14 [ ]...צ.ו.[......]...[...]

Face B

1 [ ]....................]

2 [עדיא וטבתא ז]֯י] עבדו אלהן ב[ארפד ובעמה ולישמע מתעאל]

2b ולישמען בנוה

3 [....... לישמען רבוה ולישמע עמה ולי֯]שמען כל מלכי ארפד

4 [ו.................]מ֯ן זי יעורן פהן תשמע נחת ים

5 [הן תאמר בנבשך ותעשת בלבבך גבר עדן אנה ואשמע לבר גאיה]

6 [ובנוה ועקרה פלאכהל לאשלח י֯]ד בך וברי בברך ועקרי בעקרך]

7 [ולחבזתהם ולאבדת אשמהם ו]הן יאמר מן חד בני אשב על כרסא]

8 [אבי ויבע ויזקן ויבעה ברי אנֹית להמתתי ותאמר בנבשך י]

9 [קתל מן יקתל שקרתם לכל אלהֹ]י עדיא זי בספרא זנה [.......]

TRANSLATION

Face A

..... [and should seven mares ¹suckle a colt, may it not be sated; and should seven cows give suck to a calf, may it n]ot have its fill; and should seven ²[ewes suckle a lamb, may it not be sated; and should seven goats suck]le a kid, may it not be sa[ted; ³and should seven *hens* go looking for food, may they not *kill* (anything). And if (Matî'el) should be un]faithful to Bir-Ga'yah and to ⁴[his son and to his offspring, may his kingdom become like a kingdom of sand; and may his name be for]gotten, and may ⁵[his grav]e be .... [and for se]ven years thorns, ŠB[...] ⁶[... and for se]ven years may there be [.] ⁷[...] among all the nobles of ... ⁸[...] and his land. And a cry ⁹[... and may] the mouth of a lion [eat] and the mouth of [a ...] and the mouth of a panther ¹⁰[....] (Lines 10-14 are practically illegible.)

Face B

¹........ ²the treaty and the amity whi[ch] the gods have made in [Arpad and among its people; and (if) Matî'el will not obey], and (if) his sons will not obey, ³(if) his nobles will not obey, and (if) his people will not obey, and (if) [all the kings of Arpad] will not o[bey ...] ⁴YM who *are watchful*. But if you obey, (may) tranquillity [... And] ⁵if you say in your soul and think in your mind, [" I am an ally, and I shall obey Bir-Ga'yah] ⁶and his sons and his offspring," then I shall not be able to raise a ha[nd against you, nor my son against your son, nor my offspring against your offspring], ⁷neither to strike them, nor to destroy their name. And [if one of my sons says, " I shall sit upon the throne] ⁸of my father, for he is *babbling* and grows old," or (if) my son seeks [my head to kill me and you say in your soul, ⁹" Let him kill whomever he would kill," (then) you will have been false to all the gods [of the treaty which

6

10 ‏]..[. נך ובית גש ובית צלל ו‏[
11 ‏]......[..י ופגר ..ך על פגר‏[
12 ‏]......[.י וביום חרן לכל ‏[
13 ‏........ יאתה .ל ברי ובני בנ‏ו‏י
14 ‏]............ מן יד שנאי ו.....ן שקרתם]בעדיא אלן‏[
15 ‏]. רבאב.. כמי ...שמרובשק ‏[.
16 ‏]ולאש יהוונה הן יהונה בקר‏[
17 ‏.להו·ה... הן תבעה ולת ‏[. שק‏]
18 ‏]ר[ת לכל]אלהי ע[דיא זי בספר]א זנה‏[
19 ‏].ליע‏]ן‏[.....]לך יגבר עד..‏[
20 ‏].הנ‏]ן‏[.......]זי יעז מנך ‏[
21 ‏[.....].........].[.‏[

Face C

1 ‏...............]ומן י[א
2 ‏מר להלדת ספריא]א[לן מן ב
3 ‏תי אלהיא אן זי י]ר[שמן ו
4 ‏]י[אמר אהאבד ספרי]א[ולמ]ן[.
5 ‏ן אהבד אית כתך ואית מלך
6 ‏ה ו‏יזחל הא מן לד ספר
7 ‏]י[א מן בתי אלהיא ויאמר ל
8 ‏זי לידע אנה אגר אגר ו]י[
9 ‏אמר לד]ספ[ר]י[א אלן מן בת
10 ‏י]א[להיא ובלחץ עלב י‏]מת הא[
11 ‏ובה
12 ‏....מ........את....
13 ‏]יש[א]ן[כל אלה]נ[י עד]י[א זי בספרא
14 ‏]זנ[ה אית מתעאל וברה ובר ברה
15 ‏ועקרה וכל מלכי ארפד וכל רב
16 ‏וה ועמהם מן בתיהם ומן
17 ‏יומיהם

is in this inscription....] ¹⁰[...]NK and Bêt-Gush and Bêt-ṢLL and [...] ¹¹[...] and corpse ... upon corpse [...] ¹²[...] and on a day of wrath for all [...] ¹³[...] will come to my son and [my] grandsons [...] sons of [my] sons [...] ¹⁴from the hand of my enemies and [...], you will have been false [to this treaty....] ¹⁵RB'B..KMY ... ŠMR WBŠQ. [...] ¹⁶and let *no one* oppress him. If he oppresses (him) in QR[...] ¹⁷LHW.H... if you should seek and not..[...] ¹⁸you [will have been false to] all the [gods of the trea]ty which is in [this] inscription [...] ¹⁹[.]LY⁆ [...] he will surpass *you* until ²⁰[.]HN [....] who will be stronger than you[...]

Face C

¹... ... [and whoever will] give ²orders to efface [th]ese inscriptions from the ³bethels, where they are [wr]itten and ⁴[will] say, " I shall destroy the inscriptions and *with impunity* ⁵shall I destroy KTK and its king," ⁶should that (man) be frightened from effacing the inscriptions ⁷from the bethels and say to ⁸someone who does not understand, " I shall *reward* (you) *indeed*," and (then) ⁹order (him), " Efface these inscriptions from the bethels," ¹⁰may [he] and his son die by oppressive torment. ¹²[...] ¹³and all the gods of the [trea]ty which is in [this] inscription will [   ] ¹⁴Matî'el and his son and his grandson ¹⁵and his offspring and all the kings of Arpad and all his nobles ¹⁶and their people from their homes and from ¹⁷their days.

COMMENTARY

Face A

1. The few words which are preserved on lines 1-2 suggest a text similar to that of Sf I A 21ff., the curses of the treaty. Dupont-Sommer has rightly utilized that part of Sf I for the reconstruction here; there is not exact agreement, however, so that any reconstruction of these lines will be to a certain extent conjectural. For line 1 cf. Sf I A 22-23.

2. Cf. Sf I A 23-24.

[*wšbʿ ʿzn yhy*]*nqn gdh* : " And should seven goats suckle a kid." It is possible to restore either *ʿzn* (abs. pl. fem.; vocalize: *ʿizzān*), as Dupont-Sommer has done, or *ʿzh* (abs. sg. fem.) in a collective sense, like *šwrh*. *ʿz* is the assimilated form of *ʿnz*, " goat," which occurs in *AP* 33, 10 and as the cst. st. in Syriac (*ʿanez*); cf. also Arab. *ʿanzuⁿ*. *gdh* is abs. sg. of *gadyā*, " kid." Vocalize most probably: *gadêh* (< *gaday*); see P. Leander, *LFLAA* §54 and §43w′ (*qatal*-type).

3. Cf. Sf I A 24. Note that at the end of this line Bir-Ga'yah's name is read with certainty and confirms the addition of it at the end of Sf I A 24, where it is otherwise almost certainly demanded by the context.

4. [*thwy mlkth kmlkt ḥl*] : This reconstruction depends upon my reading of Sf I A 25; Dupont-Sommer reads here *kmlkt ḥlm*.

[*w'šmh y*]*tnšy* : " And may his name be forgotten." A very plausible restoration of Dupont-Sommer: *ytnšy* is 3 sg. masc. impf. Ithpeel of *nš'*, " forget." Vocalize: *yitnašê* (< *yitnašay*); cf. *ythzh* (Sf I A 28: *yithazêh*). Nothing in Sf I A corresponds to this or the following curse.

wyhwh qb[*rh*] : " And may his grave be (or become) ...." The form *yhwh* should be noted here and contrasted with *thwy* (Sf I A 25,32; II A 6); the former points to the contraction of the final diphthong, *yihwêh*. *qbrh* should be vocalized *qabreh*, since the *a*-vowel is preserved in the first syllable in later Aram. and Syr.; cf. also Arab. *qabru^n*.

5. [*wš*]*b' šnn šyt šb*[... : This and the following line contain curses which are similar to those of Sf I A 27-28. The word, *šyt*, however, does not occur there. It is apparently otherwise unknown in Aramaic; Dupont-Sommer has related it to Hebr. *šayit*, " thorns," which certainly would suit the context as known from Sf I A.

7. *bkl rbrby* : " Among all the nobles of." Perhaps related to Sf I A 29 (*b'rpd wb'mh*); if so, supply *'rpd* after *rbrby*. We have here the reduplicated form of the plural of *rab*, which is normal in later Aramaic. Elsewhere in these inscriptions we find only *rbwh* (Sf I A 39, 40, 41; II B 3; II C 15).

8. *ṣ'*[*qh*] : " And a cry." See Sf I A 29. Cf. Gn 27 : 34; Ps 9 : 13.

9. Cf. Sf I A 30-31. *'ryh* : " Lion." Vocalize probably : *'aryêh*. Cf. S. Segert, *ArOr* 32 (1964) 124. For a lion in a treaty curse see the treaty of Esarhaddon with Ba'al of Tyre (Rev. IV 6-7); Jer 5 : 6; Hos 13 : 7-8. Cf. D. R. Hillers, *op. cit.*, pp. 54-56.

Face B

2. *'dy' wṭbt'* : " The treaty and the amity." For this meaning of *ṭbt'*, see note on Sf I C 4. Moran (*op. cit.*, p. 176) would translate, " a treaty and friendship ...."

    z[*y*] *'bdw 'lhn* : " Which the gods have made." Moran (*ibid.*) recalls the Akkad. use of *epēšu* (with *ṭābūta*) which parallels the use of *'bd* here.

    [*wlyšm' mt*"*l*] : " And (if) Matî'el will not obey." Restored by Dupont-Sommer as the logical antecedent of the following *bnwh*, *rbwh* and *'mh*. The sentence is similar to Sf I B 21-22. There is no need to restore a *waw* at the end of this line, for one precedes the first word of line 2b.

4. *-ym zy y'wrn* : " Who are watchful." This is the end of a sentence; Dupont-Sommer admits that it can also be read *y'wdn*. If *y'wrn* is to be preferred, it seems scarcely possible to give it the same meaning as the form *y'r* (Sf I A 39), " be blinded," because of the presence of the *waw*. Dupont-Sommer speaks of a Pual form of this verb; but does such a form ever occur in Aramaic? Perhaps he means only a *yuqtal* passive form (like *tu'mar* [Sf I A 33, see note there]); but these are not to be regarded as passives of the intensive stem, the idea usually conveyed by the name Pual. *y'wrn* looks more like an impf. Peal from *'wr* (cf. the form *ymwt* [Sf III 16]) with the long *u* fully written. Because of the fragmentary context it is almost impossible to determine the exact meaning of the root; perhaps it means "who are watchful." If correct, vocalize: *ya'ūrūn*.

phn : "But if." The conjunction *p-* (lit. "and") occurs also in line 6 below. It was previously thought that this conjunction was a peculiarity of the dialect of *Ya'dī*, since it occurs frequently enough in the form *p-* and *p'* in both the inscription of Hadad (*p-*: 3, 13, 14, 30, 31; *p'* 17, 33) and Panammū (*p'*: 22, 11[?]). In fact, G. Garbini ("La congiunzione semitica *pa-*," *Bibl* 38 [1957] 422, n. 2) considered its occurrence in the Bir-RKB inscription as due "al permanere di elementi ya'udici nel nuovo dialetto aramaico, di provenienza assira, che sotto Bar-Rkb venne introdotto nello stato di Šam'al." But the occurrence of the conjunction here shows that its use was more wide-spread than previously-known evidence allowed us to believe. To the evidence listed by Garbini we should now add an occurrence in the Nabataean contract from the Judaean Desert, published by J. Starcky (*RB* 61 [1954] 163, line 3).

nḥt : Though this word looks at first sight like the familiar Aramaic verb, "to descend," this meaning apparently does not fit the broken context. Dupont-Sommer may, therefore, be right in regarding it as a noun, "tranquillity, peace," related to the Hebrew *naḥat* (Is 30 : 15; Qoh 4 : 6) and the cognate Phoenician word (Aḥiram Sarc. 2; Karatepe A I 18, A II 8). Cf. Ugaritic *nḥt* (*UT* 95 : 14). This word must belong to a blessing pronounced over Matî'el on condition that he is faithful to the treaty.

5. *wt'št blbb*[*k*] : "And think in your mind." The verb *'št* occurs in *A* 25, 68; Dn 6 : 4; *BMAP* 5,3; 9,2; in the Ithpaal form: *AP* 30, 23; 31, [22]; *AD* 8,3; fr 3,13. J. C. Greenfield (*Acta orientalia* 29 [1965] 6) maintains that the verb *'št* does not simply mean to "think," but rather "to plot against." He compares Hebr. *ḥšb blbb* (Zech 7 : 10; 8 : 17) and Targumic Aramaic (on Is 32 : 6).

[*gbr 'dn 'nh*] : See Sf I B 24. We believe that this restoration makes better sense that Dupont-Sommer's *gbr 'dn h'*.

6. *l'šlḥ y*[*d bk*] : Finite complement to *pl'khl*; see note on Sf I B 24-25, 34. For the conjunction *p*, see note on line 4 above.

7. *wlḥbzthm :* " Neither to strike them ...." This verb occurs also in Sf III 24, but is otherwise unknown in Aramaic. Dupont-Sommer wrote apropos of its occurrence in Sf III 24 (*BMB* 13 [1956] 35): " Cette racine *ḥbz* semble devoir être rapprochée de la racine *ḥbṭ* " frapper ", attestée en araméen, en hébreu, en éthiopien, en arabe (*ḥbṭ*). Rapprocher encore akkadien *ḥabatu*, ugaritique *ḥbt* " piller "; judéo-araméen (et hébreu post-biblique) *ḥbs* " broyer "; syriaque *ḥbṣ* " presser," hébreu post-biblique *ḥbṣ* " battre le lait "; arabe *ḥbz* " broyer (le grain), faire le pain " (cette derniere racine est exacte-ment identique à notre *ḥbz*). Nous traduisons donc : ' quand les dieux frappèrent la maison [de mon père ...] '." Except for the last-men-tioned Arabic root we consider the other etymological connections mentioned by Dupont-Sommer as far-fetched. As far as we know, a *z* in Aramaic never represents a *t, ṭ, s* or *ṣ* in the other Semitic lan-guages. The Arabic root *ḥbz* gives enough of the idea of " striking " to admit it here as the cognate of our Aramaic word; it fits the context well too. Cf. J. C. Greenfield, *Acta orientalia* 29 (1965) 5, n. 12. In view of the inf. form which we have here, ending in *-t*, it is preferable to interpret both forms as Pael; vocalize : *ḥabbāzūthom* and *ḥabbizū*.

wl'bdt : " Nor to destroy." Pael inf.; vocalize : *'abbādūt*.

'šmhm : " Their name." The prothetic *aleph* is also found on this word in Sf I C 25; II A 4. Cf. Dt 12 : 3; 7 : 24.

w[hn ... : The conjectural restoration of this sentence by Dupont-Sommer is based on Sf III 17. The first personal form is demanded by *'by* at the beginning of the next line.

8. *wyb' wyzqn :* " For he is babbling and grows old." The meaning of the first verb is not clear; Dupont-Sommer suggests the root *nb'*, " to speak," attested in both Hebr. (Ps 19 : 3; 59 : 8) and Aram. in the causative stem. The specific nuance of " babbling " is derived from the context and the collocation of this verb with the next, *yzqn*, " grows old." It is not otherwise attested. And yet it is scarcely dittographical (*pace* D. W. Thomas, *JSS* 5 [1960] 284).

wyb'h bry '[yt r'šy lhmtty] : " Or (if) my son seeks my head to kill me." Cf. Sf III 11; but note that *'yt* does not occur there.

9. *[y]qtl mn yqtl :* " Let him kill whomever he would kill." For *qtl* instead of *qṭl*, see note on Sf I B 27. The words are a sort of soliloquy put on the lips of Matî'el, who would be secretly siding with the rebellious son of Bir-Ga'yah. Cf. Ex 33 : 19; 2 Sm 15 : 20.

šqrtm : See note on Sf I A 14; I B 23.

10. *wbyt gš wbyt ṣll :* See the note of Sf I B 3.

11. *wpgr ..k 'l pgr*[...] : See the note on Sf I B 30.

12. *wbywm ḥrn :* Dupont-Sommer relates the word *ḥrn* to the Biblical Hebr. *ḥārôn*; cf. Is 13 : 13 (*wbywm ḥrwn 'pw*).

13. Dupont-Sommer believes that this line is parallel to Sf I B 31-32. This is, however, rather problematical. *'l* is almost certainly correct as the restored preposition; cf. Sf III 1. *bn*[*yk*], read by Dupont-Sommer, is not convincing and I prefer to restore simply *bn*[*y*]; cf. Sf I A 2.

14. *mn yd śn'y :* " From the hand of my enemies." The same expression occurs in Sf III 11.

15. Unintelligible.

16. *wl'š yhwnnh :* " And let no one oppress him." Dupont-Sommer may be right in translating, " et personne ne l'opprimera," but the position of the negative is rather peculiar. One would expect *w'š lyhwnnh*. On the defective writing of *'š*, see the note on Sf I C 21. The verb is 3 sg. masc. energic impf. Haph. of *yn'*, well attested in later Aram. and Hebr. Vocalize: *yuhawninneh*. The ordinary impf. follows in the form *yuhawnêh*. The final vowel is shortened before the energic ending; cf. the Pael form *yᵉḥawwinnanī* in Dn 5 : 7.
    bqr[...] : Perhaps *bqr*[*yt'*], " in the town."

18. Cf. Sf III 4, 14, 16, 23 ; Sf I B 23 ; Sf II B 9.

19.]*lk ygbr ʿd :* " He will surpass you until ...." But it is not certain that *lk* is an independent word; it may be the suffixal ending of some noun, which is the subject of *ygbr*. Dupont-Sommer suggests [*ḥy*]*lk*, " your army." Perhaps " your army will be strong." However, this phrase may be related to the only legible one in line 20.

20. *zy yʿz mnk :* " Who will be stronger than you." *yʿz*: 3 sg. masc. impf. Peal of *ʿzz*, " be strong. Vocalize: *yaʿuz* (< *yaʿuzzu). Cf. BLA §48*b-c*. Contrast *mnk* with *mk* (Sf III 22).

Face C

2. *lhldt :* See the note on Sf I C 18. For parallels to [*y*]'*mr*, see Ex 2 : 14 ; 2 Sm 21 : 16.

spry' : "Inscriptions." One wonders about the plural here. Could it refer to Sf I and II?

bty 'lhy' : "Bethels," lit. "the houses of the gods." This expression is found below in lines 7, 9-10. Since the context shows that this expression refers to the steles themselves on which the inscriptions are written, Dupont-Sommer translates the expression into French as "bétyles," i.e. sacred stones (sometimes considered as the dwelling of a god or even as the god himself). The noun "bethel" can be used in this sense in English (see J. A. H. Murray, *A New English Dictionary on Historical Principles* [Oxford: Clarendon Press], I [1888] 829). One should contrast this expression with the use of *nṣb' znh*, "this stele" (Sf I C 17). Dupont-Sommer cites the words of Philo Byblius, quoting Sanchuniaton, about the *baitylia* invented by the god Uranus and considered to be "animate stones," ἔτι δὲ (φησιν) ἐπενόησεν Θεὸς Οὐρανὸς βαιτύλια, λίθους ἐμψύχους μηχανησάμενος (Eusebius, *Praep. Evang.*, I.10,23; ed. K. Mras, *GCS* 43/1 [1954] 48). But is this the first known instance of this expression in a Semitic text to designate the sacred stone itself? See Gn 28: 18-22, where Jacob anoints the stone he had used as a pillow, set it up as a sacred pillar (*maṣṣēbāh*), and said, *w ᵉhā'eben hazzô't 'ašer śamtî maṣṣēbāh yihyeh bêt 'ᵉlôhîm* (v. 22). On Gn 28: 18-22 see H. Donner, *ZAW* 74 (1962) 68-70; O. Eissfeldt, "Der Gott Bethel," *Archiv für Religionswissenschaft* 28 (1930) 1-30 (reprinted in *Kleine Schriften* [Tübingen: Mohr, 1962], I. 206-33); E. Meyer, *ZAW* 49 (1931) 11-12. Moreover, in the treaty of Esarhaddon with Baʻal of Tyre we find in the list of the gods after [Ištar], Gula, and Sibitti a deity named *Ba-a-a-ti-ilāni*ᵐᵉš (Rev. II, 6), "Baiti-ilāni," which Z. S. Harris (*A Grammar of the Phoenician Language* [American Oriental Series 8; New Haven: American Oriental Society, 1936], p. 86) related to *baitylos* of Hesychius and *baitylion* of Sanchuniaton. Besides C. Clemen, *Die phönikische Religion nach Philo von Byblos* (MVAG 42/3; Leipzig: J. C. Hinrichs, 1939], p. 27 (referred to by Dupont-Sommer), see K. Tümpel, "Baitylia," *Pauly-Wissowa, RE* II/2. 2779-81; N. Turchi, "Betìlo," *Enciclopedia cattolica* II. 1514-15.

3. *'n zy y[r]šmn* : "Where they are written." The interrogative adverb *'ān* is well attested in later Aramaic. *yršmn* : 3 pl. masc. impf. pass. (*yuqtal*-type) of *ršm*, "scratch, make a mark; write"; see note on Sf I A 33.

4. *'h'bd* : "I shall destroy," lit. "I shall cause to be lost." 1 sg. impf. Haph. of *'bd*, "be lost." Vocalize: *'uha'bid.*

wlm[.]*n* : Dupont-Sommer reads *wlm*[*l*]*n* and takes this word as an adverbial expression with distributive sense, " et, mot par mot(?), je supprimerai KTK et son roi." He compares the Hebr. expressions *lbqrym* (" à chaque matin," Ps 73 : 14) or *lrg'ym* (" à chaque instant," Is 27 : 3). But these are temporal expressions, which is not the case with *lmln*. Could we rather read here the adverb *mgn*, which is found in Palmyrene (see Cooke, *NSI* §116, line 4) and the Targums (as the equivalent of *ḥinnām*; see Onkelos on Gn 29 : 15) with the meaning " gratis, for nothing "? (Suggestion of G. S. Glanzman).

5. *'hbd* : This form seems to be an alternate form of *'h'bd* (line 4). Was the *aleph* in the second syllable lost by quiescence or simply by scribal omission? Donner - Röllig too confidently opt for the former (*KAI*, 2. 263).

'yt : Two clear uses of the *signum accusativi*; see note on Sf I B 32.

6. *wyzḥl* : " Be frightened." 3 sg. masc. impf. Peal of *zḥl*, " be frightened, fear." Cf. the later Aram. *dḥl*, construed with *mn* in Dn 6 : 27; see also Jb 32 : 6; Zakir a 13. See K. R. Veenhof, " An Aramaic Curse with a Sumero-Akkadian Prototype," *BO* 20 (1963) 142-44.

ld : See note on Sf I C 18.

7. *bty 'lhy'* : See note on Sf II C 2 above.

wy'mr lzy lyd' 'nh 'gr 'gr : " And say to someone who does not understand." Dupont-Sommer translates : " (et qu'il dise) à qui ne sait rien : ' Ou je serai exilé, je serai exilé.' " This interpretation cannot be right, for it does not suit the context at all. There is little difficulty with the first part of the sentence. Dupont-Sommer's interpretation of this part is certainly superior to that of Donner - Röllig (*KAI*, 2.259). The *l* is the prefixed negative; *yd'* is the Peal act. ptc. (" who does not know ").

8. *'nh 'gr 'gr* : " I shall reward (you) indeed." The first *'gr* should probably be understood as a Peal inf., intensifying the main verb *'gr*. The latter is 1 sg. impf. Peal from the root *'gr* (related to the word for " salary," cf. Jean - Hoftijzer, *DISO* 4) — Attempts to explain *'gr* as a form of *gwr*, " be afraid," are unconvincing.

9. *ld* : See note on Sf I C 18. Cf. K. R. Veenhof (*BO* 20 [1963] 144), who denies there is room for the final *t*, read by Dupont-Sommer.

10. *wblḥṣ 'lb y[mt]* : " And may he die by oppressive torment."
The noun *lḥṣ* (cst. st.) is not otherwise attested in Aramaic, but it
seems to be related to the Biblical Hebr. *laḥaṣ*, " oppression " (Ex
3 : 9 ; Dt 26 : 7). Nor is *'lb* found as a noun in Aramaic (except in
the derived form *'ulbānā*, " torment, oppression ") ; cf. 1QapGn 2, 17
(*'lyb*). The two nouns express the same idea in a cst. chain.
    y[mt] : So restored plausibly by Dupont-Sommer ; but note that
the form is written *ymwt* in Sf III 16. This restoration is more in
accord with the normal orthography of these inscriptions.

11. *wbrh* : Dupont-Sommer reads *wbnh*, marking the *nun* as a doubtful letter and translating, " et ses fils." He explains the form as
equal to *bnwh*. Similarly S. Segert, *ArOr* 32 (1964) 126, n. 111. This
defective writing of the 3 sg. masc. suff. on a plural noun is not
attested elsewhere in early Aramaic. I have refused to read it in
Sf I C 15-16 too, where it is no more certain. In this case the *nun*
is far from certain and might just as well be a *reš*. This yields a
normal form, " his son."

13. *[yš']n* : The restoration of the verb is quite problematical ; this
is the form given by Dupont-Sommer, apparently as the 3rd pl. masc.
impf. Peal of *nš'*. Whatever verb is to be restored, it should be
noted that the last letter is a *nun*, which precludes its being understood as a jussive ; it is more likely the long impf. The end of the
sentence, *mn btyhm wmn ywmyhm*, reminds one of the blessing in Sf
I C 15-16 : *yṣrw 'lhn mn ywmh wmn byth* (where the direct object of
the verb is lost). As Dupont-Sommer understands this last section
of the inscription, it deals with some crime committed in violation
of the treaty or with some damage done to the steles. This is certainly possible and in such case the restoration of *yš'n* is not wholly
improbable. But could not the last paragraph be a blessing? Admittedly, we cannot simply restore some form of *nṣr* here (as in Sf
I C 15-16), because the direct object expressed would not suit that
verb. But possibly some other verb should be restored.
    kl 'lh[y 'd]y' : See Sf I B 23, 33 ; Sf II B 9 ; Sf III 4, 14,
17, 23.

14. *mt''l wbrh wbr w'qrh wkl mlky 'rpd wkl rbwh w'mhm* : Cf. Sf III
1, 3, 14-16 for similar formulae. M. Noth (*ZDPV* 77 [1961] 132, n. 40)
believes that the suffix on *rbwh* really refers to Arpad ; and though in
form it is masc., it should really be treated as a fem.

16. *mn btyhm wmn ywmyhm* : See Sf I C 15-16.

STELE III

Stele III was acquired by the Beirut Museum in 1956 and consists of nine fragments. When pieced together, they yield an extended text of twenty-nine lines, of which the last three lines are quite fragmentary. A few letters have been lost from the middle of most of the lines but they are in most cases easily restored with certainty. Unlike steles I and II this inscription was engraved on a broad slab and apparently only on one face of it. What remains therefore of the inscription is a surface roughly 102 cm. × 72 cm.

When S. Ronzevalle published the so-called Sûjîn stele (= stele I) in 1931, he gave notice of the existence of two other fragmentary steles belonging to a group which had been set up in the neighborhood of Sefîre. Stele III is to be identified with what he then called a " seconde stèle, très fragmentaire, [qui] n'a laissé d'elle qu'une trentaine de lignes, toutes très incomplètes et mutilées." (18)

On the relation of stele III to the other two steles, see above pp. 2-3, 79. It should be recalled that though Bir-Ga'yah's name is plausibly restored in III 25, that restoration is not certain — and has, in fact, been contested. Matî'el's name does not occur in this stele either. Yet it does mention the " kings of Arpad " (lines 1, 3, 16, 27). Moreover, as A. Dupont-Sommer has remarked, there is in it " the same type of stone, the same handwriting, the same absence of word-dividers, the same mention of the ' Kings of Arpad ' and the same general contents." (19)

My transcription of this text differs only slightly from that of Dupont-Sommer: [ḥd] (3) instead of kl, ''bd (3) instead of ''br, lšlm (8) instead of lšlḥ, ngdy (10) instead of ngry, tkwh, tkh (13) instead of tpwh, tph, rḥm h' ly (8) instead of rḥmh 'ly, whwy ḥlph (22) instead of whw yḥlph, [zy lh] (20) instead of zy lhm. (20)

(18) *MUSJ* 15 (1931) 237.
(19) *BMB* 13 (1956) 24.
(20) Returning from Jerusalem to the United States via Beirut in July 1958, I was able to inspect the stele itself. In my opinion, one must read ''bd (3), w'rq (6), ngdy (10). Generally, the *daleth* is clearly distinguished from the *reš* in this inscription, the vertical shaft of the latter being longer than that of the former. In line 13 śgbwh is almost certainly to be read

Neither the beginning nor the end of the inscription has been preserved. It contains only a list of stipulations imposed on the king(s) of Arpad. Only in one instance does the suzerain promise anything: to return fugitives, provided his own are sent back.

śrbwh. Though the reading in any case is quite doubtful, we prefer *lšlm* to *lšlḥ* (8) and *tkh* to *tph* (13). See further comments on the respective lines.

TEXT : Sf III

1 או אל ברך או אל עקרך או אל חד מלכי ארפד וי[ן]מל[]ל [ע]לי או
על ברי או על בר ברי או על עקרי כים כל גב

2 ר זי יבעה רוח אפוה וימלל מלן לחית לעלי[ן..]...תקח מליא מן ידה
הסכר תהסכרהם בידי וב

3 רך יהסכר לברי ועקרך יסכר לעקרי ועקר [חד מ]לכי ארפד
יהסכרן לי מה טב בעיני אעבד להם ו

4 הן להן שקרתם לכל אלהי עדיא זי בספרא [זנה] והן יקרק מני קרק
חד פקדי או חד אחי או חד

5 סרסי או חד עמא זי בידי ויהכן חלב לתס[ו]ך ל[]הם לחם ולתאמר
להם שלו על אשרכם ולתהרם נ

6 בשהם מני רקה תרקהם ותהשבהם לי והן לי[ן]שב[ן] בארקך רקו שם
עד אהך אנה וארקהם והן תהרם נבשה

7 ם מני ותסך להם לחם ותאמר להם שבו לתחתכו[ם] ואל[] תפנו
באשרה שקרתם בעדיא אלן וכל מלכיא זי ס

8 חרתי או כל זי רחם הא לי ואשלח מלאכי או[ל]וה לשלם או לכל
חפצי או ישלח מלאכה אלי פתח

9 ה לי ארחא לתמשל בי בזא ולתרשה לי עליוה [ו]הן להן ש[ו]ק[]רת
בעדיא אלן והן מן חד אחי או מן חד בי

TRANSLATION

I. *Concerning the Surrender of Plotters*

[. . . And whoever will come to you] [1]or to your son or to your offspring or to one of the kings of Arpad and will s[pea]k [ag]ainst me or against my son or against my grandson or against my offspring, *indeed*, any man [2]who *rants* and utters evil words against me [. . . . .] you must [*not*] accept such words from him; you must hand them (i.e., the men) over into my hands and your son [3]must hand (them) over to my son and your offspring must hand (them) over to my offspring and the offspring of [any of the ki]ngs of Arpad must hand (them) over to me. Whatever is good in my sight, I shall do to them. And [4]if (you do) not (do) so, you will have been false to all the gods of the treaty which is in [this] inscription.

II. *Concerning the Surrender of Fugitives*

Now if a fugitive flees from me, one of my officials or one of my brothers or one of [5]my courtiers or one of the people who are under my control, and they go to Aleppo, you must not gi[ve th]em food nor say to them, " Stay quietly in your place "; and you must not incite [6]them against me. You must *placate* them and return them to me. And if they [do] not [dwell] in your land, *placate* (them) there, until I come and *placate* them. But if you incite them [7]against me and give them food and say to them, " Stay where [yo]u are and do not (re)turn to his region," you will have been false to this treaty.

III. *Concerning Freedom of Passage*

Now (as for) all the kings of my [8]vicinity or any one who is a friend of mine, when I send my ambassador to him for peace or for any of my business or (when) he sends his ambassador to me, [9]the road shall be open to me. You must not (try to) dominate me in this (respect) nor assert your authority over me concerning [it]. [And] if (you do) not (do) so, you will be false to this treaty.

10   ת אבי או מן חד בני או מן חד נגדי או מן חד ופ]קדי או מן חד עמיא

זי בידי או מן חד שנאי ו

11   יבעה ראשי להמתתי ולהמתת ברי ועקרי הן אי]נתי יקתלן את תאתה

ותקם דמי מן יד שנאי וברך יאתה

12   יקם דם ברי מן שנאוה ובר ברך יאתה יקם דו]ם בו]ר ברי ועקרך

יאתה יקם דם עקרי והן קריה הא נכה

13   תכוה בחרב והן חד אחי הא או חד עבדי או]חד[פקדי או חד עמא

זי בידי נכה תכה אי<ת>ה ועקרה ושג

14   בוה ומודדוה בחרב והן להן שקרת לכל אלהי וע]דיא זי בספרא

זנה והן יסק על לבבך ותשא על ש

15   פתיך להמתתי ויסק על לבב בר ברך וישא על שפתוה להמתת בר

ברי או הן יסק על לבב עקרך

16   וישא על שפתוה להמתת עקרי והן יסק על ל]ובב מלכי ארפד בכל

מה זי ימות בר אנש שקרתם לכ

17   ל אלהי עדיא זי בספרא זנה והן ירב ברו]י זי ישב על כהסאי חד

אחוה או יעברנה לתשלח לש

18   נך בניהם ותאמר לה קתל אחך או אסרה ווא]ל[תשריה ו]הן רקה

תרקה בניהם ליקתל וליאסר

19   והן לתרקה בניהם שקרת בעדיא אלן וו]מ]לכן]זי סחרו]תי ויקרק קרקי

אל חדהם ויקרק קר

20   קהם ויאתה אלי הן השב זי לי אהשב]זי לה ואו]ל תעשקני את והן

להן שקרת בעדיא א

IV. *Concerning Vengeance to be Taken in the Case of Assassination*

Now if any one of my brothers or any one of my [10]father's household or any one of my sons or any one of my officers or any one of my [of]ficials or any one of the people under my control or any one of my enemies [11]seeks my head to kill me and to kill my son and my offspring — if they kill m[e], you must come and avenge my blood from the hand of my enemies. Your son must come [12](and) avenge the blood of my son from his enemies; and your grandson must come (and) avenge the blo[od of] my grandson. Your offspring must come (and) avenge the blood of my offspring. If it is a city, you must [13]strike it with a sword. If it is one of my brothers or one of my slaves or [one] of my officials or one of the people who are under my control, you must strike him and his offspring, his *nobles* [14]and his friends with a sword. And if (you do) not (do) so, you will have been false to all the gods of the [tr]eaty which is in this inscription.

V. *Concerning Plots against the Suzerain*

If the idea should come to your mind and you should express with your lips (the intention) [15]to kill me; and if the idea should come to the mind of your grandson and he should express with his lips (the intention) to kill my grandson; or if the idea should come to the mind of your offspring [16]and he should express with his lips (the intention) to kill my offspring; and if the idea should come to the [mi]nd of the kings of Arpad, in whatever way a man shall die, you will have been false to all [17]the gods of the treaty which is in this inscription.

VI. *Concerning Duty in a Strife for Succession to the Throne*

If [my] son, who sits upon my throne, quarrels (with) one of his brothers and he would *remove* him, you shall not interfere [18]with them, saying to him, " Kill your brother or imprison him and do no[t] let him go free." But if you really *make peace* between them, he will not kill and will not imprison (him). [19]But if you do not *make peace* between them, you will have been false to this treaty.

VII. *Concerning the Reciprocal Return of Fugitives*

And as for [k]ings [of my vicin]ity, if a fugitive of mine flees to one of them, and a fugitive of theirs flees [20]and comes to me, if

21 לן ולתשלח לשן בביתי ובני בני ובני א[ו]חי ובני ע[ק]רי ובני עמי ותאמר
להם קתלו מרא

22 כם והוי חלפה כי לטב הא מך ויקם חד [ו]דמי והן ת[ו]עבד מרמת עלי
או על בני או על עקר[י]

23 [ש]קרתם לכל אלהי עדיא זי בספרא זנ[ה] ותלא[י]ם וכפריה ובעליה
וגבלה לאבי ול

24 [ו]ביתה עד[] עלם וכזי חבזו אלהן בית [ו]אבי הא ה[ו]ת לאחרן וכעת
השבו אלהן שיבת בי

25 [ת אבי ···· בית] אבי ושבת תלאים ל[ו]בר גא[י]ה ולברה ולבר ברה
ולעקרה עד עלם ו

26 [ו]הן ירב ברי וירב בר ב[ז]רי וירב עקרי [ו]עם עקרך ע[ו]ל תלאים וכפריה
ובעליה מן ישא

27 [···········] מל[ו]כי ארפד [···········[ו]לנה שקרת בעדיא אלן
והן

28 [···························] וישחדן כל מה מלך זי י[·]

29 [·· כל מה ז[י] שפר וכל מה זי ט[ו]ב ·············]

he has restored mine, I shall return [his; and] you yourself shall [no]t (try to) hinder me. And if (you do) not (do) so, you will have been false to this treaty.

VIII. *Concerning Plots against the Suzerain's Household*

²¹You shall not interfere in my house nor (with) my grandsons nor (with) the sons of my bro[thers nor (with) the sons of my off-] spring nor (with) the sons of my people, saying to them, " Kill your lord ²²and be his successor ! For he is not better than you." Some- one will avenge [my blood. If you do com]mit treachery against me or against my sons or against [my] offspring, ²³you will have been false to all the gods of the treaty which is in th[is] inscription.

IX. *Concerning the Territory of Tal'ayim*

[Tal'ay]im, its villages, its lords, and its territory (belong) to my father and to ²⁴[his house for]ever. When (the) gods struck [my father's] house, [it came to belong] to another. Now, however, (the) gods have brought about the return of my ²⁵[father's ho]use [and] my father's [house ....] and Tal'ayim has returned to [Bir Ga'y]ah and to his son and to his grandson and to his offspring forever. ²⁶[If my son quarrels and (if)] my [grand]son quarrels and (if) my offspring quarrels [with your offspring a]bout Tal'ayim and its villages and its lords, whoever will raise ²⁷[.......... the ki]ngs of Arpad [..... ....]LNH, you will have been false to this treaty.

X. *Concerning Gifts* (?)

And if ²⁸[...............] and they bribe every king who will ²⁹[.......... all th]at is beautiful and all that is go[od] ³⁰[..........].

COMMENTARY

1. *'w :* The first word, being a coordinate conjunction introducing a series, shows that we do not have the beginning of this inscription. Dupont-Sommer believes that the *verso* of the stele alone is preserved and that the formal introduction is lost.

'l : The preposition *'l*, common in Hebrew, but rare in later Aramaic, is found several times in this inscription; see lines 8 (*'lwh, 'ly*), 19 (*'l*), 20 (*'ly*). It also occurs in Zakir a 11, 12 and frequently in the address of a letter in the Elephantine texts (*AP* 40.1, 5; 41. 1,9; 30.1; *BMAP* 13.1, 6). Note that in *AD* (2.1; 3.1; etc.) it is usually replaced by *'l*. On the basis of the verb *'th* used with *'l* in line 20 we may restore: [*wmn y'th 'lyk*] *'w 'l brk*, etc. Dupont-Sommer suggests: *wkl zy y'th 'ly*; but the last word is a printing error; see his translation.

'qrk : "Your offspring." See note on Sf I A 2. The series of son, grandson, offspring, or any other king (usurper?) is significantly intended to guarantee the perpetuity of the pact that is being made. It is but another way of expressing *'d 'lm* in Sf III 25. One should recall in this connection the attempts of Esarhaddon to insure the succession of this two sons on the throne in his Vassal Treaties. Cf. 2 Sm 7: 11-14 and M. Tsevat, " Studies in the Book of Samuel, III : The Steadfast House," *HUCA* 34 (1963) 71-82.

ḥd : The indefinite use of the numeral in the sense of " a " or " one " is frequent in this stele; see line 4, 5, 9, 10, 13, 17, 19 (with a suffix), 22. It is usually construed as the *nomen regens* in a construct chain and not coupled with *mn*; cf. *A* 33; Sf I B 26 note.

mlky : This reference to kings may be to a dynasty (so Dupont-Sommer, E. Vogt); but it may also refer to kings allied in some way to the king of Arpad (so M. Noth).

'rpd : The mention of *'rpd* constitutes one of the important links between this stele and Sf I, where *Matiʿel* appears as the king of Arpad, upon whom Bir-Ga'yah, the king of KTK, imposes a treaty. See note on Sf I A 3.

wy[ml]l : Restored as in line 2.

kym : Dupont-Sommer considers this word as an adverb, " so, likewise," comparing the Accadian *kîam*; see Bezold - Goetze, *BAG* 133.

While this is quite plausible, it may however be a conjunction, like Akkad. *kīma* (cf. W. von Soden, *Grundriss der akkadischen Grammatik*, n. 114g, 116e), "just as." F. Rosenthal: "in the manner of any one man."

2. *zy yb'h rwḥ 'pwh*: "Who rants," lit. "who causes the breath of his nostrils to boil." This is an obscure expression, which Dupont-Sommer translates, "qui suppliera pour sa vie." His literal translation, "who seeks the breath of his nostrils," is understood as "qui demandera qu'on lui laisse le souffle vital ...; le texte viserait un 'suppliant', menacé de mort." He appeals to Lam 4 : 20 to support this interpretation. But such an interpretation hardly fits the context. Would one expect a *suppliant* to speak evil things against the king? The expression rather indicates the reason for the evil words; hence it is better to take the phrase as meaning a transport of arrogance or anger, as the other biblical expression mentioned by Dupont-Sommer would seem to indicate: *rwḥ 'pym* (Ex 15 : 8). Hence, " becomes enraged." F. Rosenthal (*BASOR* 158 [1960] 28, n. 1) further relates the phrase to Prv 1 : 23 (*'by'h lkm rwḥy*), explaining it as an expression of strong emotion; he notes that both here and in Prv 1 : 23 the phrase is followed by a reference to speaking. The basic meaning of the word *b'y/w* is "cause to swell, cause to boil." The phrase then would mean: "who causes his breath to boil, who breathes heavily" (as in anger or overweening pride). M. J. Dahood has shown me the difficult passage in Is 11 : 15, where the same idiom may occur. He reads *b'ym rwḥw*, "causing his wrath to well up" (an inf. absol. with enclitic *mem*; cf. H. D. Hummel, *JBL* 76 [1957] 94-95).

   rwḥ: Because of the use of this word with *'pwh*, it seems necessary to understand it as the equivalent of the biblical Hebrew *rûªḥ*, even though the *scriptio plena* of a long vowel in a medial position is peculiar in an Aramaic inscription of the eighth century. We must, it seems, reject the possibility of understanding *rwḥ* in the sense of the Hebrew *rewaḥ*, *pace* P. Nober, *VD* 37 (1959) 173-74.

   'pwh: See note on Sf I A 5 (*bnwh*) for the suffix; the form is probably a dual, "his nostrils."

   ymll: 3rd sg. masc. Impf. Pael, "utters evil words against me."

   mln: "Words." The form is abs. pl. m., but the gender is fem., as is shown by the adjective *lḥyt*. It can be vocalized *millīn*, as medial long *i* is generally not written at this period (see *lḥmtty*, line 11); or possibly *millān* (as a masculine form!), following the suggestion of H. L. Ginsberg, "Aramaic Dialect Problems," *AJSL* 52 (1936) 99-101; see also A. Goetze, "The Akkadian Masculine Plural in *-ānū/ī* and its Semitic Background," *Language* 22 (1946) 121-130, esp. 126ff.

lḥyt : " Evil," usually in a moral sense. This word is found also in Sf I A 26; C 7 (*lḥyh*), 20 (*lḥyt*); Nerab 1.10 (*lḥh*), B-M 6 (*lḥy'*), *AP* 30:7; 31:6; 32:6; *AD* 5:7 (see Driver's note). The form is the abs. pl. fem., which has preserved the archaic ending *-āt*, instead of the later *-ān*. The same ending is found on *mrmt* (line 22). J. T. Milik has shown me the occurrence of this word, not in a moral sense, in the contract, recto line 8, published by him in *Bibl* 38 (1957) 255-64; see p. 263. Cf. J. C. Greenfield, *Acta orientalia* 29 (1965) 8-9.

l'ly : Dupont-Sommer fills in the lacuna thus: *l'ly*[*lwty w*]*tqḥ*, which he translates, " relativement à ma conduite (?) et ...." This restoration is, however, hardly convincing, even though we have nothing better to suggest; we prefer to retain the lacuna as such, "against me." The form *l'ly* is a compound preposition, known in later Aramaic, that could be used here as well as the simple preposition *'l* with the verb *mll*. *l'l* appears at least three times in unpublished Aramaic texts of Qumran Cave 4. Cf. 1QapGn 2 : 26.

tqḥ : The lacuna unfortunately makes the understanding of this word quite difficult. The context would seem to demand a negative; hence " you must [not] accept." It seems to be the 2 sg. m. impf. Peal of *lqḥ*.

mly' : The emphatic masc. pl. ending occurs here in a determinate sense, since the form obviously refers to the aforementioned *mln*, hence " such words." Vocalize *millayya'*. The same ending is found on *'dy'* (4, 7, 9, 14, 17, 19, 20, 23, 27), *mlky'* (7), *'my'* (10).

mn ydh : Lit. " from his hand "; the phrase probably means simply " from him," as an immediate source.

hskr thskrhm : Lit. " you must really hand them over." The first word is a Haph. inf., used to intensify the finite form of the verb in the manner of the Hebrew inf. absol. The same use of the inf. is found in line 6 (*rqḥ trqḥm*), 12-13 (*nkh t(k)wh-t(k)h*), 18 (*rqḥ trqḥ*). Dupont-Sommer notes that this use is frequent in Hebrew and is known in Phoenician, but that it has not been met before in Aramaic. However, it very probably occurs in Nerab 2 : 6: *whwm 'thmw* (see the note in Cooke, *NSI*, p. 191). This construction is also found commonly in Ugaritic; see Gordon, *UT* 9 : 27; Driver, *CML* p. 132. — The root *skr* in the sense of " hand over," " deliver " is found in Hebrew in the Piel; see Is 19 : 4. It is possibly related to *sgr* which has the same meaning in Hebrew in the Hiphil (1 Sm 23 : 11; see *GB* 536b), in Phoenician (see Harris, *GPL*, 126), and in Qumran Aramaic (1QapGn 22 : 17). — Is *hm* really a suffix or an independent pronoun? In later Aramaic the 3 pl. suff. on verbs is avoided, while an independent form (sometimes enclitic, as in Syriac) is used. In this case we cannot tell; but see the note on *trqhm* (line 6); *-hm* occurs as a suffix on a noun in lines 6-7 (*nbšhm*) and on a pronoun in line 19 (*ḥdhm*). Cf. Zakir a 9 (*wmḥnwt-hm*); Meša' 18 (*w'šb-hm*), with word-dividers.

3. *yskr*: Dupont-Sommer remarks: " Noter la syncope de la préfor-mante *h* du hafel; cf. un peu plus haut *yhskr*." But since both Haphel and 'Aphel causative stems occur in later Aramaic (see *BLA* 36; *LFLAA*, 35i, 38k, 40s; in Qumran Aramaic: *ywš'*, 4QpsDan[a] 16.2 [*RB* 63, 413]; *tšlṭ*, 4QTest Levi 1 i 17 [*RB* 62, 400]; *yškḥ*, *'šgh*, 1Qap Gn 21.13; *ynpq*, 1QapGn 20.32; *ytybw*, 1QapGn 20.25; etc.), would it not be better to regard this form as an early instance of an Aphel imperfect? S. Segert (*ArOr* 32 [1964] 121) regards *yskr* as a mere " Schreibfehler."

'qr ... yhskrn: " The offspring of [any of the ki]ngs of Arpad must hand (them) over." Dupont-Sommer finds this construction strange, as the subject is sg., while the verb is pl. Though he trans-lates, " et la descendance [de tous les r]ois d'Arpad devra me (les) livrer," he thinks that *'qr* might be the result of dittography. Then *mlky 'rpd* would become the subject of *yhskrn*, " ce qui serait plus conforme à la syntaxe et donnerait un sens meilleur." But there is nothing wrong with a plural verb being construed with a collective singular subject. Hence *'qr ... yhskrn* is to be retained.

ḥd: Restored according to line 1. Dupont-Sommer prefers to read *kl*; M. Noth (*ZDPV* 77 [1961] 133, n. 42) also prefers *ḥd*.

''bd: Dupont-Sommer reads *''br* and says, " Le *r* est tout à fait sûr." He translates: " je leur pardonnerai." For such a meaning of the verb *'br* he appeals to Am 7 : 8; 8 : 2 and to the aforemen-tioned suppliants, to whom the vassal is supposed to show mercy. Granted that such a meaning of *'br* does fit the passages in Amos (see *GB* 559a), it is not yet attested in Aramaic, as far as I am aware. Secondly, it scarcely fits the construction of the subordinate clause, *mh ṭb b'yny*, where it would be necessary to twist the meaning of *mh* to " if," to suit such a conclusion: " I shall pardon them, if it seems good in my sight." But with the normal meaning of the compound relative pronoun *mh*, used in a generic sense, one would expect something like, " I shall pardon or punish " — or better still, " I shall do." Thirdly, the context of " suppliants," to which Du-pont-Sommer refers is quite questionable, as we have already remarked. Fourthly, from a careful examination of the photos, the squeeze, and the stone itself, it is clear that one must read a *daleth*. The vertical shaft of the letter is rather broad down to a certain point

(making a good *daleth*); after that it thins out. The thin part belongs to a chipping of the stone produced probably when the stone was damaged. The chipped spot is visible in Pl. IV published by Dupont-Sommer, just above the *yodh* of *'hy* (line 4). When *''bd* is read, the compound relative functions normally: as the subject of the nominal relative clause and the object of the main transitive verb. It is then the Aramaic equivalent of the expression in 2 Sm 19 : 38: *w'šh lw 't 'šr ṭwb b'ynyk*; see also Jos 9 : 25 ; 2 Sm 3 : 19 ; 1 Kgs 14 : 8 ; 2 Kgs 10 : 5 ; Esth 3 : 11.

4. *whn lhn :* See note on Sf I B 36.

šqrtm : " You will have been false." See note on Sf I A 14. The verb is followed by the preposition *l* when persons are the object of the treachery (see lines 4, 14, 16, 23 ; Sf I A 24,[14, 15] ; Sf I B 23 ; Sf II A 3 ; B 9, 18 ; and cf. Gn 21 : 23), but by *b* when the treaty itself is the object (see lines 7, 9, 19, 20, 27 ; Sf I B 38 ; Sf II B 14 ; and cf. Ps 44 : 18). The same verb is found in Sf I A 14, but in the protasis of the conditional sentence and used in the imperfect. Dupont-Sommer translates the form here as 2 pl., and this can be defended on the score that the king and his descendants are being addressed. But in the majority of cases in this stele the king is addressed in the singular; see the suffixes in lines 1 and 3 and the verbs in line 5. Moreover, *šqrtm* (which also occurs in lines 7, 16, 23) should be compared with *šqrt* in lines 9, 14, 19, 20, 27. In lines 7 and 23, is *šqrtm* the plural, since the vassal alone is addressed? Formerly, I thought that this form was 2 pers. sg. with an enclitic *mem*. Such an enclitic is well-attested in Ugaritic and Bibl. Hebrew; cf. *UT* 11 : 7 and H. D. Hummel, " Enclitic *mem* in Early Northwest Semitic, especially Hebrew," *JBL* 76 (1957) 85-107. His remarks on the scarcity of this enclitic in Aramaic (p. 88) are significant. See my further observations in *JAOS* 86 (1966) 295-96. Interesting for the light it sheds on several OT passages (especially Ps 89:34 ; also 44:18 ; Is 63,8) is the use of the root *šqr*, meaning to break faith in a covenant. — Throughout the inscription *šqrt(m)* is preferably to be taken as Pael.

'dy' : " Treaty." Only the emph. pl. of this word occurs in this inscription, but the cst. pl. *'dy* is found frequently in Sf I. See note on Sf I A 1.

spr' : The emph. state before the demonstrative adjective is supplied on the basis of the same expression in lines 14, 17, 23 and Sf I B 28, 33 ; C 17 ; Sf II B 18 ; C 13. See the note on Sf I B 23.

yqrq : " Flees." Dupont-Sommer notes that the same form is found in *AD* 3 : 5 and in AšOstr (lines 9, 13, 16, 17, 18). See M. Lidzbarski, *Altaramäische Urkunden aus Assur* (Leipzig: J. C. Hinrichs, 1921), 8; *KAI* 233; D. H. Baneth, *OLZ* 22 (1919) 55-58. In later Aramaic the form is *'rq*, as in Syriac. Now that this etymology is established, there can no longer be any question of a relation between *'rq* and Arabic *'araqa* (see C. Brockelmann, *Lexicon syriacum*, p. 550), nor probably with Jb 30 : 3, 17, as I. Caine has pointed out to me.

qrq : Though Dupont-Sommer prefers to regard this form as an inf. absol., he does mention another possibility which seems to me more probable, viz., a participle, " fugitive " (*qāriq*). Cf. *qrqy* and *qrqhm* on lines 19-20, which must be regarded as participles. Moreover, in the other cases of an intensifying infinitive in this inscription, it always precedes the finite verb; see note on *hskr* (line 2). For provision concerning fugitives in earlier Syrian treaties, see D. J. Wiseman, *The Alalakh Tablets* (London, 1953), 3.5-15 (p. 31); 1 Kgs 2 : 39-40.

pqdy : " Officials." See lines 10, 13 for the same word. Cf. Hebrew *pāqîd*, Akkadian *pāqidu* and *paqūdu*, Aramaic *pqyd* (*AD* 2 : 2, 3 ; 4 : 1 ; 6 : 1, etc.). Note the *scriptio defectiva* of the medial long *i*.

5. *srsy :* " My courtiers or eunuchs " ; cf. Hebrew *sārîs*, Aramaic *srs* (*NSI* 150 : 2 ; *CIS* 2 : 75). The word is sometimes explained as related to Akkad. *ša rēsi šarri*, " he who is by the head of the king."

zy bydy : " Who are under my control," lit. " who are in my hands."

yhkn : 3 pl. masc. impf. Peal either of *hlk* (so Dupont-Sommer) or preferably of *hwk*. Thus T. Nöldeke (*ZA* 20 [1907] 142), and *BLA* 46*b*. The latter root is thought to be related to the Ethiopic *hôka*. Other occurrences of this verb are in line 6 (*'hk*) and in Sf I A 24 (*yhkn*). Cf. the forms *tqh* (line 2) and *ysq* (line 14) for the assimilation (?) of *lamedh*, if it is preferable to derive the form from *hlk*.

hlb : " Aleppo," a town probably belonging to the kingdom of Arpad at this period. It is also mentioned in Sf I A 10-11. For the spelling and derivation of the name of the town, cf. H. T. Bossert, *Orientalia* 30 (1961) 319-20, n. 3. *hlb* is used with a verb of motion toward it, but without a preposition. See Pad I v 5, I r 3; *BMAP* 13 : 3; *AP* 42 : 7; 83 : 2; *AD* 6 : 2, 4, 5. Contrast *AP* 37 : 11. Cf. *JNES* 21 (1962) 20.

lts[k l]hm : Restored according to line 7; cf. Sf I B 38. The verb must come from the root *nsk*, which normally means to " pour a libation." But it is used here in a generic sense with *lhm* " to provide food." F. Rosenthal (*BASOR* 158 [1960] 29, n. 3) compares Akkad. *nasāku*, " throw down food, meals." Cf. Dn 2 : 46. The prefixed *l* is the negative *lā*, always written thus in this inscription; see *lt'mr, lthrm* (line 5), *ly*[*šb*]*n* (line 6), *ltršh, ltmšl* (line 9), *ltšlḥ* (line 17,21), *lyqtl wly'sr* (line 18), *ltrqh* (line 19).

šlw : " Stay quiet "; pl. impv. Peal of *šl'*. Cf. Jer 12 : 1 ; Ps 122 : 6 ; Lam 1 : 5.

thrm : 2 sg. masc. impf. Haph. of *rwm*. Dupont-Sommer translates, " tu ne me soustrairas pas leur âme." The literal meaning seems to be, " you shall not make their soul higher than me," hence you must not incite or embolden them. Cf. *rm lbw* of Jer 48 : 29 ; Hos 13 : 6 ; Dt 8 : 14 ; Ez 31 : 10 ; and especially Dt 17 : 20, which uses the prep. *mn* (as here) with a person toward whom the bold insolence would be displayed. F. Rosenthal (*BASOR* 158 [1960] 29) would translate, " you must not cause them to be disdainful of me." The expression is one of reckless elation and disdain. Cf. Dn 5 : 20 (*kᵉdî rim libᵉbeh*).

6. *nbšhm :* For the form *nbš* instead of the normal *npš* see BirRKB 8 :7 ; Hadad 17, 21, 22 ; Panammū 18 ; Sf I A 37 ; I B 39, 40, 42 ; Sf II B 5.

rqh trqhm : " You must placate them." On the use of the inf. see note on *hskr* (line 2). The same root is also found in *rqw* and *'rqhm* of this line and in lines 18-19. But Dupont-Sommer prefers to regard the root of the verbs in this line as *rqq*, " broyer, contraindre," whereas that of the verbs in lines 18-19 as *rqh*, " être bienveillant, vouloir." In favor of such a distinction one should note the transitive use of the verbs in line 6 and the use with *bn* in lines 18-19. Here he translates, " tu devras les capturer ... capturez(-les) là bas, jusqu'à ce que j'(y) aille moi-même et que je les capture." The form *rqh* is explained as an infinitive, without the preformative *m*, but with the feminine ending *-h* (cf. the now certain reading of Sf I A 13 : *lḥzyh*). However, we fail to see how one can regard *rqh* as the Peal inf. of *rqq* (related to the Hebrew *rṣṣ*), " crush " in this context. The forms *rqh* and *trqh* certainly indicate a *tertiae infirmae* root ; the form *rqw* seems to show that it was an original *lamedh waw* verb, as suggested to me by F. M. Cross, Jr., who compares the Moabite forms *wy'nw* and *''nw* (see Mešaʿ 5, 6 ; *KAI* 181:5-6 ; S. R. Driver, *Notes on the Hebrew Text and the Topography of the Books of Samuel* [Oxford : Clarendon Press, 1913] lxxxv) and the South Arabic *rḍw*. Hence, the Aramaic verb here must be *rqh*, related to the Hebrew *rṣh* " to be acceptable, pleasing." The forms are probably Pael, " to make acceptable to them," hence " to prevail " upon their wills. F. Rosenthal (*BASOR* 158 [1960] 29) compares the Pael usage in Syriac and translates " placate " or " pacify." Therefore, vocalize *rqw* as *raqqiw*, *trqhm* as *turaqqīhom*, and *'rqhm* as *'uraqqīhom* (< *'uraqqiy/w-hom*). — For the inf. without preformative *m* in Peal cf. *l'mr* (*AP* 2 : 3 ; 5 : 3, 12 et passim ; *BMAP* 1 : 3 ; 2 : 3 et passim ; contrast *lmmr*, *AP* 32 : 2 ; 43 : 2). Further examples in this stele : *rqh* (line 18), *nkh* (lines 12-13). See also Hadad 10 (*lnṣb*, *lbny*). But since this use of the inf. in this Aramaic inscription is probably due to Canaanite influence, it may be that the infinitives here should be vocalized as Phoen. or Hebr. Thus *raqqēh* (like Hebr. Piel *gallēh*), *haskir* (line 2), *nakeh* (?). See G. Garbini, *RSO* 34 (1959) 50-51.

thšbhm : Haph. impf. of *šwb*, " return." For a parallel to the apodictic form used here, cf. the Hittite treaty of Mursilis II with Manapa-Dattas col. I, 52ff. (see J. Friedrich, *Staatsverträge des Hatti-Reiches in hethitischer Sprache* [MVAG 31/1]).

ly[*šb*]*n* : Dupont-Sommer rightly regards this as Peal impf. of *yšb* ; vocalize *yiššibūn* and cf. Bibl. Aram. *yittib* (*BLA* 45j) ; see *yšb* (line 17), *šbw* (line 7).

rqw : Vocalize *raqqiw* ; see above. The direct object is understood.

šm : " There," as in Hebr. *šām*. Later Aramaic is *tmh*, Syriac *tmn*.

'rqhm : Though I hesitated at first between *r* and *d* here, having seen the stele I am convinced that Dupont-Sommer is correct in reading *r*. The same chipping that makes the *lamedh* of *šlw* (5) difficult has effaced the top of the *reš*. But the long vertical shaft remains. Hence, we have a suffixal form of the Pael, *'uraqqīhom*.

7. *šbw* : The masc. pl. impv. of *yšb*. Dupont-Sommer : " Résidez au lieu où vous êtes." The substantival use of *tḥt*, meaning " place," together with the verb *yšb* occurs in Ex 16 : 29, *šbw 'yš tḥtyw* (as pointed out to me by J. Strugnell) ; cf. Jos 5 : 8. Cf. J. C. Green-field, *ZAW* 73 (1961) 226-28. As Dupont-Sommer notes, the context excludes the sense of " return " (root *šwb*) ; so the verb must be *yšb*.

'l : In addition to the negative prefix *l-* we also find in this inscription *'l* as the negative of a prohibition ; see lines 18 (*w'*[*l*]), 20 ([*w'*]*l*). Possibly it also occurs in line 9 (*'l tmšl*) ; see note there. Cf. Sf I A 21, 22, 23, 24, 28, 29, 33, 36 ; I B 8 ; I C 24 ; Sf II A 2.

w'l tpnw b'šrh : " Do not (re)turn to his region." F. Rosenthal (*BASOR* 158 [1960] 29) would translate this phrase, " and pay no attention to him," noting that " to turn after him " means " to look after him." He compares the use of *pnh* in Hebr. with the corre-sponding prep. *'ḥry*, " to turn, look behind oneself." But the meaning of this phrase is not quite the same (with the suffix of a different person), and the meaning of the Hebr. parallel scarcely fits the present context.

wkl mlky' : A new section begins here, but there is no verb with which *mlky'* is to be construed. Hence we must have a *casus pendens*.

zy : Whereas *zy* is used elsewhere in this inscription as a relative, it appears here as a determinative expressing a genitive relationship, as a substitute for a construct chain.

8. *shrty* : This word is probably related to the later Aramaic *saḥrānīn* (m. pl.), which Dalman (*ANHW* 287b) translates, " Umgebung, Nachbarschaft." It has recently turned up also in a fragment of Qumran: [*wl'*] *yshrwn shrthw*[*n*] *l'lm* (4Q Tob aram[b] 3 i 14), which I cite here with the permission of J. T. Milik. The word " vicinity " undoubtedly refers here to those lands which were contiguous to that of Bir-Ga'yah, with whose rulers he had made a pact of trade and commerce, and consequently of friendship or amity. See J. J. Rabinowitz, *Bibl* 39 (1958) 401; cf. Gn 34 : 9-10; 42 : 34; Is 47 : 15; Ez 27 : 12, 21. Compare Akkadian *saḥāru*, Hebrew *shr*.

kl zy rḥm h' ly : " Anyone who is a friend of mine." Dupont-Sommer breaks up the letters differently: *kl zy rḥmh 'ly*, and explains *rḥmh* as " graphie défective pour *rḥmwh*, du nom pluriel *rḥmyn*;" he translates, " quiconque dont l'affection (se portera) vers moi." Similarly S. Segert, *ArOr* 32 (1964) 126, n. 111. But the defective writing of such an ending is impossible in this inscription; see note on *'pwh* (line 2). Consequently, *rḥm* must be a participle, *h'* the personal pronoun serving as copula, and *ly* the object of *rḥm. — h'* (= *hu'*): cf. Hadad 22; Panammū 11; Meša' 6.

w'šlḥ : " When I send." As in line 17, a *waw* follows a *casus pendens*, which may have conditional force (so E. Vogt, *Bibl* 39 [1958] 272), or — even better — temporal force. Cf. Meša' 4-5 (*KAI* 181 : 4-5). For the idiom *šlḥ ml'ky*, cf. AšOstr 19; 1 Kgs 20 : 2.

'[l]wh : Restored on the basis of *'ly*, which is parallel to it.

lšlm : " For peace." The reading here seems quite doubtful. Dupont-Sommer reads *lšlḥ*, translating " pour (lui) envoyer (un message)," noting that *šlḥ* is attested in Aramaic in the sense, " to send a message, order." Aside from the fact that the expression is cumbersome, the last letter is quite doubtful, judging both from the photos and the squeeze. J. T. Milik has suggested the reading *šlm*, which fits the context well. J. Starcky has told me that this was his original conviction, but that he yielded to Dupont-Sommer who returned to Beirut to verify several readings and maintains that the *ḥ* is certain. Having seen the stele, I think the letter is quite doubtful. There is a vertical line on the left and a horizontal one on the top, but it is hard to say whether these are primary or secondary cuts.

ḥpṣy : " Business " ; see Is 58 : 3 ; Qoh 3 : 1, 17 ; 8 : 6.

9. *ptḥh* : Pe'îl participle fem. sg., *patīḥā*, lit. " opened." Dupont-Sommer, while preferring this explanation, mentions another " moins probable " ; impv. with paragogic *h*. However, he gives no parallel for this in Aramaic ; it is rather unlikely.

'rḥ' : " The road." Dupont-Sommer reads, as we do, *ptḥh ly 'rḥ' ltmšl by*. Since the negative in this inscription is either the prefix *l-* or *'l*, it is difficult to say whether we should read instead *'rḥ 'l tmšl*. The context seems to demand the emphatic state of *'rḥ*. Though all other cases of the emph. sg. are followed by a demonstrative adjective in this stele, we do find the emph. pl. alone (*mly'*, line 2). Hence it is better to retain Dupont-Sommer's division of the words. On the fem. gender of the masc. form, see G. Garbini, *RSO* 34 (1959) 46. Note the apodictic form of the stipulation here, which throws light on the forms in the OT Decalogue.

bz' : " On it," i.e., on the road, since *'rḥ'* is feminine.

wltršh : " Nor assert your authority over me concerning it." Dupont-Sommer notes that the root *ršh* is frequent in the Elephantine papyri in the sense " to sue for " or " to lay a claim to " and in Syriac in the meaning " to reproach." But the meaning of *tršh* is rather that found in Nabataean, " to have authority over." Cf. *ršy* (*NSI* 89.4), *ršyn* (*NSI* 90.3). It seems to occur also in this sense in Hadad 27 ; Karatepe A III 26. Cf. also the Hebrew *ršywn*, " permission," Ezr 3:7. In Rabbinical Aramaic one finds *rš'y*, " allowed, authorized."

[w]hn lhn : See note on Sf I B 36.

mn ḥd : " Any one." Compound indefinite pronoun ; *mn* = *man*. See note on Sf II B 9.

'ḥy : " My brothers." Is this intended to mean " blood brothers" or " kinsmen " ? See *JNES* 21 (1962) 17 ; E. Y. Kutscher, *Lešonenu* 26 (1962) 8-9.

10. *ngdy* : " My officers," or " my military commanders." Dupont-Sommer reads *ngry*, comparing the Akkadian *nāgiru*. But a careful examination of the squeeze and the stele suggests rather that *ngdy* was originally written and that the lengthened vertical shaft of the letter is either a slip or a secondary cut. It is neither as deep as the upper first part nor does it continue in the same direction. Cf. Hebrew *nāgîd*, the interesting parallel use of *pqyd ngyd* in Jer 20 : 1, and its use as applied to Saul (1 Sm 9 : 16) and David (1 Sm 13 : 14). What is important is to note the position occupied by the *nagīd* (= later

Aram. *n ᵉgīdā*) between the royal princes and the " officials " (*paqīday*).
See further W. F. Albright, *Samuel and the Beginnings of the Prophetic
Movement* (Cincinnati: Hebrew Union College Press, 1961) 15-16; cf.
M. Noth, *ZDPV* 77 (1961) 150, who looks with skepticism on the
reading *ngdy*. Any attempt to support the reading *ngry* by an appeal
to the Adon Letter, line 8, is nothing more than an explanation of
ignotum per ignotius; see *Bibl* 46 (1965) 44, 54-55. Cf. R. A. Bowman,
AJSL 58 (1941) 303 (B7).

[*p*]*qdy* : " My officials." Cf. *AD* 1.2; 2.3; 4.1; *RES* 1798 A.
The form is basically passive (*qatīl*-type), expressing one who is under
a command; but he is a commander or officer of some sort. Cf.
Mt 8:9.

ᶜmy : " People." The form of the noun is plural here, whereas
in lines 5, 13 (which are parallel) the singular occurs.

w- : I had proposed to delete this conjunction, but J. Hoftijzer
(*VT* 9 [1959] 316, n. 2) has tried to identify it as a " *waw* of apodosis."   J. Koopmans (*AC*, p. 66) has objected to this explanation of
it, and I agree. It is scarcely a *waw* of apodosis because it intro-
duces, not the verb in the apodosis, but the verb in the conditional
clause itself after a long series of subjects. More than likely it should
be explained as anacoluthon, with the *waw* added because of a similar
conditional use of *waw* found elsewhere in these texts.

11. *lhmtty* : " To kill me." Vocalize: *la-hamītūtī*, or possibly *hamātūtī* (cf. *BLA* §46z). The Haph. inf. appears here with the fem. ending *-ūt* before the pronominal suffix; the same form occurs also on
a non-suffixal infinitive, *hmtt*. Cf. *BLA* §65p. These forms are found
again in III 15-16; cf. II B 8. For a similar Hebrew idiom, see Jer
26:21; Ps 37:32; and for possible Akkadian parallels, see J. C.
Greenfield, *Acta orientalia* 29 (1965) 7.

ᵓy[*t*]*y* : " Me," with the *signum accusativi*; see the comment on
Sf I B 32.

wtqm : 2 sg. masc. impf. Peal of *nqm*, " to avenge." Cf. 2 Kgs
9:7.

yqtln : " They kill me." 3 pl. masc. impf. Peal of *qtl* (with non-
emphatic *t*); see note on Sf I B 27.

ᵓt : " You." The emphatic use of the independent personal
pronoun before the verb; cf. lines 6, 20 (after the verb).

12. *yqm* : " Will avenge." Note the asyndetic collocation of the
verbs here, in contrast to *ᵓth wtqm* in line 11.

hᵓ : Vocalize *hīᵓ*; it serves as the predicate-copula.

nkh : " You must strike." The Peal inf. is used as an intensifier; see note on *hskr,* Sf III 2.

13. *t(k)wh :* Dupont-Sommer reads *tpwh,* taking the form as the pl.
impv. with suffix (3 sg. fem.) of the root *tpp,* " to strike." This
form must be considered with *tkh* further on in the line. In the latter
case the reading *tph* is, in our opinion, quite doubtful. On the other
hand, *tpwh* at the beginning of the line is certain. As the inf. which
precedes the finite verb in both cases is clearly *nkh* and we can read
tkh in the second instance, we prefer to read *tkwh* at the beginning
of the line also, regarding *tpwh* as an engraver's error. All the other
cases of the intensifying inf. in this inscription are of the same root
as the finite form that they modify. This reason is not, of course,
absolutely conclusive, but it does strengthen an otherwise doubtful
reading. Cf. Dt 13 : 16 ; Jos 11 : 11 ; 1 Sm 22 : 19. But what form
is *tkwh?* If from *nkh,* it looks like a 2 sg. impf. Pael with a fem.
suffix, perhaps *takkiwah* (suggestion of F. M. Cross, Jr.). See above
the note on *rqh trqhm* (line 6).

tkh : " You must strike." 2 sg. masc. impf. Peal of *nkh.* Dupont-Sommer explains the *tph* which he reads here as a defective
writing for *toppeh* (sg. impv. with suffix) or for *toppūhī* (pl. impv.
with suffix). But this cannot be right. First of all, the *yodh* is
always found in this inscription for a final *i* ; hence his latter vocalization is excluded. Secondly, we see no reason for explaining *h* as
a suffix, if his explanation of the following word (*'yh*) is correct.

'yh : " Him." " Tel quel, ce mot ne nous semble offrir ici aucun
sens. Nous supposons qu'un *t* a été accidentellement omis : *'y<t>h,*
eum (cf. 1.11 : *'yty*), reprise du pronom suffixe *-h* devant l'énumération
w'qrh wśgbwh wmwddwh." Thus Dupont-Sommer. But is it not better
to regard the corrected *'y<t>h* as the first element of the compound
direct object, thus eliminating the doubtful suffix?

śgbwh : " Ses grands." Dupont-Sommer compares the Hebr. root
śgb, " to be lofty," and takes the word as a synonym for *rbwh* (Sf
I A 40). The reading of *g* at the end of the line is doubtful and
should be read as *r.* In favor of *śgbwh* one can cite the Akkadian
word *sagbû,* " garde, protection " (G. Dossin, *ARM,* 5.1, 12 and
p. 124 n. ; see also M. Noth [*ZDPV* 77 (1961) 150], " Wächter ". If
śrbwh, " nobles," must be read, then one can compare Akkadian
šurbū, " gross, hoch, erhaben " (*BAG* 253) or Syriac *šarbtā* (see F.
Rosenthal, *BASOR* 158 [1960] 29, n. 8).

14. *whn lhn :* See note on Sf I B 36.

ysq 'l lbbk : " The idea should come to your mind," lit. " it
should ascend to your heart." On the form *ysq,* see note on Sf I A

5; cf. Ps. 139:8. Cf. the Hebrew equivalent *'lh 'l lb* (Is 65:17; Jer 3:16); and 1 Cor 2:9. Note the use of the 3 sg. masc. here as impersonal; cf. Sf I A 42.

wtś' : "You should express with your lips (the intention)," 2 sg. masc. impf. Peal of *nś'*; lit. "if you should raise to your lips"; cf. Zakir a 11 and Aḥiqar (*passim*) for the same verb in Aramaic. Cf. Ps 16:4.

15. *śptwh* : See note on *'pwh*, Sf I A 5 (*bnwh*).

16. *kl mh* : See note on Sf I A 26. Here the expression is pronominal and neuter.

ymwt : "Shall die." Vocalize *yamūt* and note the *plena scriptio* of a medial long vowel; see the note on *rwḥ*, Sf III 2.

br 'nš : "A man." This inscription attests the early use of this expression in a very generic sense. Cf. Dn 7:13; 1QapGn 21:13; see F. Vattioni, "La prima menzione aramaica di ' figlio dell'uomo '," *Biblos-Press* 6/1 (1965) 6-7. E. Sjöberg (*Acta orientalia* 21 [1950-53] 57-65, 91-107) cites no instance of *br 'nš* in Aramaic texts between the 8th cent. B.C. and the 3rd cent A.D. Cf. G. Garbini, *RSO* 34 (1959) 47.

17. *yrb* : "Quarrels with." Vocalize *yarīb* and contrast this form with *ymwt* of line 16; it is 3 sg. masc. Peal impf. of *ryb*.

yšb : See note on *yšbn*, Sf III 6.

khs'y : "My throne." The reading of this word is certain. Dupont-Sommer regards the *h* as a stonecutter's error for *r*. This would give *krs'y*, "my throne," a meaning that is favored by the context. The word *krs'* is found in the Bir-RKB inscription 7. *BLA* (p. 233, n. 1) explain *korsê* as a word taken over directly from the Akkadian *kursē*: through a false analogy *kursê > kursay* and with a suffix *korse-yeh* (Dn 7:9). The form with the *aleph* preserved is also found in *AP* 6.2. The Arabic form is *kursiyuⁿ*, whereas Hebrew and Phoenician have *ks'*, and Akkadian has a second form *kussu*. Dupont-Sommer suggests that if the form *khs'y* is not to be regarded as an error, then it must represent a transitional form between the Aramaic-Arabic word and that of Phoenician-Hebrew. Cf. the form *dbhh* in Sf I A 31 — another doubled consonant resolved by use of *he*? S. Segert (*ArOr* 32 [1964] 121) is undoubtedly right in saying that these two isolated instances scarcely argue for a weakened or uvular articulation of the *r*.

zy yšb ... : "Who sits upon my throne." We have taken this clause as a relative attributive to *bry*; so too F. Rosenthal (*ibid.*). But possibly it is causal, "because one of his brothers sits upon my throne." In any case *yšb* is scarcely a ptc. (so G. Garbini, *RSO* 34 [1959] 49), given the impf. forms in the vicinity (*yrb* and *y'brnh*).

y'brnh : "And he would remove him." This form seems to be the 3 sg. masc. energic impf. Aphel (not Haphel) with a suffix, from the root *'br*, "pass over." Cf. Jon 3 : 6 ; Zech 13 : 2 ; 2 Chr 15 : 8. This seems to be a explanation of the form preferable to that proposed by F. Rosenthal (*BASOR* 158 [1960] 30), "conceives a hatred of him," relating the word to Hebrew *'brh* and Arabic *ġibru^n*.

ltšlḥ lšnk : "You shall not interfere with them," or lit. "you shall not send your tongue." For the figurative use of the tongue as an instrument of slander, see Hadad 9 ; Ps 140 : 12 ; 101 : 5 ; 15 : 3 ; Ugaritic *lšn* (Driver, *CML*, 158). Cf. Ps 50 : 19. Is the idiom an adaptation of the more common *šlḥ yd*?

18. *bnyhm :* The same word occurs twice again in this inscription : once in this line and once in the following. The reading is certain in each case. From the context the meaning seems to be "between them." Dupont-Sommer takes it thus too. But if it is a form of the preposition *byn-*, then we have here a case of a medial diphthong contracted and written defectively, whereas one would expect *bynyhm* according to the usual explanation of the orthography of Aramaic at this period (see Cross and Freedman, *EHO*, p. 24, no. 4). The same spelling is found later, of course, in *AP* 13.14 ; 25.7 ; *BMAP* 4.10,11 (see P. Leander, *LFLAA* §4g). J. T. Milik believes that we rather have here a form of the adverb/preposition *bn* which is found in Phoenician (meaning "inside, within") ; see Karatepe Portal Inscription 2.18 ; 3.8 ; Ešmun'azor (*CIS* 3) 5 ; J. Friedrich, *PPG*, §254 Ia. For the time being, at least until further evidence is forthcoming that this word is also used in Aramaic, we prefer to regard the form *bnyhm* as the well-known preposition *byn-*, even if it is written defectively.

wt'mr : "Saying to him," lit. "and you shall not say to him." The negative is to be supplied from the previous, coordinated verb, *ltšlḥ* ; see line 21.

'ḥk : "Your brother." Vocalize *'aḥūk*.

'srh : "Imprison him," masc. sg. impv. Peal with suff. of 3 sg. m.

w'[l] : Restored as in line 7. Part of the *aleph* is still visible on the stele.

tšryh : "Do not let him go free." Vocalize *tišrayeh* ; 2 sg. masc. impf. Peal of *šry*, "to loose, set free." Note that the suffix is not added here to the energic form of the imperfect. This is a clear case of a suffix added to a *tertiae infirmae* verb, which should be considered in the analysis of *trqhm* (line 6).

rqh : See note on *hskr* (Sf III 2) and on this root in Sf III 6. "You really make peace."

lyqtl wly'sr : "He will not kill and will not imprison." The direct object to be supplied from the context. Dupont-Sommer has an alternate explanation : impf. passive *yuqtal* forms. But this is less likely as it would demand a change of subject in this otherwise very dense style.

19.　*w[m]lkn [zy shr]ty* : "As for kings of my vicinity," a *casus pendens*. This restoration of Dupont-Sommer has proved to be the best, despite the difficulty of the absol. pl. form instead of the expected emphatic (not " les rois ").

wyqrq : "If a fugitive of mine flees." The *waw*, used after the *casus pendens*, must have conditional force, as suggested by E. Vogt, *Bibl* 39 (1958) 273, comparing line 8.

qrqy, qrqhm : Participles (used substantively) with suffixes ; see line 4.

hdhm : "One of them." The numeral with a suffix is not extraordinary in view of the fact that *hd* in this inscription is regularly construed in a construct chain (and not with *mn* the preposition). For the use of suffixes on numbers in Aramaic, see C. Brockelmann, *Grundr* I, 249b.

20.　*hšb, 'hšb* : "He has restored ... I shall restore." Haph. act. of *šwb* ; note the change of tense from perfect to imperfect. G. Garbini (*RSO* 34 [1959] 48) thinks that the first word (*hšb*) is a passive form of the Haphel perfect.

zy ly : "Mine." Perhaps these words should be written as one, *zyly*, for the expression has all the earmarks of the stereotyped possessive so familiar in the Elephantine texts (*AP* 5.4 ; *BMAP* 3.16, 19 ; *A* 172), Arsames correspondence (*AD* 1.2 ; 2.2, 3) and in Syriac (*dyl-*).

[zy lh] : "His." Dupont-Sommer restores *zy lhm*, " clairement suggéré par le contexte." But it is rather the sg. suffix that the context demands — *hdhm* (" one of them "), *hšb* (3 sg. masc. pf. Haph.).

t'šqny : "You yourself shall not try to hinder me." 2 sg. masc. impf. Peal of *'šq*, " to oppress, wrong," plus the suffix of 1 sg. Do we have here an energic form? Cf. Agbar 8.

21.　*ltšlh lšn* : See note on Sf III 17.

bbyty : "In my house." The preposition is to be repeated in sense with the nouns coordinated to this one. Literally, the expression means, " you shall not send your tongue against my house nor (against) the sons of my sons, nor (against) the sons of my brothers, etc." But Dupont-Sommer takes the first *bny* of each group as a form of the preposition *bên-*, " between," and translates, " Et tu ne mettras pas la langue dans ma maison ni entre mes fils ni entre [mes] frè[res ni entre] ma [des]cendance ni entre mon peuple." Such an interpretation is not impossible; moreover, if it is correct, then we have three (or four, counting the restoration which is certain) more cases of the defective writing of a contracted diphthong. However, it is strange to see a shift from one preposition (*b*) to another (*bny*) with the same verb in the same sentence. My own interpretation seems more natural, but it is admittedly more cumbersome; however, in view of the line-up of kin found in the earlier part of the inscription such a cumbersome expression does not seem to be impossible. Moreover, see the note on Sf I A 2.

wt'mr : " Saying to them," lit. " you shall not say." Understand the negative prefix here from the preceding coordinated verb, as in lines 17-18.

mr'km : " Your lord." In the Hazael inscription of Arslan-Tash, in Panammū (13, 16, 17) and in Bir-RKB (5, 6, 9) we find the word *mr'* used as a title for a sovereign.

22. *whwy ḥlph* : " And be his successor." The division of the letters into words is crucial here. Dupont-Sommer reads them thus: *whw yḥlph*, translating, " et qu'un tel le remplace." G. Garbini (*RSO* 34 [1959] 44-45) and S. Segert (*ArOr* 32 [1964] 124) also take *hw* as a pronoun, though with some hesitation. Since the usual orthography of the 3rd sg. masc. pronoun at this period is *h'* (see Sf III 13; Hadad 22, 30; Panammū 11, 22; Bir-Rakkab 17, 18, 19), while *hw* occurs in later Aramaic texts (especially at Elephantine), this reading cannot be right. J. T. Milik suggested the reading used here. *hwy* is the masc. sg. impv. Peal and *ḥlph* is probably the act. ptc. with a suffix, *ḥālipeh*, " his successor " (cf. F. Rosenthal *BASOR* 158 [1960] 30). Another possibility was suggested by Rosenthal, to understand *ḥlph* as suffixal form of the prep. *ḥlāp* " and be in his place." Either of these is better than our original suggestion (followed by Donner - Röllig, *KAI*, 2.270) to take *ḥlph* as a noun, " and let there be a change " (*ḥalīpāh*); cf. 1 Kgs 5 : 28; Ps 55 : 20; Jb 10 : 17; 14 : 14. Cf. Jean - Hoftijzer, *DISO*, p. 63. See note on Sf I A 21.

ky ṭb h' mk : " For he is not better than you." This is Rosenthal's solution (*BASOR* 158 [1960] 30) to this difficult phrase. The assimilated suffixal form of the prep. *mn* is most peculiar. Should we really write *m<n>k*? Cf. 1 Kgs 19 : 4.

wyqm : If this is the same verb as in lines 11-12, then Dupont-Sommer is right in restoring a form of *dm-*.

ḥd : " Someone." This seems to be the absol. state of this pronoun, whereas all the other instances of it in this inscription are in the construct.

mrmt : " Treachery." Fem. absol. pl., as in the case of *mln lḥyt* (line 2); the idea is indefinite. Cf. Hebrew *mirmāh*; see Dn 11 : 23.

23. [*wtl'y*]*m* : Restored according to lines 25-26. From the words that follow it must be the proper name of a place, belonging to the royal house of the suzerain. M. Noth (*ZDPV* 77 [1961] 156) has plausibly suggested the identification of *tl'ym* with *Talḥayim*, repeatedly mentioned in the Mari letters, but whose location is still uncertain (see *ARM* 2.4,9; 5.51,12-15; 1.53,11; C.-F. Jean, *Semitica* 1 [1948] 18-21). It would seem to have lain in the Khabur region, but a location in the more westerly Balikh area is not excluded.

wkpryh : " And its villages." This word occurs again in line 26 and in Hadad 10, Panammū 10. In both of the last two instances it is spelled *kpyr*; see also Neh 6 : 2. M. Noth (*ZDPV* 77 [1961] 155) would understand this word to mean the " storehouses " (" ihre Vorratshäuseranlagen ") in which the semi-nomads stored their harvests.

b'lyh : " Its lords." See note on Sf I A 4.

gblh : " Its territory." Vocalize *gabūlah*. G. Garbini (*RSO* 34 [1959] 47) wrongly takes *gblh* as a fem. noun; it must be a suffixal form, given the preceding words *kpryh* and *b'lyh*.

24. *wkzy* : This is a common conjunction in the Elephantine texts; *AP* 6.1; 13.4; 27.2; etc.

ḥbzw : " Struck." See note on Sf II B 7.

'lhn : " Gods." Vocalize *'ilāhīn* (or possibly *'ilāhān*); see note on Sf III 2, *mln*.

[*h*]*wt* : " It came to belong." 3 sg. fem. pf. Peal of *hw'*, the subject of which is *h'* (vocalize *hī'*), referring to Tal'ayim.

l'ḥrn : This " other " person is unknown. For the idiom, see Dt 24 : 2 (*hyth l'yš-'ḥr*).

hšbw : " Have brought about the return." Haph. pf. of *šwb*, which is followed by a cognate accusative, *šybt*. Dupont-Sommer compares Ps 126 : 1; *b ᵉšûb Yahwēh šîbat Ṣiyyôn*. In this verse several commentators have wanted to read *š ᵉbût* or *š ᵉbît* (cf. Jer 33 : 7) instead of *šîbat*, which is to be retained, being now supported by this extrabiblical attestation of the same expression (even though in Aramaic). Moreover, the significance of this expression for the understanding of the biblical Hebrew expression *šûb* or *hēšîb š ᵉbût* should not be missed.

The Hebrew noun has always been puzzling to scholars, some wanting
to derive it from *šbh*, " to capture," others from *šwb*, " to return."
The Aramaic expression shows that the noun is a cognate accusative
and so supports the derivation of *š ᵉbût* from *šwb*.   The context, moreover, is one of restoration.   See J. C. Greenfield, *Acta orientalia* 29
(1965) 4.   Cf. Meša' 8-9, where one should read *w[yš]bh kmš*, "and
Kemoš restored it."   S. Segert (*ArOr* 32 [1964] 126) suggests the
possibility of vocalizing *šybt* as *šayyābat*.

25.   *wšbt* : " Has returned."   Vocalize *šābat*, 3 sg. fem. pf. Peal.
      tl'ym l[brg'y]h : Dupont-Sommer supplies *br g'y*, thus reading the
name *Bir-Ga'yah*, known to us from Sf I.   Here only the last letter
is preserved of what is obviously a proper personal name, to judge
from the following phrases.   There is just space for five letters and
the conjecture is quite plausible.   M. Noth (*ZDPV* 77 [1961] 118-72)
is quite skeptical about this restoration made by Dupont-Sommer;
it is not accepted by F. Rosenthal, but has been used by Donner -
Röllig (*KAI* 2.271).   Even though it is not certain, there is no better
restoration, in my opinion, for the present.   If correct, it establishes
a relation between Sf III and Sf I and II.   On the etymology of the
name, see note on Sf I A 1.

26.   The first part of this line is restored according to line 17.
      mn : " Whoever."   The interrogative pronoun is here used as an
indefinite relative.
      yš' : " Will raise."   3 sg. masc. impf. Peal of *nš'*, the same verb
as in line 14ff.

27.   Dupont-Sommer suggests as a possible restoration: *mn yš'* [*'l
šptwh lhšbth lhd ml*]*ky 'rpd* [*tqtlnh whn ltqt*]*lnh šqrt*, etc.

28.   *yšḥdn* : " They bribe."   Could this giving of presents refer to
bribes?   Dupont-Sommer thinks that this last section (beginning with
whn) expresses a hope for the prosperity of the vassal, provided that
he remains loyal to the suzerain.   See J. C. Greenfield, *Acta orientalia*
29 (1965) 10.
      kl mh mlk : " Every king."   See note on Sf I A 26.

29.   *špr* : Vocalize *šappīr*.

THE AFFINITY OF THE SEFIRE INSCRIPTIONS TO HITTITE AND ASSYRIAN TREATIES

During the course of the foregoing discussion the comments on various lines of the Aramaic treaties called attention to parallels in Hittite and Assyrian treaties of a similar nature. Since these Aramaic treaties come from a general area where the Hittites once had influence and the Assyrians were neighbors, it is not surprising that a certain amount of similarity should be found in the Aramaic, Assyrian, and Hittite treaties. However, because the latter are several centuries earlier than the former, there are also differences.

The classical analysis of the Hittite treaties was published by V. Korošec in 1931.([21]) He distinguished treaties of two sorts: *parity* treaties, in which both parties are mutually bound to obey similar stipulations, and *suzerainty* treaties, in which an inferior king is bound by oath as a vassal to obey the stipulations imposed on him by the suzerain or great king. It is to the suzerainty or vassal treaty that A. Dupont-Sommer compared the Sefîre inscriptions.([22]) Korošec described the general form of the Hittite suzerainty treaty as follows: (1) the preamble which identifies the author of the covenant (the " great king ") and gives his titles and attributes; (2) the historical prologue which recounts the benevolent deeds of the suzerain on behalf of the vassal, because of which the latter is obligated forever to obey the suzerain's stipulations; (3) the stipulations which set forth in detail the obligations imposed on the vassal; (4) the provisions for the deposit of the treaty in a shrine or temple and for periodic public readings of it; (5) the list of the gods who are summoned as witnesses of the pact; (6) a formula of curses and blessings invoked on the vassal. The various subheadings which are interspersed throughout my translation of the Aramaic treaties will enable the reader to make

---

([21]) *Hethitische Staatsverträge: Ein Beitrag zu ihrer juristischen Wertung* (Leipziger rechtswissenschaftliche Studien, 60; Leipzig: T. Weicher, 1931).

([22]) See *BMB* 13 (1956) 36: Sf III is characterized " comme un *traité de vassalité*," and is compared (pp. 37-38) with the Hittite treaty of Mursilis II and Duppi-Tessub of Amurru from the fourteenth century B.C. (see *ANET*, pp. 203-5).

a quick comparison with the above list of details which characterize the Hittite suzerainty treaty. The Aramaic treaties are unfortunately fragmentary and it is difficult to say whether they ever contained all six parts, a scheme which was not rigidly followed in any case even in the Hittite treaties.

One element in particular is significantly absent, the historical prologue. Whatever reason may be assigned for the omission of this element in the Aramaic treaties, the absence of it constitutes a major difference between the Aramaic and Hittite treaties. This element is basic to the Hittite conception of the covenant; it constitutes the " legal framework " of the Hittite suzerainty treaty. Hittite suzerains recalled their favors toward the vassals as well as those of their predecessors in order to establish the obligation of the vassal's loyalty and service.

Indeed, it is precisely this element which is absent from covenants of the first millennium B.C., whether they be Aramaic or Assyrian. This qualification seems to be necessary in view of the claim made by D. J. Wiseman ([23]) that the covenant form " remained basically unchanged through Neo-Assyrian times."

W. L. Moran has pointed out that more recently published material has confirmed the thesis which G. E. Mendenhall tried to establish by his comparison of certain covenants described in the Old Testament with the legal form of the Hittite treaties.([24]) Basing his investigations mainly on the Hittite treaties of the 15th to 13th centuries, Mendenhall made out a good case for the derivation from them of a form of covenant-relationship which characterizes much of the Yahweh-Israel relationship in the Old Testament. In particular, he pointed to the covenant tradition containing the Decalogue (Ex 20) and the narrative of the renewal of the covenant at Shechem (Jos 24). In the case of the Decalogue, specific obligations are imposed on the tribes of Israel without Yahweh being bound to any at all. As for Jos 24, " It is very difficult to escape the conclusion that this narrative rests upon traditions which go back to the period when the treaty form was still living, but that the later writer used the materials of the tradition which were of importance and value to him, and adapted them to his own contemporary situation." ([25])   It is crucial to Menden-

([23]) *Iraq* 20 (1958) 28.
([24]) See G. E. Mendenhall, *Law and Covenant in Israel and the Ancient Near East* (Pittsburgh : Biblical Colloquium, 1955) ; see *BA* 17 (1954) 26-46, 50-76. Cf. the review by W. L. Moran, *Bibl* 41 (1960) 297-99.
([25]) *BA* 17 (1954) 67. — Further support for Mendenhall's thesis can be found in the independent work along the same lines conducted by K. Baltzer,

hall's thesis that the Old Testament covenant forms are related to the Hittite style of the suzerainty treaty. For him this is an indication of the date of the tradition and the legal pattern which are being used — they must have been introduced into the history of Israel at an early date. In stressing the influence of such an early literary form derived from Hittite sources, Mendenhall stands in sharp contrast to the usual Wellhausenian explanation of the origin of the covenant relationship (that it was the product of prophetic religious thought in the eighth and seventh centuries B.C.).([26]) Moran has also made much of the difference in the Hittite and later treaties, precisely in their absence of the historical prologue.([27]) The more recently published material from the second millennium B.C. to which he appeals are Ugaritic and Akkadian texts; see J. Nougayrol, *Le palais royal d'Ugarit IV* (Mission de Ras Shamra 7; Paris: Imprimerie nationale, 1956); D. J. Wiseman, *The Alalakh Tablets* (London: British Institute of Archaeology at Ankara, 1953).

It is also significant that in the Assyrian treaties of Esarhaddon, dating from the first millennium B.C., there is no historical prologue, just as there is none in the Aramaic treaties of Sefîre. Another difference which characterizes the later first millennium treaties is the tendency to use more elaborate and colorful curses. ([28])

When, however, one prescinds from these differences, one cannot fail to notice the otherwise striking similarity existing between the Aramaic treaties of Sefîre and the Hittite and Assyrian vassal treaties. The detailed comparison has been made in many cases in the com-

Das Bundesformular (Wissenschaftliche Monographien zum Alten und Neuen Testament, 4; Neukirchen: Neukirchener Verlag, 1960). It is beyond the scope of my work here to go into a detailed discussion of the relevance of these treaty-forms for the Old Testament covenants. While Mendenhall's thesis has found widespread acceptance, there are some dissenting voices which raise difficulties in certain areas. The reader may consult the following discussions for further details: E. Gerstenberger, " Covenant and Commandment," *JBL* 84 (1965) 38-51; D. J. McCarthy, " Covenant in the Old Testament: The Present State of Inquiry," *CBQ* 27 (1965) 217-40; also his *Treaty and Covenant* (see bibliography, p. 7 above); H. B. Huffmon, " The Exodus, Sinai and the Credo," *CBQ* 27 (1965) 101-13, esp. pp. 109-10; P. B. Harner, " Exodus, Sinai and Hittite Prologues," *JBL* 85 (1966) 233-36.

([26]) For the espousal of a view which is very close to that of J. Wellhausen, see C. F. Whitley, " Covenant and Commandment in Israel," *JNES* 22 (1963) 37-48.

([27]) *Bibl* 41 (1960) 298-99.

([28]) See H. B. Huffmon, *op. cit.*, p. 109, n. 41. Greater detail for the purposes of comparison can be found in D. J. McCarthy, *op. cit.*, part I, chs. 7-8.

ments on the lines in the foregoing treatment. It may be useful to
recall some of the similarities here. Several of the stipulations in the
Hittite treaty between Mursilis and Duppi-Tessub of Amurru end with
a formula which is quite similar to the concluding clauses in these
steles : " If you do (or do not do) such things, you act in disregard
of your oath." This is the Hittite counterpart of the Aramaic *whn
lhn* clause. Still more significant is the alternate formula : " you act
in disregard of the gods of the oath." Cf. Sf I B 27, 33 ; II B 9 ;
III 4, 14, 17, 23. Dupont-Sommer has also called attention to the striking parallel in Sf III 4-7 to the Hittite treaty of Mursilis with Duppi-
Tessub, (§13) : " If anyone of the deportees from the Nuhassi land
or of the deportees from the country of Kinzu whom my father removed
and I myself removed escapes and comes to you, (if) you do not
seize him and turn him back to the king of the Hatti land, and
even tell him as follows : ' Go ! Where you are going to, I do not
want to know,' you act in disregard of your oath " (see *ANET*,
pp. 203-5).

For further comparative study of the Aramaic, Hittite, and Assyrian treaties, one can find abundant material in D. J. McCarthy,
*Treaty and Covenant : A Study in Form in the Ancient Oriental Docu-
ments and in the Old Testament* (Analecta Biblica, 21 ; Rome : Biblical
Institute, 1963).

There is the final question whether the Sefîre treaties are really
vassal treaties at all. The question has been raised by M. Noth,[29]
who recalls that we have only the texts found in the area of Matî'el
of Arpad. Sf I and II may really represent the " treaty of Bir-Ga'-
yah, king of KTK " and set forth only his understanding of the pact
with the stipulations that he is imposing on Matî'el. It is not impossible that a similar text was drawn up from the standpoint of the
latter, imposing similar (but not identical) stipulations on Bir-Ga'yah
— a text which is unfortunately lost to us. If so, then the Sefîre
inscriptions would really represent a parity treaty, and not a vassal
treaty. Moreover, Noth insists that four essentials are needed in the
vassal treaty and that these appear in the study of the Hittite treaties carried out by V. Korošec.[30] They can be summed up as follows : (a) the setting up (or confirmation) of the vassal by the overlord ; (b) the imposition of an obligation on the vassal to appear
regularly before the overlord ; (c) a regularized payment of tribute

(29) *ZDPV* 77 (1961) 138-45. A similar stand is taken by Donner - Röllig,
KAI, 2. 271-72.

(30) Noth (p. 139) refers to the following pages of Korošec's *Hethitische
Staatsverträge* : 8-10, 72-85.

to the overlord; (d) the supply of a number of armies or troops by the vassal to the overlord in the case of a war. According to Noth, the first three elements in this list are lacking in the Sefîre inscriptions; (d) appears in Sf I B 28-33, II B 5-7.

But part of the difficulty is that Noth is falling into the same fault that he complains about in the case of others who are using the Hittite treaties as norms to say that the Sefîre inscriptions are vassal treaties; he derives certain elements from the Hittite treaties and not finding them present in the later Aramaic treaties questions whether they are really vassal treaties. It seems to me that the relationship of Matî'el to Bir-Ga'yah cannot be understood — at least on the basis of the material now available — in any other way than as that of a vassal to his overlord, or " great king." D. J. McCarthy has also disagreed with Noth's estimate of the Sefîre treaties in this regard. He insists that " Mati'el's throne clearly depends on KTK (Stele I, B, 24-25; II, B, 5-7) and this is the essential thing. Furthermore, Noth mentions that parity treaties appeared in different editions for each party, and he thinks Sfiré is Mati'el's edition, while there might have been another with more emphasis on the king of KTK's duties. However, each edition of the typical parity treaty, Ramses II-Hattusilis III, details the obligations of both parties. There is no question of different texts of the clauses for each, and we have seen that the parity treaty normally applied an obligation now to one, now to the other party, and only then moved on to the next obligation. The obligations of each were not listed separately. There is an instance of a double edition of a vassal treaty (Mattiwaza) and there each edition makes clear the inferiority of the lesser party." [31]

Until further evidence is brought to light to change this judgment, we prefer to regard the Sefîre inscriptions as examples of vassal or suzerainty treaties.

---

[31] *Op. cit.*, p. 64, n. 39. It might also be well to recall here McCarthy's more general thesis that there is basically no difference in the vassal and parity treaty from the standpoint of their *form* : " Formally, parity and vassal treaty are one " (*op. cit.*, p. 27). The judgment, therefore, shall have to be made on the contents and the stipulations, and the general treatment of the underling.

THE LAND OF *KTK*

The major problem in the interpretation of the Sefîre inscriptions is undoubtedly the identification of the land of *KTK* over which the suzerain Bir-Ga'yah ruled in the middle of the eighth century B.C. Various attempts to identify it have been made by writers since the first publication of the Sefîre I inscription in 1931. The present discussion of it is an attempt to survey the various proposals and to assess them.

(1) The original editor of Sf I, S. Ronzevalle, sensed the problem and gave only a generic description of the locality where *KTK* should be found.([32]) Shortly after his publication J. Cantineau proposed the interpretation that *KTK* was Assyria and understood Bir-Ga'yah as a second name for Aššurnirāri V.([33]) The main reason for this interpretation was the existence of an Assyrian treaty between Aššurnirāri V and Mati'ilu of Arpad.([34]) Since the latter is certainly to be identified with Matî'el, son of 'Attarsamak, the vassal in the Sefîre inscriptions, Cantineau suggested that Sf I was an Aramaic version of the same pact. Accordingly, he regarded *KTK* as " une graphie volontairement fautive " for Kalaḫ. This sort of interpretation of *KTK* was pushed still further by G. Dossin who proposed that it was a cryptogram for *KUR.A Š.KI*, equalling *māt Aššur*. ([35])

([32]) Ronzevalle wrote, " L'emplacement exact du pays de KTK reste à trouver : toutes mes recherches à cet égard ont échoué. La prononciation même de ce nom reste indécise : *Katak, Katouk, Koutik, Kattoûk*, etc. Mais on ne se trompera pas beaucoup en le situant dans la région ayant pour limites, au nord, Alep et son district, à l'est et au sud-est, les collines de Ḥass, le lac salé de Gabboûl et l'Euphrate, (sinon le Khaboûr, si Ḥaṣeka doit être identifiée avec la Ḥaseka moderne = Hassetché) ; à l'ouest, les collines du Djebel Sema'ân, et au sud et au sud-ouest la plaine qui donne accès à la région alépine " (*MUSJ* 15 [1930-31] 252).
([33]) *RA* 28 (1931) 178.
([34]) See E. F. Weidner, *AfO* 8 (1932-33) 17-34.
([35]) *Muséon* 57 (1944) 151-53. See also G. Contenau, " La cryptographie chez les Mésopotamiens," *Mélanges bibliques rédigés en l'honneur de André Robert* (Travaux de l'Institut Catholique de Paris, 4 ; Paris : Bloud et Gay, 1957), pp. 17-21.

The obvious difficulty which such an interpretation encounters is to explain why *KTK* should be a cryptogram or a deliberately false writing of the name of the suzerain's country in the text of a state treaty. This is scarcely the sort of document in which one conceals the identity of the country or of the king involved. Moreover, if Assyria were really the major partner to the treaty, it is difficult to explain the absence of the god Asshur from the list of deities who are witnesses to the pact in Sf I A 8-13. Again, if Sf I A 25 is correctly read and interpreted now, then " Assyria " (*'šr*) is explicitly mentioned and seems to be distinct from *KTK*.[36]

(2) A. Alt proposed the vocalization of the name as *Katikka* and located it in the region around Lake Jebbûl, to the east of Aleppo in Syria.[37] He maintained that the steles had been erected by the Aramaean princeling Bir-Ga'yah in his own territory. He sought to identify *KTK* with the name of an area mentioned in one of the inscriptions of Tiglathpileser III. Unfortunately, the text is broken and one has only the beginning of the geographical name to which he refers, *Ka*[   ].[38] On the basis of the spelling of the Aramaic name *KTK* he proposed to restore "*Ka-[ti-ik-ka]*, a name which would resemble *Ḥatarikka*, the Akkadian form of the biblical Hadrach. Indeed, Alt apparently regarded the territory as " ein unselbstständiger Teil des Reiches Arpad."

This proposal has not met with much acceptance because of the many problematical elements in it : the broken text of Tiglathpileser III, the likelihood that the region around Lake Jebbûl belonged rather to the territory of Matî'el, and the implication of Sf I C 1-3, which suggests that it was rather Matî'el who had erected the steles in his territory.

(3) B. Landsberger, on the other hand, equated *KTK* with Ḥatarikka, which is the same as Ḥazrak of the Zakir stele (a 4, 9, 10 ; b 1, 4) and Ḥadrach of Zech 9 : 1.[39] He suggested that Bir-Ga'yah was the king over the double kingdom of Ḥamath and Ḥatarikka, just as Zakir had been king over Ḥamath and Lu'ash, according to the Zakir stele.

The difficulty in this suggestion, however, is to show that there is any linguistic connection between *KTK* and Ḥatarikka or any political connection between *KTK* and Hamath in this period.

---

[36] See further the remarks of A. Dupont-Sommer, *BMB* 13 (1956) 39.

[37] *ZDMG* 88 (1934) 237 ; *Kleine Schriften* 3 (1959) 216.

[38] See P. Rost, *Die Keilschrifttexte Tiglat-Pilesers III.* (Leipzig : E. Pfeiffer, 1893), Kleinere Inschriften II, line 28 (p. 85).

[39] *Sam'al*, p. 59, n. 147.

(4) A. Dupont-Sommer at first identified *KTK* with *Kaska*, the king of which is mentioned in the Annals of Tiglathpileser III as *Da-di-i-lu* ᵘʳᵘ*Kas-ka-ai*.(⁴⁰) In this context Kaska (or more properly *Kašk*) is mentioned after Sam'al, Gurgum, and Melidh, but before Tabal, Tuna, and Tuḫana. From this collocation Dupont-Sommer concluded that Kašk lay somewhere between Gurgum, Melidh, and Tabal. It points to a northern locality which is plausible in the light of the references to Muṣr (= Muṣri), Arpad, and " all Aram " in Sf I A 5. The name Dadi-ilu is Aramaic and suggests that the dynasty of Kašk was Aramean. Since the name Bir-Ga'yah is also Aramaic, Dupont-Sommer suggested that possibly he was the father of Dadi-ilu in the time of Aššurnirāri V (or possibly that he was even the same person, Dadi-ilu bir Ga'yah).

Aside from the last element in this proposal, this identification encounters only one major difficulty. Dupont-Sommer was apparently aware of it, when he later wrote,(⁴¹) " Du point de vue linguistique, la graphie *KTK*, au lieu de KSK-KŠK, ne ferait pas difficulté ; c'est ainsi, par ex., que, dans les documents assyriens, le mot *Luḫuti* (avec *t*), designant une région située en Syrie, correspond au mot L'Š (avec Š) de l'inscription araméenne de Zakir." Aside from the fact that the place *l'š* in the Zakir stele is most probably to be identified with Nuḫašše and not Luḫuti, there is the problem of the Aramaic *t* and the Assyrian *s* (pronounced *š*). If the Aramaeans heard the name *Kašk*, why would they not have written it *KŠK*? After all, it is the Proto-Semitic *tha*, apparently still pronounced as such by the Arameans who wrote these inscriptions,(⁴²) who used the *š* to represent it. When the *ṯ* > *t* eventually, it was then written as *t*, as in Imperial Aramaic

---

(⁴⁰) *Les Araméens*, pp. 59-60. See P. Rost, *op. cit.*, p. 26 (*Annals*, lines 152-53) ; D. D. Luckenbill, *ARAB*, 1. §772 ; *ANET*, p. 283. A place called Kasku is mentioned along with Tabal, Ḫilakku (Cilicia), Musku, and Muṣur in an inscription of Sargon II ; see H. Winckler, *Die Keilschrifttexte Sargons* (Leipzig : E. Pfeiffer, 1889), I. 148-49 ; II, pl. 38 ; D. D. Luckenbill, *ARAB*, 2. §99 ; *ANET*, p. 284. — The identification of *KTK* with Kašk was also adopted by W. F. Albright, " Syrien, Phönizien und Palästina," *Historia mundi* (ed. F. Kern ; Munich : L. Lehnen), II (1953) 370-71. He located it at Sakcegözü, east of Zinjirli, where Garstang partially excavated a Syro-Hittite royal city. S. Segert (*ArOr* 32 [1964] 112, n. 21) still prefers the identification of *KTK* with Kašk (" wohl mit dem Königreich Kasku [Kašku] nördlich von Syrien identisch ").

(⁴¹) *MPAIBL* 15 (1958) 22, n. 1.

(⁴²) Two exceptions apparently occur in these inscriptions, in which the shift from *ṯ* to *t* seems to have taken place : *yrt* (I C 24) ; *btn* (I A 32).

9

and later. M. Noth has also questioned the identification of *Luḥuti* and Lu'ash but he tries to justify the *š-t* shift by pointing to the identification of *ḥzrk* (in the Zakir stele) with *ḥdrk* (in Zech 9 : 1) and with Assyrian *Ḥa-ta-rik-ka*.([43]) But this is not very convincing either, for the anomaly is the Assyrian *t* for the West Semitic *z-d*; the parallel limps. If one objects and says that the Aramaeans heard the Assyrian *Kašk* precisely as *Katk*, then the problem still remains to explain why they did not write this as *Kšk*, as in the majority of cases in these inscriptions. The only way that this could be saved would be to postulate that in this instance too there is another case of the shift of *ṭ* to *t*.([44])

(5) More recently, however, Dupont-Sommer has adopted another identification on a conjectural basis.([45]) He now prefers to regard Bir-Ga'yah as a second or imperial throne name of Sardur III, the son of Argišti I, the king of Urartu. Being Aramaic in form and meaning "son of majesty," it was preferred by the Urartian king in his dealings with his Aramaean allies; in this sense, then, it can be regarded as the *Deckname* for Sardur. Having brought his kingdom of Urartu to the peak of its power, Sardur consolidated his rule over the Araxus area, collected tribute from Melidh and Commagene, and conquered Aleppo. He then sought to influence the king of Arpad despite the latter's treaty with Assyria to revolt from the latter and to join him in a coalition against Assyria. Dupont-Sommer thinks that he must have succeeded in this because in the third year of his reign Tiglathpileser III (ca. 743 B.C.) recorded : " Sardur of Urartu revolted against me and joined Mati'ilu." ([46]) Apropos of the same year we read in the Eponym List, " In the city of Arpad : the army of Urartu defeated." ([47]) These two texts show Arpad and Urartu were leagued against Assyria and were defeated by Tiglathpileser III. Dupont-Sommer concludes that the Sefîre steles may well have been the treaty between Mati'ilu and Sardur III of Urartu. In this proposal *KTK* would be the name of an important city in Urartu in SE Asia Minor, possibly a city founded by Sardur himself, but not attested elsewhere. The name *KTK* would equal *Kasku-i* or *Kašku-i*.

([43]) *ZDPV* 77 (1961) 166.

([44]) See note 42 above ; and then another example must be added to the list in the Appendix, B. Phonology, 1.

([45]) *BMB* 13 (1956) 39-40 ; *MPAIBL* 15 (1958) 22.

([46]) *Annals*, line 59 ; see P. Rost, *op. cit.*, p. 12 ; D. D. Luckenbill, *ARAB*, 1. §769, 785, 813.

([47]) See A. Ungnad, *Reallexikon der Assyriologie*, 2 (1938) 430 ; H. Tadmor, *Scripta hierosolymitana* 8 (1961) 252-58.

Once again we are confronted with the difficulty that the list of gods who witness the pact in Sf I A 8-13 contains none that are Urartian. E. Vogt points out a further difficulty which this identification encounters, when account is taken of Sf III 24. The king there says that his father's house had been struck by the gods and that Tal'ayim had been lost to it. This town, whose locality is not certain, was almost certainly in northern Syria.([48]) The situation, described in Sf III 24 and involving it, would scarcely suit the reign of Argišti I, the father of Sardur III and former ruler of Urartu.

(6) M. Noth has made still another attempt to establish the locality of *KTK*. He identifies it with *Kisik* (= [*Ki-is*]-*sik^{ki}*), which is mentioned in the *Annals* of Tiglathpileser III (line 13).([49]) Though very little can be learned from these Annals about the place, the name appears elsewhere in a stereotyped list of cities in southern Mesopotamia (along with Ur, Uruk, Eridu, etc.).([50]) This would suggest that Kisik was a not unimportant eighth century town in the lower or middle region of Mesopotamia, on either the Euphrates or the Tigris. But its precise location is apparently impossible to establish.([51]) The Eponym List (C^b 1 and C^b 2) indicates that Aššurnirāri III had earlier (ca. 786 B.C.) undertaken a campaign against Kiski (= Kisik), just as he had done against Arpad and Damascus. To the obvious question whether a king with an Aramaic name would be ruling in an area in southern Mesopotamia in the eighth century B.C., Noth answers confidently that Tiglathpileser III records his campaign against " all the Arameans " in the plains of that region. Again, he argues that the list of gods in Sf I A 8-13 is Mesopotamian in part and that the name of the obscure god Mullesh is particularly decisive.

It is, however, an identification which is not very convincing. The distance of some 625 mi. between the two places is a factor that

([48]) *Bibl* 39 (1958) 270. M. Noth (*ZDPV* 77 [1961] 161) has recognized the validity of Vogt's argument. But he links to it his own objections to the Sefîre inscriptions as examples of vassal treaties and to the identification of the main king of Sf III as Bir-Ga'yah. If the latter is not the king of Sf III who is contracting the pact with the " king(s) of Arpad " (see the problematic restoration of Sf III 25), then the pertinence of this inscription to the land of Urartu is even less. See his remarks on p. 167, n. 154.

([49]) *ZDPV* 77 (1961) 166-67 ; see P. Rost, *op. cit.*, p. 4 ; D. D. Luckenbill, *ARAB*, 1. §764.

([50]) For instance, in the records of Sargon II ; see H. Winckler, *op. cit.*, 1.54-55, 60-61 ,96-97, 124-25, 146-47, 158-59 ; A. Ungnad, *Reallexikon der Assyriologie* 2 (1938) 429, 431.

([51]) See now A. Falkenstein, " Zur Lage des südbabylonischen Dūrum," *AfO* 21 (1966) 50-51.

must be considered.   There is, further, the linguistic difficulty which
is similar to that mentioned above (under §4).

(7) W. F. Albright has pointed out to me still another attempt
to identify *KTK*.   It was called to his attention by a Mr. Manuel
Kassouni of Fresno, Cal., who recalled that his brother, the Rev.
Y. S. Kassouny, had suggested the identification of *KTK* with a
place called *Katuk* in Syriac and Armenian sources.[52]   The source of
this information is the Syriac *Chronicle* of Michael the Great, the
Jacobite patriarch of Antioch (A.D. 1126-99).[53]   This work was utilized
by Gregory Abû'l Faraj (= Bar Hebraeus) in his *Chronography*.[54]
There exists also an Armenian translation of the *Chronicle* of Michael
the Great, the work of a priest Ischok.[55]   Unfortunately the manuscript
on which the modern edition of Michael the Great's *Chronicle* depends
lacks the page in which Book 18, ch. 11 should appear, and the
editor J.-B. Chabot has substituted for it the corresponding passage
of Bar Hebraeus's *Chronography*, which runs as follows in Wallis
Budge's translation: " And in the year fourteen hundred and seventy-
six of the Greeks (= A. D. 1165), Kelej 'Arslan, Sûltân of Iconium,
reigned over Gâdûg and 'Ablestîn, and Tûrandâ, and he began to
persecute the sons of Dânishmand.   And Nûr ad-Dîn reigned over
Bânyâs and he fortified it strongly.   And Tôrôs the Armenian pillaged
Mar'âsh and captured four hundred Turks." [56]   Though Kassouny

---

[52] *Nakhahaygagan Hayastan* (Beirut, 1950), p. 417 [= *Prearmenian Armenia : A Critical History of Armenia from the Neolithic Age to 600 B.C.*].   Kassouny writes the name as *katouk*.

[53] J.-B. Chabot (ed.), *Chronique de Michel le Syrien, patriarche jacobite
d'Antioche* (1166-1199) (4 vols. ; Paris : E. Leroux, 1899, 1901, 1905, 1910 ;
réimpression anastatique : Brussels : Culture et Civilisation, 1963).

[54] See E. A. Wallis Budge, *The Chronography of Gregory Abû'l Faraj the
Son of Aaron, the Hebrew Physician commonly known as Bar Hebraeus, Being
the First Part of His Political History of the World, Translated from the Syriac*
(2 vols. ; London : Oxford University Press, 1932) ; P. J. Bruns and G. G.
Kirsch, *Bar-Hebraei chronicon syriacum* (2 vols. ; Leipzig : A. F. Boehm, 1788-
89) ; P. Bedjan, *Gregorii Barhebraei chronicum syriacum* (Paris : Maisonneuve,
1890).

[55] See V. Langlois, *Chronique de Michel le Grand, patriarche des Syriens
jacobites, traduite pour la première fois sur la version arménienne du prêtre
Ischôk* (Venice : Académie de Saint-Lazare, 1868).

[56] See E. A. Wallis Budge, *Chronography*, 1. 289.   The Syriac text can
be found in the photo of fol. 103r, col. 1, line 9 of the Bodleian Ms. Hunt
No. 52 in the second volume of Wallis Budge's edition.   The other editions
of Bar Hebraeus give the same spelling of the name, *g'dwg* ; see P. Bedjan,
p. 331 ; Bruns and Kirsch, 1. 354.

states that *KTK* is to be identified with the name *Katuk*,([57]) the Syriac text of Bar Hebraeus reads the name as *g'dwg*, which most of the translators have transcribed as *Gâdûg*. Even the French version of the Armenian, done by V. Langlois, gives the name as *Gadoug*.([58]) The difference may simply be a phonetic shift from the voiced to the unvoiced velar and dental. But which came first? Did *KTK > GDG*, or vice versa? There is, moreover, a time lapse of almost 2000 years between the Sefîre inscriptions and these sources which must not be forgotten.

Kassouny has, moreover, suggested that this *Katuk* is to be identified with the town called in Byzantine Greek sources Ἀδατϑᾶ, in Syriac *Ḥadeth* or *Ḥadatta*, and in Arabic *al-Ḥadath*.([59]) It lay on the Lake Göinük Göl (Arabic *Buḥairat al-Ḥadath*), near modern Inekly, about 50 km. NE of Mar'ash. It was a town in the eastern Taurus Mountain passes leading from Syria to Anatolia. But what is the ancient evidence for the identification of *Katuk* with *Adattha*? ([60])

([57]) *Op. cit.*, pp. 417-18. Kassouny also calls attention to the fact that the Armenian patriarch, Constantine II (1286-89), was from Katuk, and that Arab writers noted that the important town of Ḥadath at Goelbashi was called Kaytuk by the Armenians. But unfortunately he gives no references to support the latter statement.

([58]) *Op. cit.*, p. 324. This French version of the Armenian seems to indicate that the latter is based on a slightly different text. Since I cannot find the Armenian text of the *Chronicle*, I must leave this question to more competent persons. Langlois' translation runs as follows : " En l'année 1476 de l'ère syrienne et 592 des Arméniens, le sultan Kilidj-Arslan triompha des fils de Danischmend, et s'empara avec l'aide de l'émir (p. 324) mir [sic !] Danoun (Dsoulnoun) des villes de Gadoug, d'Ablasta et de Daranda, (Laranda). La même année, le baron Thoros envoya à Alep une ambassade avec des présents pour réclamer les captifs arméniens qui se trouvaient dans cette ville. Sa demande ne fut pas accueillie. Thoros indigné envahit le territoire de Marach et le saccagea. Nour-Eddin expédia contre lui des troupes ; mais Thoros les battit et leur fit un grand nombre des prisonniers." — Cf. F. Haase, " Die armenischen Rezension der syrischen Chronik Michaels des Grossen," *Oriens christianus* NF 5 (1915) 60-82, 271-84.

([59]) On the town of Adattha see E. Honigmann, " Historische Topographie von Nordsyrien im Altertum," *ZDPV* 46 (1923) 149-93, esp. p. 153 ; *Die Ostgrenze des byzantinischen Reiches von 363 bis 1071* (Corpus bruxellense historiae byzantinae, 3 ; Brussels : Editions de l'institut de philologie et d'histoire orientales, 1935), pp. 86-87. See also G. Hirschfeld, in Pauly-Wissowa, *Real-Encyclopädie der classischen Altertumswissenschaft*, 1. 348.

([60]) Is there any connection between the town called *Ḥadatta*, mentioned by Asshurbanipal (Cylinder B, VIII. 30 ; see *ANET*, p. 299) and Adattha? B. Mazar (*BA* 25 [1962] 100) locates a place called Hadatta to the east of the Euphrates, almost due east of Sam'al, in the Assyrian world of this period.

Even though this attempt to identify *KTK* in the Sefîre inscriptions with a place called *Katuk* (or Gadug) in sources almost two millennia later encounters the linguistic and historical difficulties already pointed out, it is attractive because of the plausible location which it brings into the discussion. It is, in effect, identifying *KTK* with an area in Gurgum. Our entire discussion has so far presumed that *KTK* is the name of a " land," but it may just be that it is the name of a town, and the name of a town in Gurgum. If Bir-Ga'yah were the king of *KTK* in the territory of Gurgum, how would this fit into what we otherwise know about Gurgum?

Our knowledge of Gurgum in the ninth and eighth centuries B.C. is skimpy indeed. Among those who paid tribute to Shalmaneser III in his first regnal year (= 858 B.C.) was a certain Mutallu of Gurgum.[61] Then in his sixth regnal year (= 853 B.C.) we learn of a ruler named Kalparuda of Gurgum, who also paid tribute along with " the kings of the other side of the Euphrates — that is, of Sanagara from Carchemish, Kundashpi of Commagene, of Arame, man of Gusi [= Arpad?], of Lalli from Melitene (*Melid*), of Haiani, son of Gabari, of Kalparuda from Hattina ".[62] In the first quarter of the eighth century " the king of Gurgum and his army " formed part of the coalition of Bir Hadad, the son of Haza'el, the king of Aram, who with other kings opposed Zakir the King of Hamath and Lu'ash.[63] Unfortunately the name of this king of Gurgum is not given. In the same coalition there appears Bir Gush, and indeed the first of the kings named after Bir Hadad himself. This implies the distinction of Gurgum and Arpad again, but also the proximity of the two areas. In the time of Tiglathpileser III a certain Tarḫulara reigned in Gurgum; he is mentioned in connection with Tiglathpileser's third regnal year (= 743 B.C.) and again in what seems to be the equivalent of 738 B.C.[64] " Cities in the region of Gurgum " are mentioned in the time of Tiglathpileser III in the Panammu inscription from Zenjirli, but the broken context makes it impossible to derive any further information from it.[65] Later on in the time of Sargon II we

(61) See the *Monolith Inscription.*, 1. 40-41 ; D. D. Luckenbill, *ARAB*, 1. § 599 ; *ANET*, p. 277.

(62) See the *Monolith Inscription*, 2. 84 ; D. D. Luckenbill, *ARAB*, 1. § 610 ; *ANET*, p. 278.

(63) Cf. the Zakir stele, a 6 (= *KAI* 202.6 ; *ANET*, p. 501).

(64) See *Annals*, lines 61, 88, 152 ; D. D. Luckenbill, *ARAB*, 1. § 769, 772, 797, 801 ; *ANET*, p. 283. Note that in these *Annals* Tarḫulara of Gurgum is mentioned alongside of Dadi'ilu of Kaska.

(65) See *KAI* 215.15. This Aramaic inscription is dated roughly between 733-27 B.C.

learn of a son of Tarḫulara, Mutallu of the tribe of Bit-Pa'alla. Sargon annexed the whole land of Gurgum, putting an end to the kingdom of Tarḫulara, of the city of Marqasu, and bringing all Gurgum into the territory of Assyria.[66]

Into such a picture Bir-Ga'yah could fit as the king of *KTK* in the land of Gurgum, if he were to precede Tarḫulara. Since we do not know when the latter began his reign, it is impossible to be sure. Since, as we have already pointed out, Matî'el was already the king of Arpad in 754 B.C. and concluded a treaty with Aššurnirāri V in the spring of 754-53 B.C., it is not impossible that Bir-Ga'yah could have been reigning in *KTK* about this time. We have already mentioned the various opinions which attempt to date the Sefîre inscriptions before and after 754 B.C. Even if they should be subsequent to that date, as is more likely in my opinion, this would not make it impossible that Bir-Ga'yah was the king in *KTK* around 750 B.C. and was the predecessor of Tarḫulara. But most of this is conjecture and we cannot be too apodictic about it.

A further question might arise, if this last solution finds any probability, and that is the relation of Bir-Ga'yah, king of *KTK*, to Sardur III of Urartu. In this connection possibly one could admit the suggestion of B. Mazar that " the ruler of *Ktk* most likely was a vassal of the mighty state of Ararat (Urartu) which from 749 ruled over southern Anatolia and began to compete with its enemy Assyria for dominion over northern Syria." [67]

[66] See *Annals* 209-11 (ed. H. Winckler, 1. 34-37) ; *Prunkinschrift*, 83-84 (ed. H. Winckler, 1. 112-13) ; Pavé des portes inscription, 28-31 (ed. H. Winckler, 1. 148-49) ; D. D. Luckenbill, *ARAB*, 2. §29, 61, 79, 92, 99. Cf. A. G. Lie, *The Inscriptions of Sargon II, King of Assyria : The Annals* (Paris : P. Geuthner, 1929), pp. 38-39.

[67] *BA* 25 (1962) 116. — I am indebted to Prof. W. F. Albright for having called this last attempt at an identification of *KTK* to my attention, for having allowed me to use the extensive notes which he had collected on this question, and for discussing the matter with me at length. The formulation in the above discussion, however, must be attributed to me alone. Unfortunately, I came across too late the discussion of KTK = Kaška as a designation for Phrygia to incorporate it in the above treatment. See E. von Schuler, *Die Kaškäer : Ein Beitrag zur Ethnographie des alten Kleinasiens* (Untersuchungen zur Assyriologie und vorderasiatischen Archäologie, 3 ; Berlin : de Gruyter, 1965), pp. 67-70.

THE GRAMMAR OF THE SEFÎRE INSCRIPTIONS

APPENDIX

In this appendix we present a comprehensive view of the main grammatical features of the Sefîre inscriptions. We attempted this already in the articles (in the *CBQ* and *JAOS*) on which this work is based. But the items were isolated and what is now needed is a comprehensive survey of these features of the Sefîre inscriptions. Even though these inscriptions scarcely reflect all the aspects of Aramaic grammar in the period of " Old Aramaic " (for my understanding of this term, the reader is referred to *The* Genesis Apocryphon *of Qumran Cave I : A Commentary* [Biblica et Orientalia, 18; Rome: Pontifical Biblical Institute, 1966], pp. 19-20), they are quite representative because of their length. There is, therefore, reason to study the Aramaic language of these inscriptions, which represent an important group in the division of " Old Aramaic " texts.

A.   ORTHOGRAPHY

An explanation of the orthography of these inscriptions of Sefîre depends to some extent on the vocalization of the words appearing in them. We shall say a word here about the method used to determine the vocalization of the words in the inscriptions. In general, the vocalization of later Aramaic is the norm, especially when this exists in a vocalized form which can be predicated of the consonantal text of these inscriptions. In particular, we are referring to what is known as Aramaic in the Bible, in Rabbinical literature, and in Syriac. Yet it must be emphasized that this later Aramaic has often developed forms which cannot be easily transferred to this early period; it is necessary to make an effort to discern what is late and secondary. There are indeed times when the full consonantal writing of words gives us a clue to the vocalization of these early texts; and when this vocalization not only agrees with later patterns but also with contemporary (early) data from the cognate Semitic languages, it should be regarded as highly probable. But the norm for vocalization should be a judicious mixture of the indications derived from later Aramaic and the early cognate material. This is why we have so often cited in the commentary cognate forms of the words which appear in the text.

We persist in regarding the Aramaic family as a unit in that we give preference to forms of words according to the later Aramaic vocalization rather than to Hebrew or Phoenician or Ugaritic forms. For instance, because the word for " night " turns up almost always in the various stages of Aramaic either as a form *layl* or as the reduplicated form *laylay*, we regard this as a distinctive Aramaic development, and accordingly vocalize the consonants *lylh* as a form of the latter (*laylay* > *laylê*, with the dissimilation of the diphthong and the representation of it by final *h*) rather than as a form similar to the Hebrew *laylāh*. The Aramaic of this period is definitely under Canaanite influence, and a priori one cannot exclude the possibility that the word for " night " in Aramaic could be a Canaanite borrowing, but it seems advisable to defend the forms as Aramaic, when this can be done — even if it means appealing to later Aramaic vocalizations. In this case, there is no real principle that is being compromised by the appeal. For it is obvious that, while the vast majority of diphthongs in " Old Aramaic " are uncontracted, there are exceptions. No thesis about the vocalization of the Aramaic of this period should create a Procrustean bed.

When the evidence for a particular word is lacking in the Aramaic family, then we are forced to have recourse to cognate languages.

The main difference which the reader will note between the vocalization of the Aramaic of these early texts attempted below and later Aramaic is the reluctance to make use of the vocal *shewa*. It is a well established principle in Aramaic phonetics that a short vowel in an open pretonic syllable is reduced to *shewa*. The only difficulty is that we do not know at what period this reduction to *shewa* became operative. I have already discussed this question briefly in the sketch of Qumran Aramaic, which forms part of *The* Genesis Apocryphon *of Qumran Cave I : A Commentary* (see Appendix II, pp. 173-174). Because of this difficulty I have preferred to retain the full short vowel for convenience; those who prefer to reduce the vowel even at this period can easily make the slight adjustment which that entails. But then the principle should be carried out consistently; and one should avoid using, now the full short vowel, now the *shewa* without any apparent reason for the difference (cf. Cross and Freedman, *EHO*, pp. 21-34).

In the following lists the number within parentheses behind the suggested vocalization of the form refers to *one* instance in which the given form can be found; the references are not meant to be exhaustive for each form. But the *list of forms* occurring in these inscriptions is intended to be complete.

In the earlier form of this grammatical study we made frequent use of the circumflex accent in the attempted vocalizations. In what follows we have made a slight difference. The circumflex is now restricted to those vowels which arise from a contraction of a diphthong. Otherwise the macron is used to designate a long vowel. The reason behind this decision to use the macron is that there is really no evidence in Aramaic — aside from Masoretic Hebraisms in Biblical Aramaic — of tonal long vowels. Tonal and pretonic lengthening is a characteristic of Hebrew. The macron, therefore, designates what would be an original long vowel in Proto-Semitic or in the Aramaic noun or verb types which are being used. In this regard, one should beware of interpreting the *ṣere* in Biblical Aramaic as a long *e*. Such an interpretation might seem plausible in the light of the tonal lengthening in Hebrew, e.g., in the Pi'el. But the corresponding form in Aramaic is either Pa'el or Pa'il, showing that in reality the *e* and *i* are merely allophones of the same basic phoneme, which in this case is short. The same is to be said for the Pe'al ptc., *qātel* or *qātil*; both forms are found in Biblical Aramaic and correspond to the Hebrew *qôtēl*.

(1) FINAL LONG A IS INDICATED BY HE:

br g'yh (Bir-Ga'yāh I A 1); *znh* (zināh I A 6); *kd'h* (? I A 10); *rḥbh* (Raḥbāh I A 10); [*mṣ*]*lh* (maṣūlāh I A 11); *ḥzyh* (ḥazzāyāh I A 13); *ssyh* (sūsyāh I A 22); *šwrh* (šawrāh I A 23); *bkth* bakkatāh? I A 24); *mh* (māh I A 26); *lḥyh* (laḥyāh I A 26); *twl'h* (tawla'ah I A 27); *ṣ'qh* (ṣa'aqāh I A [29]); *yllh* (yalalāh I A 30); *ḥwh* (ḥiwwāh I A 31); *dbhh* (dubhāh? I A 31); *nmrh* (nimrāh I A 31); *'qh* ('aqāh? I A 33); *mrbh* (Maribāh? I A 34); *mzh* (? I A 34); *mblh* (? I A 34); [*z*]*n*[*yh*] (zāniyāh I A [41]); *'ykh* ('aykāh I A 37); *ḥdh* (ḥadāh I B 8); [*'nh*] ('anāh I B 24); *lbkh* (? I B 35); [*m*]*lh* (millāh I B [41]); *kh* (kāh I C 1); *ptḥh* (patīḥāh III 8); *qryh* (qiryāh III 12).

In the case of the negative *lā* we find only *l-*, without any consonant, which suggests that it does not have a final *a* and is therefore to be considered as a prefix; Cf. *lhn* (lāhen III 4); *ltsk* (lātissuk III 5); *lṭb* (lāṭāb III 22). Two forms should be noted here, *'mrn* and [*k*]*tbn* (I C 1), which lack the final *he* and therefore probably were not pronounced *'amarnāh* and *katabnāh*.

(2) Final Long ī Is Indicated by YODH:

zy (zī I A 5); *twy* (? I A 28); [*ṣy*] (ṣī I A 32); *y'd*[*y*] (Ya'dī
I B 9); *bry* (barī or birī I B 25); *'qry* ('iqqārī I B 25); *'rqy*
('arqī I B 27); *b*[*y*]*ty* (baytī I B 32); *'my* ('immī or 'ammī I B
33); *lḥmy* (laḥmī I B 38); *ly* (lī I B 38); *nbšy* (nabšī I B 40);
[*'šr*]*y* ('ašrī I C 4); *m*[*lky*] (mulkī I C 6); *'by* ('abī II B 8);
[*r'šy*] (ri'šī II B 8); [*ḥmtty*] (ḥamītūtī or ḥamātūti II B 8);
sḥrty (saḥratī III 7); *ml'ky* (mal'akī III 8); *ḥpṣy* (ḥapṣī III 8);
dmy (damī III 11), *qrqy* (qāriqī III 19), *khs'y* (kuhsa'ī? III 17),
mny (minnī III 4); *by* (bī III 9), *ky* (kī III 22); *kzy* (kazī III
24); *'yty* ('iyyātī III 11), *t'šqny* (ta'šuqinnī III 20); *'my* ('ammī
III 21).

(3) Final Long ū Is Indicated by WAW:

[...]*w* (? I A 5 ; *pqḥw* (paqaḥū I A 13); *śmw* (śamū I B 6);
'rqw ('Arqū I B 9); *yb*[*rdw*] (yabrudū I B 9-10); *'rw* ('Arū I
B 10?); *m..w* (? I B 10); *y'bd*[*w*] (ya'bidū I C 5); *yṣrw* (yiṣṣarū I C 15); *yhpkw* (yahpukū I C 21); *yśmw* (yaśīmū I C 23);
'bdw ('abadū II B 2); *šbw* (šibū III 7); *qtlw* (qitlū or qitulū?
III 21); *ḥbzw* (ḥabazū III 24); *hšbw* (hašībū III 24).

(4) Final aw Is Represented by WAW:

'w ('aw I B 26); [*yhww*] (yihwaw [I A 31]); *tpnw* (tipnaw III 7),
šlw (šilaw III 5).   G. Garbini (*RSO* 34 [1959] 42) prefers to
vocalize *'w* as ô.

(5) Final ay Is Indicated by YODH:

'dy ('aday I A 1); *bny* (banay I A 2); *b'ly* (ba'alay I A 4);
[*mlky*] (malakay I A 5); *'lhy* ('ilāhay I A 10); [*'bny*] ('abanay
I A 26); *'py* ('appay I A 28); *nšy* (našay I A 41); *ṭby* (ṭūbay
I B 6); *mly* (millay I B 8); *'ly* ('alay I B 26); *śn'y* (śāni'ay
I B 26); *mqny* (miqnay I B 27); [*'ly*] ('elay I B 29); *yqpy*
(yāqipay I B 29); *my* (may I B 33); *srsy* (sarīsay I B 45);
rbrby (rabrabay II A 7); *bty* (bāttay II C 7); *ydy* (yaday III 5),
'yny ('aynay III 3), *'ḥy* ('aḥay III 4), *pqdy* (paqīday III 4),
ngdy (nagīday III 10), *'bdy* ('abaday III 13).

The gentilic ending -āy (e. g., *'ly* ['illāy I A 6]) should not be
confused with this final -ay, for the *yodh* there is most likely consonantal.

(6) FINAL LONG e IS APPARENTLY REPRESENTED BY BOTH HE AND YODH:

(a) *HE* :

lylh (laylêh < laylay I A 12); *'rbh* ('arbêh I A 27); *ythzh* (yithazêh < yithazay I A 28); *ṣdh* (ṣadêh I A 33); *'rnh* (? I A 34); *y'th* (yi'têh I B 28); *t'th* (ti'têh I B 31); *tb'h* (tib'êh I B 39); *gdh* (gadêh II A 2); *yhwh* (yihwêh II A 4); *'ryh* (? 'aryêh II A 9); *yb'h* (yib'êh II B 8); *yhwnh* (yuhawnêh II B 16); *trsh* (tiršêh III 9); *trqh* (turaqqêh III 18), *tkh* (tikkêh III 13), *rqh* (raqêh? III 6), *nkh* (nakêh? III 13).

G. Garbini (*RSO* 34 [1959] 42) strangely lists the verb forms *yb'h*, *trsh*, *t'th*, *y'th*, *rqh* and *trqh* under *he* as a *mater lectionis* for long *a*.

(b) *YODH* :

thry (tihrê < tihray I A 21); *thwy* (tihwê I A 25); *ṣby* (ṣabê I A 33); *[y]tnšy* (yitnašê II A 4); *hwy* (hawê III 22). On the problem which these forms present for the study of early Aramaic orthography, see the note on *thry* (I A 21). See, however, the dissertation of a student of F. M. Cross, Jr., who concludes that "all in all, a mixed paradigm seems called for by the evidence" (M. E. Sherman, *Systems of Hebrew and Aramaic Orthography : An Epigraphic History of the Use of Matres Lectionis in Non-Biblical Texts to ca. A.D. 135* (Cambridge : Harvard Divinity School, 1966), p. 23 [cf. *HTR* 59 (1966) 455-56]. Perhaps the form *'lh* (I A 32) should be considered here too ; but see below §11. Dupont-Sommer has restored *krs'* (II B 7); if correct, this would be a case of final *ē* represented by *aleph*.

N. B.   In the following sections dealing with medial vowels the form is not repeated if it occurs merely with a different suffix.

(7) MEDIAL LONG a IS NEVER REPRESENTED BY A VOWEL LETTER:

'rm ('Arām? Or is it 'Aram < 'Aramm? I A 5); *'ly* ('illāy I A 6); *'ll* ('ālil I A 6); *śm* (śām I A 7); *qdm* (qudām I A 8); *'lhy* ('ilāhay I A 10); *'lyn* ('elyān I A 11); *m'ynn* (ma'yānīn I A 12); *śhdn* (śāhidīn I A 12); *hzyh* (hazzāyāh I A 13); *[mhy]-nqn* (muhayniqān I A 21); *ymšhn* (yimšahān I A 21); *yhynqn* (yuhayniqān I A 22); *š'n* (śa'ān I A 23); *yhkn* (yahākān I A

24); *yhrgn* (yihragān I A 24); *ḥl* (ḥāl I A 25); *ql* (qāl I A 29); *knr* (kinnār I A 29); *mrq* (māriq I A 29); *'lhn* ('ilāhīn I A 30); *'kl* ('ākil I A 30); *ss* (sās I A 31); *qq* (qāq? I A 32); *yšmn* (yašīmān I A 32); *šrn* (šurān I A 33); *bnth* (banātah I A 35); *gnb'* (? I A 36); [*z*]*n*[*yh*] (zāniyāh I A [41]); *y'rrn* (yu'rarān I A 41); *yqḥn* (yuqqaḥān I A 42); *śmw* (śāmū I B 6); [*'l*]*mn* ('ālamīn I B 7); [*ytšm'n*] (yitšama'ān I B 9); *lbnn* (Libnān I B 9); *bk* (bāk? I B 25); *br*[*k*] (barāk I B 25); *'qrk* ('iqqārāk I B 25); *śn'y* (śāni'ay I B 26); *yqpy* (yāqipay I B 29); *ḥylk* (ḥaylāk I B 31); *'yt* ('iyyāt I B 32); *'bdt* ('abbādūt I B 36); *zkrn* (zikrān I C 2); [*'lm*] ('ālam I C 9); *ṭbt'* (ṭābāta' [perh. sg.] I C 4); *lḥyt* (laḥyāt I C 20); *tḥtyth* (taḥtāyteh I C 23); ['*]lyth* ('illāyteh I C 24); [*'zn*] ('izzān II A 2); *p* (pā-? II B 4); *ḥbzthm* (ḥabbazut-hum II B 7); *ḥrn* (ḥarān II B 12); *mnk* (minnāk II B 20); *hldt* (halādūt II C 2); *bty* (battay? II C 2); *'n* ('ān II C 3); *ld* (lād II C 6); *šlm* (šalām III 8); *śptyk* (šapā-tayk III 14); *'nš* ('unāš III 16); *mrmt* (mirmāt III 22); *'ḥrn* ('uḥrān III 24); *qrq* (qāriq III 4); *rḥm* (rāḥim III 8); perhaps *hmtty* (hamātūtī III 11); *ḥlph* (ḥālipeh, or possibly ḥalāpeh III 22); *šbt* (šābat III 25).

The only apparent exception to this list is *'hbd* (II C 5), which is not clearly a case of a long *a*. It must be contrasted with *'h'bd* (II C 4), in which the *aleph* of the stem is preserved. It is difficult to say whether it has disappeared in the first form due to quiescence or to mere scribal omission. Dupont-Sommer notes (*ad loc.*) that in later Aramaic the Haph. of *'bd* appears as *t'hôbed*, etc. (a form built on analogy with Pe Waw verbs).

(8)   MEDIAL LONG ı IS USUALLY NOT INDICATED:

mt''l (Matī''el I A 1); *n*[*ṣb'*] (naṣība' I A 6); *zrpnt* (Zarpanīt I A 8); *m'ynn* (ma'yānīn I A 12); *śhdn* (śāhidīn I A 12); *'l* ('īl I A 22); *šmyn* (šamayīn I A 26); *šnn* (šanīn I A 27); *ḥsr* (ḥasīr I A 28); *'lhn* ('ilāhīn I A 30); *yšmn* (yašīmān I A 32); [*h'*] (hī' I A 33); *mrbh* (Marībāh? I A 34); [*'l*]*mn* ('ālamīn I B 7); *'dn* ('adīn? I B 24); *mlkn* (malakīn I B 26); *hy*[*n*] (ḥayyīn I B 41); *srsy* (sarīsay I B 45); *'hld* ('uḥalīd I C 18); *'śm* ('aśīm I C 19); *'š*['] ('iša' I C 21); *yśmw* (yaśīmū I C 23); [*hmtty*] (hamītūtī; or is it hamātūtī? II B 8); *mln* (millīn, or possibly millān; see note on III 2); *ngdy* (nagīday III 10); *pqdy* (paqīday III 4); *srsy* (sarīsay III 5); *ptḥh* (patīḥāh III 8); *špr* (šappīr III 29); *kpryh* (kapīrayh III 23); *yrb* (yarīb III 17);

hšbw (hašībū III 24); *hšb* (hašīb III 20); *'hšb* ('ahašīb III 20);
thšbhm (tuhašībhum III 6); *'rqhm* ('uraqqīhum III 6); *trqhm*
(turaqqīhum III 6); *thrm* (tuharīm III 5,6).

But *šybt* (III 24) stands for *šībat* and medial long *i* is here written
with *yodh.*   *kym* (III 1) is probably to be understood as *kīma* (though
we cannot exclude Dupont-Sommer's connection with *kīam*).   In any
case, it is a compound word in which the *yodh* represents the final
i of *kī.*   The word *šhlyn* creates a problem.   Is it *šahlīn* (with medial
long *i* fully written) or *šahlayin* (I A 36)?   A clear case of the full
writing of medial long *i* is found in *byr'* (I B 34).

(9)   MEDIAL LONG U IS USUALLY NOT INDICATED:

ysqn (yissaqūn I A 5); *nb'* (Nabū' I A 8); *[mṣ]lh* (maṣūlāh I
A 11); *yšqrn* (yušaqqirūn I A 16); *ssyh* (sūsyāh I A 22); *mlkt*
(malkūt I A 25); *'šr* ('Aššūr I A 25); *yšlhn* (yišlahūn I A 30);
ygzrn (yugzarūn I A 40); *tby* (ṭūbay I B 6); *yṣrn* (yiṣṣarūn I
B 8); *[yšm'n]* (yišma'ūn I B 21); *ymlkn* (yamlukūn I B 22);
[tšm'n] (tišma'ūn I B 24); *[tš]lmn* (tašlimūn I B 24); *h'* (hū'
I B 24); *lygz[rn]* (lā-yigzarūn I B [41]); *hbzthm* (habbāzūt-hum
II B 7); *'bdt* ('abbādūt II B 7); *[hmtty]* (hamītūtī II B 8);
hldt (halādūt II C 2); *y[r]šmn* (yuršamūn II C 3); *ld* (lūd II
C 9); *y[mt]* (yamūt II C 10; cf. III 16); *[yš']n* (yiśśa'ūn? II
C 13); *yhskrn* (yuhaskirūn III 3); *yhkn* (yahākūn III 5); *yšbn*
(yiššibūn III 6); *yqtln* (yiqtulūn III 11); *yšhdn* (yišhadūn III
28); *hmtt* (hamītūt III 11); *'hk* ('ahūk III 18).

But medial long *u* is represented by *waw* in several cases: *tw'm*
(Tū'im? I A 34); *rwh* (rūh III 2); *ymwt* (yamūt III 16); *y'wrn*
(ya'ūrūn II B 4; but S. Segert [*ArOr* 32 (1964) 125] would take the
form as Pu'al !).   These forms must now be considered in connection
with *'šwr* ('Aššūr) in Panammū 7, 11, 12, 13, 15, 16, 17, 17; Bir-RKB 9;
Agbar 7 (*šmwny*); Zakir a 17 (*šwr'*, " wall," in contrast *šr* to a 10).
The form *'šwr*, being a proper name, is precious evidence for the fact
that the phenomenon of representing an internal long vowel by a
vowel-letter was known to the Aramaeans of this period.   For in
writing a foreign name they would be expected to record it in accord-
ance with their own orthographic habits.   In none of these cases is
there any reason to look for a diphthong; we simply have an extension
of the use of vowel-letters from the final position to a medial position.

(10)   MEDIAL AW IS REPRESENTED BY WAW:

bnwh (banawh I A 5); *ywm* (yawm I A 12); *šwrh* (šawrāh I A
23); *twl'h* (tawla'āh I A 27); *š'wt'* (ša'awta' I A 37); *rbwh*

rabbawh I A 39); [*t*']*twn* (ti'tawn I B 32); *mlwh* (millawh I C 18); *yhwnnh* (yuhawninneh II B 16); *yhwnh* (yuhawnêh II B 16); *ywmyhm* (yawmayhum II C 17); *'pwh* ('appawh III 2); *śn'wh* (śāni'awh III 12); *śgbwh* (śagabawh? III 13); *mwddwh* (mawdidawh III 14); *'hwh* ('ahawh III 17); *'lwh* ('elawh III 8); *śptwh* (śapātawh III 15). — But cf. *hm*[*wn*] (I A 29, correctly restored?). Does *mwt* (I B 30) belong here?

(11) MEDIAL AY IS REPRESENTED BY YODH:

byt (bayt I A 6); *'dy'* ('adayya' I A 7); *lylh* (laylêh I A 12); *šmyn* (šamayīn I A 11); *'ynykm* ('aynaykum I A 13); [*mhy*]*nqn* (muhayniqān I A 21); [*śdyhn*] (šadayhen I A [21]); *'lym* ('ulaym I A 22); *byt'l* (bayt'el I A 34); *'yk* ('ayk I A 35); *šhlyn* (šahlayin? [see note above after section 8]); *'ykh* ('aykāh I A 37); *hṣy'* (hiṣṣayya' I A 38); *'pyh* ('appayh I A 42); [*'lhy*]*'* ('ilāhayya' I B 8); *mlky'* (malakayya' I B 22); *hylk* (haylāk I B 31); *mrhy'* (? I B 31); *hy*[*n*] (hayyīn I B 41); *šyt* (šayt II A 5); *spr*[*y*]*'* (siparayya' II C 4); *btyhm* (battayhum II C 16); *ywmyhm* (yawmayhum II C 17); *mly'* (millayya' III 2); *'yny* ('aynay III 3); *byt* (bayt III 21); *'my'* ('ammayya' III 10); *śptyk* (śapātayk III 14); *kpryh* (kapīrayh III 23); *b'lyh* (ba'alayh III 23); *'lyh* ('alayh III 9).

But *bnyhm* (III 18-19) creates a problem here. According to Cross and Freedman (*EHO*, p. 24, no. 4), "There is no evidence for the contraction of diphthongs, *ay* and *aw*, in Old Aramaic under any circumstances." That would prevent us from vocalizing this word as *bênayhom* and from deriving it from the preposition *bên-*. Yet the sense of the context forces us to regard the word as a form of this preposition (and not of *bn-* known in Phoenician and suggested to me by J. T. Milik). Consequently, the statement of Cross and Freedman will have to be modified. Together with this word one should consider the form *tgltplsr* in Panammū 13, 15, 16 and *tgltplysr* in Bir-RKB 3, 6. The remarks of G. Garbini (*AA*, p. 246) concerning their treatment of *tgltplsr* now seem justified. There is the further case of *'lh* ('alêh I A 32; cf. III 9 *'lyh*). Compare *BMAP* 4.10, 11 (*bnyhm* for *bynyhm*). The reason for maintaining that the diphthong was normally uncontracted in both the case of *ay* and *aw* is the general thesis of Cross and Freedman who have gathered the pertinent orthographical evidence for the various Northwest Semitic languages. The material of the Sefîre inscriptions confirms their general thesis, although it has brought to light some scattered Aramaic examples which show that the treatment of the final diphthong *ay* (especially on *tertiae infirmae* roots) and of medial long vowels and diphthongs was beginning to fluctuate somewhat.

(12) CONSONANTAL ALEPH:

On the existence of consonantal *aleph* in Old Aramaic there is a difference of opinion between Cross and Freedman on the one hand, who maintain that final *aleph* is consonantal, and Garbini and Segert on the other, who regard it as a *mater lectionis*. See also M. Tsevat, "A Chapter on Old West Semitic Orthography," *The Joshua Bloch Memorial Volume*: *Studies in Booklore and History* (New York: Public Library, 1960), pp. 82-91. Commenting on a form like *nṣb'*, Cross and Freedman say, "The article is indicated by *aleph*, which is of course consonantal. As will be seen, there is no evidence for the early quiescing of *aleph* in Aramaic" (*EHO*, pp. 24,33-34). This position is criticized by Garbini who maintains that "l'aramaico antico usava la ' come *mater lectionis* in fine di parola col valore di -*â*, e che conseguentemente lo stato determinato, almeno nel periodo della lingua a noi noto, consisteva in una determinazione di natura vocalica" (AA, p. 247). Most of the examples cited by Garbini on p. 247 to support his contention are quite doubtful (e.g., *'rbh* certainly represents *'arbêh* [< *'arbay*; cf. Ugaritic *'irby*] and has nothing to do with the emphatic state; *'rqh* is not the emphatic state but the 3 sg. masc. suffixal form; the enigmatic *rḥbh* is most likely a proper name [cf. R. Dussaud, *CRAIBL* 1930, 155-56]; *š'wth* is simply not written with final *he*, but with *aleph* [cf. the plates]!). Indeed, not one of these cases is valid evidence to show that the word was written with a final long *a*.

In these inscriptions, prescinding from cases in which *aleph* is used as the first consonant of a word (like *'l*, negative or preposition), we find it in both the final and medial position.

(a) *In the final position*:

n[*ṣb'*] (naṣiba' I A 6); *'dy'* ('adayya' I A 7); *nb'* (Nabū' I A 8); *qr*[*yt'*] (qiryata' I A 33); [*h'*] (hī' I A 33); *mdr'* (? I A 34); *š'wt'* (ša'awta' I A 35); *z'* (za' I A 35); [*nbš'*] (nabša' I A 36); *h'* (hū' I A 37); *qšt'* (qašta' I A 38); *ḥṣy'* (ḥiṣṣayya' I A 38); *'gl'* ('igla' I A 40); *ymḥ'* (yimḥa' I A 42); [*'lhy'*] ('ilāhayya' I B 8); *spr'* (sipra' I B 8); *mlky'* (malakayya' I B 22); *mrhy'* (? I B 31); *tš'* (tiśśa' I B 39); [*mlk*]*'* (malka' I B 35); *'pl'* (? I B 43); *ṭbt*[*'*] (ṭābāta' I C 4); *šmš'* (šamša' I C 5);

'š['] ('iša' I C 21); *spry*' (siparayya' II C 2); '*m*' ('amma' III
5); '*rḥ*' ('urḥa' III 9); *mly*' (millayya' III 2); '*my*' ('ammayya'
III 10); *yš*' (yiśśa' III 15).

(b) *In the medial position :*

br g'yh (Bir-Ga'yah I A 1); *kd'h* (? I A 10); *š't* (śa'at I A 21);
š'n (śa'ān I A 23); *y'kl* (yi'kul I A 27); *t'kl* (ti'kul I A 27);
t'mr (tu'mar I A 33); *tw'm* (Tū'im I A 34); *y'dy* (Ya'dī I B 9);
t'mr (ti'mar I B 24); *śn'y* (śāni'ay I B 26); *y'th* (yi'têh I B
28); *t'th* (ti'têh I B 31); [*t*']*twn* (ti'tawn I B 32); *t'zl* (ti'zil I
B 39); *y'mr* (yi'mar I C 18); '*ḥ'bd* ('uha'bid II C 4 — cf. '*ḥbd*
II C 5 [see note above §7]); [*yš*']*n* (yiśśa'ūn II C 13); *r'šy*
(ri'šī III 11); *khs'y* (kuhsa'ī, see note on III 17); *y'sr* (yi'sar
III 18); *śn'wh* (śāni'awh III 12).

In the case of *h*' (hū' or hī') the *aleph* is clearly consonantal.
The same seems to be true of *z*'. As far as the other words with
final *aleph* are concerned, it might seem at first sight that it is impossible to decide whether the *aleph* is consonantal or not. Here we
must consider the evidence of the negative *lā*, which is never written
with an *aleph* in this inscription. The fact that it seems to be a
prefix does not militate against our argument here. If final long *a*
were represented by *aleph*, we would certainly find it in the negative
(judging from later Aramaic and cognate languages).

In the case of *śn'y* and *śn'wh* the medial *aleph* is clearly consonantal. In most of the other medial cases listed it appears at the end
of a closed syllable, where it seems to have retained its character as
a radical. Moreover, there are a number of cases of medial long *a*
not represented by a vowel letter (see §7 above). Hence, we find no
reason to regard *aleph* in this stele as anything but consonantal, and
consequently the emphatic ending as -*a*'.

(13) CONSONANTAL HE :

(a) = *EH :*

['*qr*]*h* ('iqqāreh I A 2); '*šrh* ('ašreh I A 5); *brh* (bireh I A 25);
mlkth (malkūteh I A 25); *nbšh* (nabšeh I A 37); *yqtlnh* (yiq-
tulinneh I B 27); *ydh* (yadeh I B 27); *ywmh* (yawmeh I C 15);
byth (bayteh I C 16); [*b*]*h* (beh I C 22); *tḥtyth* (taḥtāyteh I C
23); ['*]lyth* ('illāyteh I C 24); *šr*[*š*]*h* (šuršeh I C 24); ['*šmh*]
('ašumeh II A 4); *qb*[*rh*] (qabreh II A 4); '*rqh* ('arqeh II A 8);
'*mh* ('ammeh II B 3); *yhwnnh* (yuhawninneh II B 16); *ml'kh*

(mal'akeh III 8); *lh* (leh III 18); *'y<t>h* ('iyyāteh III 13); *tšryh* (tišrayeh III 18); *'srh* ('asureh III 18); *y'brnh* (yi'barinneh III 17); *ḫlph* (ḫālipeh or ḫalāpeh III 22).

(b)   = *AH :*

klh (kullah I A 5); *tḫth* (taḫtah I A 6); *'rqh* ('arqah I A 28); *'ḫwh* ('aḫwah I A 29); *'mh* ('ammah I A 29); *mlkh* (malkah II C 5); *gblh* (gabūlah III 23); *tkwh* (takkiwah? III 13).

(c)   = *AWH :*

bnwh (banawh I A 5); *rbwh* (rabbawh I A 39); *mlwh* (millawh I C 18); *'pwh* ('appawh III 2); *śn'wh* (śāni'awh III 12); *śgbwh* (śagbawh? III 13); *mwddwh* (mawdidawh III 14); *'ḫwh* ('aḫawh III 17); *'lwh* ('elawh III 8); *śptwh* (śapātawh III 15).

(d)   = *AYH :*

'pyh ('appayh I A 42); *kpryh* (kapīrayh III 23); *b'lyh* (ba'alayh III 23); *'ly[h]* ('alayh III 9).   See note on *'lh* above, §11.

As is evident from the above survey, most of the orthographical features of these inscriptions are quite regular and fit into the patterns set up by previous studies.

B. PHONOLOGY

(1)   INTERDENTALS : The treatment of the interdentals in these inscription conformss entirely to that found in the other Old Aramaic inscriptions.   Cf. G. Garbini, *AA*, p. 248; S. Moscati, *Il sistema conso-nantico delle lingue semitiche* (Roma : Pont. Ist. Bibl., 1954), pp. 46-47.

Protosemitic	Old Aramaic	Later Aramaic	Canaanite
ḏ	z	d	z
ṯ	š	t	š
ḍ	q	'	ṣ
ṭ	ṣ	ṭ	ṣ

ḏ :   *zy, znh, z', zkrn, zqn, zḫl*
ṯ :   *'šr, šwb, yšb, šm, šybt, šwrh, šbr, š'l, šḫlyn(?), [šdyhn]*
ḍ :   *qrq, 'rq, rqh (?), qq, [rbq], prq (?), mrq*
ṭ :   *ḫpṣ, ṣby, ḫṣ, nṣr*

It is most likely that at the period of these inscriptions the Aramaeans were still using the Proto-Semitic sounds, d̠, t̠, ṭ, which they represented by the closest sounding letters of the borrowed Phoenician alphabet. This feature gives to Old Aramaic orthography a peculiar Canaanite quality, which it lost later on as the pronunciation of the interdentals evolved. However, there are certain anomalies to be noted; for instance:

zrpnt instead of the usual Akkadian Ṣarpanītu; see note on Sf I A 8. If Dupont-Sommer's reading and interpretation of *yrt* (I C 24) are correct, and we are right in dividing *btn* (Sf I A 32) and explaining it as related to Ugaritic *bt̠n*, then we have here the earliest known examples of a Proto-semitic *tha* turning up in an Aramaic text as *t*. Cf. AšOstr 11 (*yhtb = yhšb*). There is also the uncertain case of *lwd* (instead of *lwz*) in Sf I C 18 (see note). They are exceptions to the otherwise consistent treatment of the interdentals in these (and other early Aramaic) inscriptions. Perhaps the name of Matīʿel's father, *ʿtrsmk*, should be considered here too, for it may be an assimilation of *ʿṭtrsmk* (< *ʿštrsmk*).

(2) ASSIMILATED CONSONANTS: In the case of Pe Nun verbs the first consonant is always assimilated: *ysk*, *tsk* (nsk); *ypq* (npq); *yṣr*, *yṣrw*, *yṣrn* (nṣr); *yś*', *tś*' (nś'); *ybʿ* (nbʿ); *tkh* (nkh); *tqm* (nqm). The only exception is *tntʿ* (I B 29, if our division of the letters is correct; see note). Pe Yodh verbs form their impf. on an analogy with the Pe Nun verbs, as in certain cases in later Aramaic: *tqd*, *yqd* (yqd); [*'šb*] (yšb); *thb* (yhb); *tqp* (yqp); *yrt* (yrt). In each case the second radical must be considered doubled. Assimilation is also found in *'pwh* ('np). It is hard to say whether analogy or real assimilation is at work in the following forms: *ysq*, *ysqn* (slq); *yqḥ*, *tqḥ*, *yqḥn* (lqḥ), with which compare *ylqḥ* (I B 35). On *'hk*, *yhkn*, see note on Sf III 5. *ʿtrsmk* (I A 1) probably belongs here too; see above.

(3) VARIA: We have already called attention in the notes to the peculiar word *khs'y* (III 17), which may be a stone-cutter's error or possibly a transitional form. We have likewise noted the form *nbš* for the usual *npš* (III 5-6) and *qtl* for the usual *qṭl* (III 11, 18, 21); see G. Garbini, *RSO* 34 (1959) 43; *Antonianum* 31 (1956) 310-11. A new instance of the *b/p* shift is found in *btn* for later Aram. *ptn* (I A 32); *šḥt* occurs instead of *šḥt* of later Aramaic (I A 32). There is also the lack of metathesis of *š* and *t* in the reflexive forms of verbs (I A 29; I B 9) to be contrasted with [*yš*]*tḥṭ* (I A 32).

C. MORPHOLOGY

I. Pronouns

(1) PERSONAL

(a) *Independent forms*

'*nh* (I B [24]; I C [2]; II B [5]; II C 8; III 6); '*t* (I B [39]; III 11,20); *h*' (hū' I B 24,42ter?; III 8, 13,22); *h*' (hī' I A 37; III 12,[24]); '*tm* (I B [31]); *hm* (I B 6,[42]). We consider *hw* (as read by Dupont-Sommer, Garbini, et al. in III 22) to be erroneous.

(b) *Suffixal forms*

on nouns :

-*y* (I B 25bis,27bis,32,[33],38,40bis,44,45 ; I C 3bis,4, [6]; II B [6bis],8bis,[8],13 ; III 1,3); -*k* (I B [25],31, [32],39,40,41,42 ; II B 5,[5],[6bis],[8] ; III 1bis,3,6,11); ---; -*h* (-eh I A [5],25ter,28,41 ; I B 3,11,[21-22],27 ; I C [8],8,16bis,22,23,24,25 ; II A [4quater],[5],8 ; II B 3,6 ; II C 14bis,15 ; III 7,8); -*h* (-ah I A 5,6,28,29bis, [35]; I B [4],5 ; II B [2]; II C 5 ; III 23); ---; -*km* (I B 21,32); ---; -*hm* (I B 45 ; II B 7 ; II C 16). -*y* (-ay I B 26,27,29?,45 ; II B [13],14 ; III 4,10, etc.); -*yk* (-ayk III 14); ---; -*wh* (-awh I A 5,39,40,[41]; I B [21]; I C 18-19 ; II B 2,3,6 ; II C 15 ; III 2,13, 14,15,16); -*yh* (-ayh I A 42 ; III 23,26); ---; -*km* (I A 13 ; III 5,7,21); ---; -*hm* (II C 16,17 ; III 5,6); -*hn* (I A [21]).

on prepositions :

-*y* (I B 29?,33,38 ; III 3,4,6,7,8,9); -*k* (I B 25,39?,43 ; II B [6],19?,20 ; III 22?); ---; -*h* (-eh I C 22 ; III 18, [20]); ---; -*y* (-ay I B 26,[29]; III 1,2,8,20,22); ---; -*wh* (III 8); -*yh* (III 9); ---; ---; -*hm* (III 3,5,7, 18,19,21); -*hn* (I A 36).

on verbs :

-*ny* (nī I B <28>; II B [8]; III 20); ---; ---; -*h* (-eh I B 27 ; II B 16 ; III 17,18,18); -*h* (III 13?); ---; ---; ---; -*hm* (II B 7 ; III 26ter); ---.

(2) DEMONSTRATIVE

znh (" this " masc.): I A 7,36,40; I B 8,[23],28,33,37;
I C 17; II B 9,[18]; II C [14]; III [4],14,17,23.
z' (" this " fem.): I A 35,[36],37,[42]; III 9.
'ln (" these "): I A 7bis,38; I B 7,[8],11,24,38; II B
[14]; II C 2,9; III 7,9,19,20,27.
h' (" that " masc.): I C [22]; II C 6,[10].
h' (" that " fem.): I A [33]; I B [34].

(3) DETERMINATIVE-RELATIVE

determinative: *zy* (III 7,[19]).
relative: *zy* (I A 5,7; I B 2,6,22,23,28,31,33,34,35bis;
I C 3,17,20,22; II B 2,4?,18,20; II C 8,13; III 2,4,5,8,
10,13,14,16,17bis,20bis,23,28,29bis).
compounded: *mzy* (I A 25); *'yk zy* (I A 35,38,39bis,
[40],[41]); *'ykh zy* (I A 37); *'n zy* (II C 3); *kzy* (III
24); *zyly* (III 20).
Conjunction: *zy* (I B 41?; I C 6).

(4) INDEFINITE

interrogative used as indefinite: *mn* (I B 30; I C 16;
II B [7],9; II C [1]; III 9bis,10quinquies,26); *mh* (I
A 26bis,30; I B 2,26bis,29?; I C 1; III 3,16,28,29).
'ḥrn (III 24).
kl (cst. st.): I A 6bis,10,12,26bis,30; I B 2,[8],22,23,[26],
29bis,34,40; I C 6,22; II A 7; II B 3,9,12,18; II C 13,
15bis; III 1,4,7,8bis,14,16bis,23,28,29,[29].
klh (suffixal): I A 5; I B [4].
kl mh : I A 26bis,30; I B 2,26,29; III 16,28,29.
ḥd (abs. st.): III 22; *ḥdh* (fem.): I B 8.
ḥd (cst.): I B 26bis,28,30,45; II B [7]; III 1,[3],
4ter,5,9bis,10quinquies,13quater,17.
ḥdhm (suffixal): I B 45; III 19.

II. Nouns and Adjectives

(1) STATES

Masc. forms

	Sg.	Pl.
Abs.	*mlk* (I A 6)	*mlkn* (I B 26)
Cst.	*mlk* (I A 1)	*mlky* (I B 41)
Emph.	*spr'* (I B 8)	*mlky'* (I B 22)

Fem. forms

	Sg.	Pl.
Abs.	*ssyh* (I A 22)	*š'n* (I A 23)
	š't (I A 21)	*lḥyt* (I C 20)
Cst.	*qšt* (I A 39)	-----
Emph.	*qšt'* (I A 38)	*ṭbt'* (II B 2)
	bkth? (I A 24)	

N. B.   The archaic ending (*t*) is found for both the abs. fem. sg. (= at) and pl. (= āt).

Abs. sg. : (masc.) *mlk* (I A 6; I B 2,7,26,30?; III 28); *'rq* (I A [11],26); *ywm* (I A 12; I B 31; I C 20); *lylh* (I A 12); *'lym* (I A 22); *'l* (I A 22; II A [1]); *'gl* (I A 23; II A [1]); *'mr* (I A 23; II A [2]); *lḥm* (I A 24; I B 38,39; II A [3]; III 5,7); *ḥl* (I A 25bis; II A [4]); *'ml* (I A 26); *brd* (I A 26); *'rbh* (I A 27); *twy?* (I A 28); *ḥṣr* (I A 28); *yrq* (I A 28); *knr* (I A 29); *mrq* (I A 29); *'qrb* (I A 31); *ss* (I A 31); *qml* (I A 31); *btn* (I A 32); *yšmn* (I A 32); *tl* (I A 32); *ṣy* (I A [32]); *š'l* (I A 33); *'rnb* (I A 33); *šrn* (I A 33); *ṣdh* (I A 33); *'š* (I A 35,37,[37]); *mlḥ* (I A 36); *rb* (I B 7); *yd* (I B [25],25,[27],34; II B [6]); *pgr* (I B 30bis; II B 11bis); *byr* (I B [34]); *zkrn* (I C 2); *'lm* (I C [9]; III 24,25); *'šm* (I C 25); *gdh* (II A 2); *šyt* (II A 5); *'ryh* (II A 9); *nḥt* (II B 4?); *ḥrn* (II B 12); *'lb* (II C 10); *gbr* (III 1); *šlm* (III 8); *ḥrb* (III 13,14); *'nš* (III 16); *lšn* (III 21); *ṭb* (III 3,22,29); *špr* (III 29); *qrq* (III 4); *rḥm* (III 8). -- (fem.) *mṣlh* (I A [11]); *š't* (I A 21); *ssyh* (I A 22); *šwrh* (I A 23; II A [1]); *bkth?* (I A 24; II A [3]); *lḥyh* (I A 26; I C [6]); *twl'h* (I A 27);

ṣ'qh (I A [29]; II A [8]); yllh (I A 30); ḥwh (I A 31); dbhh (I A 31); nmrh (I A 31; II A [9]); 'qh (I A 33); bq't (I B 10); mlh (I B [25]); qryh (III 12).

Cst. sg. :　(masc.) mlk (= malk I A 1bis,3,[13],14,[15]; I B [1]); br (I A 1,3,14; I C [3],[8]; II C 14; III 1,12bis,15bis, 16,25,[26]); 'qr (I A 3,15,[15]; I B 2bis; III 3); ḥbr? (I A 4); 'ly (I A 6); byt (I A 6; I B 3; I C [6],7; II A 12?; II B 10bis; III 9,24bis,[25]); šṭ (I A 24); II A [3]); ql (I A 29); hml (I A 29); hmwn (I A [29]); pm (I A 30,31ter; II A 9ter); qq (I A 32); rbq (I A 32); gbr (I A 39; I B 24; II B [5]); mlk (= mulk I B 6); b'l I B [29]); nbš (I B 40); krs' (II B [7]); ywm (II B 12); yd (II B 14; III 11); lḥṣ (II C 10); rwḥ (III 2); dm (III 12ter); lbb (III 15bis,16). -- (fem.) mlkt (I A 25bis; II A [4]); qšt (I A [38],39); gbrt (I A [42]); qryt? (I B 36); šybt (III 24).

Emph. sg. :　(masc.) nṣb' (I A [6]; I C 17); spr' (I A [6]; I B 8,[23],28,33; I C 17; II B [9],18; II C 13; III 4,14, 17,23); gnb' (I A 36); nbš' (I A [36]); 'gl' (I A 40); mlk' (I B [35]); ngd' (? I B 36); 'pl' (I B 43); šmš' (I C 5); 'š' (I C [21]); byr' (I B 34bis); 'm' (III 5,13). -- (fem.) qryt' (I A [33]); š'wt' (I A 35, 37,39,[42]); qšt' (I A 38); 'rḥ' (III 9).

Suff. on sg. :　bry (I B 25,27,45; I C 3bis; II B [6],8,13; III 1bis,3,11,12bis,15,17,26bis); 'qry (I B 25,[32]; II B [6]; III 1,3,11,12,16,21,22,26); 'rqy (I B 27); byty (I B 32,40,44; III 21); lḥmy (I B 38); nbšy (I B 40); 'šry (I C [4]); mlky (I C [6]); 'by (II B 8; III 10,23,[24],[25],25); r'šy (II B [8]; III 11); sḥrty (III 7); ḥpṣy (III 8); ml'ky (III 8); qrqy (III 19); dmy (III 11,[22]); khs'y (III 17); 'my (III 21). — brk (I B 25,41; II B [6]; III 1,2,11,12,15); 'qrk (I B [25],32; II B [6]; III 1,3,12,15,[26]); ḥylk (I B [28], 31); nbšk (I B 39,42; II B 5,[8]); bytk (I B 40); lbbk (II B [5]; III 14); lšnk (III 17); 'ḥk (III 18); 'rqk (III 6). — 'qrh (I A [2],25,41; II A [4]; II B 6; II C 15; III 13,25); 'šrh (I A [5]; I B 3; III 7); thth (I A 6); brh (I A 25; I C 8bis; II A [4]; II C 11,14bis; III 25bis); mlkth (I A 25; II A [4]); nbšh (I A 37); 'mh (I B 11,[21]; II B 3); ydh (I B 27;

III 2); *ywmh* (I C 15); *byth* (I C 16,22; III [24]); *ṭhtyth* (I C 23); *'lyth* (I C 24); *šršh* (I C [24]); *'šmh* (II A [4]); *qbrh* (II A [4]); *'rqh* (II A 8); *ml'kh* (III 8). — *'rqh* (I A 28); *'hwh* (I A 29,32); *'mh* (I A 29,30; I B 5; II B [2]); *gblh* (III 23). — *bytkm* (I B 21); *hylkm* (I B 32); *'šrkm* (III 5); *mr'km* (III 21); *ṭhtkm* (III 7). — *'šrthm* (I B 11); *'šmhm* (II B 7); *'mhm* (II C 16); *nbšhm* (III 5,6); *qrqhm* (III 19).

Abs. pl. : (masc.) *šmyn* (I A 11,26; I B 7); *m'ynn* (I A 12); *šnn* (I A 27bis,[27]; II A 5,6); *'lhn* (I A 30; I B 6bis,31; I C 15,21; II B 2; III 24bis); *šhlyn* (I A 36); *'lmn* (I B [7]); *'dn* (I B 24,41; II B [5]); *mlkn* (I B 26,28); *hyn* (I B [41]). — (fem.) *š'n* (I A 23; II A [2]); *lhyt* (I C 20; III 2); *'zn* (II A [2]); *mln* (III 2); *mrmt* (III 22).

Cst. pl. : (masc.) *'dy* (A I 1bis,2,3,[3],4ter,13; I B 1bis,4quater, 5bis,6); *bny* (I A 2quater,[16]; I B 1bis, [1],[2],3; II B 13; III 21quater); *b'ly* (I A 4bis; I B 4,[5]); *mlky* (I A [5]; I B 41; II B 3; II C 15; III 1,3,16, 27); *'lhy* (I A 10,[12bis]; I B 5,[5],23,33; II B [9], [18]; II C [13]; III 4,14,17,23); *'bny* (I A [26]); *'py* (I A 28); *nšy* (I A 41ter,[42]); *ṭby* (I B 6); *mly* (I B 8; I C 17); *my* (I B 33,34); *rbrby* (II A 7); *bty* (II C 2,7,9).

Emph. pl. : (masc.) *'dy'* (I A 7bis; I B 7bis,11,23,24,[28],33,38; II B 2,[9],[14],18; II C [13]; III 4,7,9,14,17,19,20,23, 27); *hṣy'* (I A 38; I B 29); *'lhy'* (I B [8]; II C 3,7, 10); *mlky'* (I B 22; III 7); *mrhy'?* (I B 31); *spry'* (II C 2,4,6,[9]); *mly'* (III 2); *'my'* (III 10). — (*fem.*) *ṭbt'* (I C [5 — possibly sg.],19; II B 2).

Suff. on pl. : *śn'y* (I B 26; II B 14; III 10,11); *mqny* (I B 27); *srsy* (I B 45; III 5); *bny* (II B [7],[13]; III 10,21, 22); *pqdy* (III 4,10,13); *'hy* (III 4,9,13,21); *ngdy* (III 10); *'bdy* (III 13); *'yny* (III 3); *ydy* (III 2,5,10,13). — *śptyk* (III 14). — *bnwh* (I A 5; I B [21]; II B 2,6); *rbwh* (I A 39,40,[41]; II B 3; II C 15); *mlwh* (I C 18); *śn'wh* (III 12); *śgbwh* (III 13); *mwddwh* (III 14); *'hwh* (III 17); *'pwh* (III 2); *śptwh* (III 15, 16). — *'pyh* (I A 42); *bnth* (I A [35]); *kpryh* (III

23,26); *b'lyh* (III 23,26). — *'ynykm* (I A 13) — *btyhm* (II C 16); *ywmyhm* (II C 17).

(2) GENDER

Some feminine nouns have masculine forms: *yd* (I B 25; III 11); *ydy* (III 2,5,10,13); *ydh* (I B 27; III 2); *'yny* (III 3); *'ynykm* (I A 13); *'rq* (I A 26); *'rqk* (III 6); *nbš* (I B 40); *nbšy* (I B 40); *nbšk* (I B 39); *nbšh* (I A 37); *nbšhm* (III 5,6); *mln* (III 2); *mly* I B 8); *mlwh* (I C 18); *nšy* (I A 41); *šnn* (I A 27); *byr'* (I B 34); *'rḥ'* (III 9).

III. Verbs

(1) CONJUGATIONS AND FORMS ATTESTED

PEAL

Pf.	Impf.	Impv.	Inf.	Ptc.
gzr (I A 7)	*ymlk* (I A 25)		*śgb* (I B 32)	Active:
hwt (III 24)	*tštq* (I B 8)		*mšlḥ* (I B 34)	*'kl* (I A 30)
	tmšl (III 9)	*qtl* (III 18)	*nkh* (III 12,13)	*znyh* (I A [41])
				śhdn (I A 12)
ktbt (I C 2)	*'šlḥ* (I B 24)			*yqpy* (I B 29)
śmw (I B 6)	*y'bdw* (I C 5)			Passive:
	tpnw (III 7)			*ptḥh* (III 8)
	ymlkn (I B 22)			
	ymšḥn (fem. I A 21)			
	tšm'n (I B [24])	*qtlw* (III 21)		
ktbn (I C 1)				

YUQTAL

ygzr (I A 40)
tšbr (I A 38)
ygzrn (I A 40)
y'rrn (I A 41)

ITHPEEL

ytšm' (I A 29)
tt'bd (I C [7])
ytšm'n (I B [9])

PAEL

ymll (III 1,2)   *ḥzyh* (I A 13)
                                       'bdt (I B 36)

šqrt (I B 38)   *trqh* (III 18,19)
                    'rqhm (III 6)
ḥbzw (III 24)
šqrtm (III 4)   *rqw* (III 6)

ITHPAAL

yštḥṭ (I A [32])

HAPHEL

hšb (III 20) *yhskr* (III 3)   *hskr* (III 2)   *mhynqn*
                  yhwnh (II B 16)   *hmtt* (III 11) (I A [21])
                  thrm (III 5,6)   *hmtty* (III 11)
                  'hld (I C 18)

hšbw (III 24) *yhskrn* (III 3)
                   yhynqn (fem. I
                       A 22)

APHEL

yskr (III 3)
y'brnh (III 17)
tšlmn (I B 24)

'OPHAL

y'r (I A 39)

(2) **SUFFIXAL FORMS**

Peal: *yqtlnh* (I B 27); *ysbn<y>* (I B 28); *y'brnh* (III 17); *t'šqny*
(III 20?); the foregoing forms are energic imperfect. But
the suffix is also found on the ordinary impf.: *tkwh* (III

13?);   *tšryh* (III 18).   On the impv.:   *'srh* (III 18);   on the ptc.:   *qrqy* (III 19);   *qrqhm* (III 19-20).

Pael: *trqhm* (III 6);   *'rqhm* (III 6);   *ḥbzthm* (II B 7).

Haphel: *thšbhm* (III 6);   *thskrhm* (III 2);   *yhwnnh* (II B 16);   on the infinitive: *hmtty* (III 11,15; II B [8]).

(3)   CLASSES OF VERBS REPRESENTED

(a)   *Strong Verbs:*

gzr (I A 7);   *ygzr* (I A 40bis);   *ygzrn* (I A 40);   *tgzr* (I B 43);   *šqrt* (I B [27],[33],[36],38; II B [17]; III 9,14,19,20,27);   *šqrtm* (I B 23; II B 9,14; III 4,7,16, 23);   *yšqr* (I A 14,15,24; II A [3]);   *yšqrn* (I A [16]);   *ymlk* (I A 25; I B [3]);   *ymlkn* (I B 22);   *yqtl* (II B 9bis; III 18);   *yqtln* (III 11);   *yqtlnh* (I B 27);   *qtlw* (impv. III 21);   *ktbt* (I C 2);   *ktbn* (I C [1]);   *yšbr* (I A 38);   *tšbr* (I A 38);   *tštq* (I B 8);   *tšlmn* (I B [24]);   *śgb* (I B 32bis);   *prq* (I B 34);   *yqrq* (I B 45; III 4, 19bis);   *qrq* (ptc. III 4);   *qrqy, qrqhm* (ptc. with suffix, III 19);   *yzqn* (II B 8);   *ygbr* (II B 19);   *yršmn* (II C 3);   *yhskr* (III 3);   *yhskrn* (III 3);   *thskrhm* (III 2);   *hskr* (inf. absol. III 2);   *yskr* (Aphel III 3);   *tmšl* (III 9).

(b)   *Pe Nun Verbs:*

ysk (I A [25],26);   *tsk* (I B 38; III 5,7);   *ypq* (I A 28);   *yṣrn* (I B 8);   *tnt'?* (I B 29);   *yṣr* (I C 17);   *yṣrw* (I C 15);   *yš'* (III 15,16,26);   *tš'* (I B 39; III 14);   *yš'n* (II C [13]);   *yb'* (II B 8);   *nkh* (inf. III 12,13);   *tkh* (III 13);   *tkwh* (III 13);   *yqm* (III 12ter,22);   *tqm* (III 11).

(c)   *Pe Laryngalis Verbs:*

'bdw (II B 2);   *t'bd* (I B [26]; III 22);   *''bd* (III 3);   *y'bdw* (I C 5);   *tt'bd* (I C [7]);   *yhrgn* (I A 24; II A [3]);   *'hpk* (I C 19);   *t'št* (II B 5);   *ḥbzw* (III 24);   *ḥbzthm* (II B 7);   *y'brnh* (III 17);   *t'šqny* (III 20).

(d)   *Pe Yodh Verbs:*

mhynqn (I A [21]);   *yhynqn* (I A 22bis,23bis);   *tqd* (I A 35bis,37);   *tqp* (I B 29);   *yqpy* (I B 29);   *thb* (I B 38);   *yrt* (I C 24);   *'šb* (II B [7]);   *yšb* (III 17);   *yšbn* (III 6);   *šbw* (III 7);   *yhwnnh* (II B 16);   *yhwnh* (II B 16);   *yd'?* (II C 8);   *yqd* (I A 37).

(e) *Pe Aleph Verbs :*

y'kl (I A 27,[30]) ; *t'kl* (I A 27) ; *'kl* (I A 30) ; *'mrn*
(I C 1) ; *y'mr* (I C 18 ; II B [7] ; II C [1],4,7,[8]) ;
t'mr (= ti'mar I A 36? ; I B 24,26 ; II B 5,[8] ; III 5,
7,18,21) ; *t'mr* (= tu'mar I A 33) ; *'bdt* (I B 36 ; II
B 7) ; *'h'bd* (II C 4) ; *'hbd* (II C 5) ; *y'th* (I B 28bis,
32,[45] ; II B 13 ; III 11,12bis,20) ; *t'th* (I B 31 ; III
11) ; *t'twn* (I B [32]) ; *t'zl* (I B 39) ; *y'sr* (III 18) :
'srh (impv. III 18) ; *'gr* (II C 8).

(f) *Ayin Laryngalis Verbs :*

śhdn (I A 12) ; *yšṭḥṭ* (I A [32]) ; *'khl* (I B [24],33 ; II
B 6) ; *ykhl* (I B 25,[34]) ; *yzḫl* (II C 6) ; *tkhl* (I B
[39]) ; *yb'h* (III 2,11) ; *rḥm* (ptc. III 8) ; *yšḥdn* (III
28).

(g) *Ayin Waw Verbs :*

y'r (I A 39bis) ; *y'wrn* (II B 4) ; *ymt* (II C 10) ; *ymwt*
(III 16) ; *hmtt* (III 11,15,16) ; *hmtty* (II B [8] ; III 11,
15) ; *ld* (II C 6,9) ; *hldt* (II C 2) ; *'hld* (I C 18) ; *yhkn?*
(I A 24 ; III 5 ; II A [3]) ; *hšb* (III 20) ; *'hšb* (III 20) ;
hšbw (III 24) ; *thšbhm* (III 6) ; *šbt* (III 25) ; *'hk* (? III
6) ; *thrm* (III 5,6).

(h) *Ayin Yodh Verbs :*

śm (I A 7) ; *śmw* (I B 6) ; *'śm* (I C 19) ; *yśmw* (I C
23) ; *yrb* (III 17,[26bis],26).

(i) *Ayin Ayin Verbs :*

'll (I A 6) ; *t'rr* (I A [40]) ; *y'rrn* (I A 41) ; *ysbn<y>*
(I B 28) ; *ysb* (I B 34) ; *y'l* (I B 35) ; *y'zz* (I B 44) ;
y'z (II B 20) ; *ymll* (I B [26] ; III [1],2).

(j) *Lamedh Laryngalis Verbs :*

tqḥ (I A [42] ; III 2) ; *yqḥ* (I B 27) ; *ylqḥ* (I B 35bis) ;
yqḥn (I A 42) ; *yšlḥn* (I A 30) ; *'šlḥ* (I B 24 ; II B 6 ;
III 8) ; *yšlḥ* (I B 25,[26],27 ; III 8) ; *mšlḥ* (I B 34) ;
tšlḥ (I B 37 ; III 17,21) ; *tšm'* (II B 4) ; *'šm'* (II B
[5]) ; *yšm'* (I B 21,[21] ; II B [2],3) ; *yšm'n* (I B
[21],[22] ; II B 2,3bis) ; *tšm'n* (I B [24]) ; *ytšm'* (I A
29) ; *ytšm'n* (I B 9) ; *yzr'* (I A 36) ; *yśb'* (I A 22bis,
23bis ; II A [1],1,[2bis]) ; *pqḥw* (I A 13) ; *ymšḥn* (I A
21) ; *ptḥh* (III 8).

(k)   *Tertiae Infirmae Verbs :*

hwt (III 24) ; *hwy* (III 22) ; *thwy* (I A 25,32 ; II A [4],6) ; *yhwh* (II A 4) ; *yhww* (I A [31] ;)*ḥzyh* (I A 13) ; *ytḥzh* (I A 28bis) ; *ybʻh* (II B 8 ; III 2,11) ; *tbʻh* (I B 39 ; II B 17) ; *thry* (I A 21) ; *ytnšy* (II A 4) ; *yʼth* (I B 28bis,32,[45] ; II B 13 ; III 11,12bis,20) ; *tʼth* (I B 31 ; III 11) ; *tʼtwn* (I B [32]) ; *šlw* (III 5) ; *rqh* (inf. III 6,18) ; *trqh* (III 18,19) ; *rqw* (*impv.* III 6) ; *trqhm* (III 6) ; *ʼrqhm* (III 6) ; *nkh* (III 12,13) ; *tkh* (III 13) ; *tkwh* (III 13) ; *tršh* (III 9) ; *tpnw* (III 7) ; *tšryh* (III 18) ; *znyh* (I A [41].

(l)   *Lamedh Aleph Verbs :*

ymhʼ (I A 42) ; *yšʼ* (III 15,16,26) ; *tšʼ* (I B 39 ; III 14) ; *yšʼn?* (II C [13]) ; *ʼrbʼ* (I B 30).

(m)   *Special Verbs :*

ysq (I A 27 ; I B [3] ; III 14,15bis,16) ; *ysqn* (I A 5 ; I C 4) ; *yhkn* (I A 24 ; II A [3] ; III 5) ; *ʼhk* (III 6).

IV. Adverbs and Particles

(1)   Negative *ʼl :* I A 21,22bis,23bis,24,28,29,33,36 ; I B 8 ; I C 24 ; II A [1bis],[2],2,[3] ; III 7,18,[20].
(2)   Negative *l- :* I A 28bis ; I B 21,[21bis],[22],[24bis],25,[25], 31,[32bis],34,36,38bis,[39],39,41 ; I C [7],17 ; II B [2],2,3ter, 6bis,16?,17 ; II C 8? ; III 4,5ter,6,9ter,14,17,18bis,19,20,21, 22 (?).
(3)   *ʼyk :* I A 35,38,39,[39],[40],[41].
(4)   *ʼykh :* I A 37.
(5)   *kn :* I A 35,37,38,39,40,41,42 ; I B 43 ; I C 21.
(6)   *ʼyt* (signum accusativi): I B 32 ; II B [8] ; II C 5bis,14 ; *ʼyty* (III 11) ; *ʼy<t>h* (III 13).
(7)   *hn* (emphatic): I B 36 ; III 4,9,14,20.
(8)   *kh :* I C 1,[1].
(9)   *ʼn :* II C 3.
(10) Enclitic *-m :* *kym* (III 1).
(11) *kʻt* (temporal): III 24.
(12) *šm* (local): III 6.
(13) *l-* (signum accusativi?): I C 4.

V. Prepositions

(1) *'el* : *'l* (II B [13] ; III 1ter,19) ; *'ly* (I B [29] ; III 8,20) ;
     'lwh (III 8).

(2) *'al* : *'l* (I A 26,28,42 ; I B 44,[45],45 ; I C [7] ; II B [7],
     11 ; III 1ter,5,14bis,15ter,16bis,17,22bis,26) ; *'ly* (I B 26:
     III 1,22) ; *l'ly* (III 2) ; *'lh* (I A 32) ; *'lyh* (III 9) ; *m'l*
     (compound, I B 30).

(3) *b* : I A 5,24,26bis,29bis,30bis,35,37bis ; I B 3,12,22,[23],
     25ter,[27],[28],28,30,31bis,32,33,34,36,38 ; I C 4,17,20 ; II A
     [3],7 ; II B 2,[2],5bis,6bis,[8],[9],12,[14],16,18 ; II C 10,13 ;
     III 2,3,4,5,6,7bis,9bis,10,13bis,14bis,16,17,19,20,21,23,27 ; *by*
     (III 9) ; *bk* (I B 25 ; II B [6]) ; *bh* (I C [22]) ; *bhn* (I B 36).

(4) *bên* : *bnyhm* (III 18bis,19).

(5) *l* : I A 13,[14],[15],[24],25,32bis ; I B [7],13,21,23bis,26,
     32bis,33,[34],34,[36],40ter,42 ; I C 2,3,[3],[6],[20],[23] ; II
     A 3bis,[4] ; II B [5],7bis,[8],9,12,18 ; II C 2,4,7 ; III 2,3bis,
     4,7,8bis,11bis,14,15bis,16bis,23 ter,24,25quater ; *ly* (I B 29,
     38 ; III 3,6,8,9bis,20) ; *lk* (I B 39 ; II B 19?) ; *lh* (III 18,20) ;
     lhm (III 3,5bis,7bis,21).

(6) *mn* : I A 20,30 ; I B 8,[9],9,[10bis],27bis ; I C 15,16,18 ; II
     B 14 ; II C 2,6,7,9,16bis ; III 2,11,12 ; *mny* (III 4,6,7) ; *mk*
     (III 22) ; *mnk* (II B 20) ; *mnhm* (I B 41) ; *m-* (I B 7?,30).

(7) *'d* : I B 9bis,10bis ; I C [8] ; II B 19? ; III [24],25.

(8) *'m* : I A 1,2,3bis,4,5quater,6bis,[13] ; I B 1,2bis,3ter,4bis,
     5bis,11,[29] ; III [26] ; *'my* (I B 33) ; *'mk* (I B 43).

(9) *k* : I A 25 ; II A [4].

(10) *qdm* : I A [7],8ter,9quater,10bis,11quater,12.

(11) *tht* : I C [5].

VI. Conjunctions

(1) *'w* : I B 26,27,35,45 ; I C 19 ; III 1sexies,4bis,5,8ter,9,10
     quinquies,13ter,17,18,22bis.

(2) *hn* : I A 14,[15],[16],24 ; I B [23],[25],28,31,[32],36,37,38,
     43 ; II A [3] ; II B 4,5,[7],16,17 ; III 4bis,6bis,9bis,11,
     12,13,14bis,15,16,17,18,19,20bis,[22],[26],27.

(3) *mzy* : I A 25.

(4) *p* : II B 4,6.

(5) *w* : passim.

(6) *'d* : III 6.

(9) *ky* : III 22 ; *kym* (III 1).

(8) *kzy* : III 24.

D. SYNTAX

I. Pronouns

(1) PERSONAL

(a) *Independent forms :*

(i) As subject : It may either precede or follow the verb ; often it scarcely supplies any emphasis. Thus *'nh 'gr 'gr,* " I shall reward (you) indeed " (II C 8) ; *mh ktbt '[nh mt']'l lzkrn,* " what I, Matî'el, have written (is to act) as a reminder " (I C 2). Similarly : *'d 'hk 'nh w'rqhm* (III 6) ; *'t t'th* (III 11) ; *w'l t'šqny 't* (III 20) ; *w'[tm lt']twn* (I B 31) ; *[w't ltk]hl lts̆'* (I B 39) ; *wyzḫl h' mn ld* (II C 6) ; *y[mt h'] wbrh* (II C 10) ; *[h' h]wt* (III 24).

A special function of the independent form is that of subject of a nominal sentence : *whn ḥd 'ḥy h',* " if it is one of my brothers " (III 13) ; *ky lṭb h' mk,* " for he is not better than you " (III 22). Similarly : *wnbšh h'* (I A 37) ; *whn wqryh h'* (III 12) ; *zy 'dn ḥy[n hm]* (I B 42) ; *[w]'dy 'lhn hm* (I B 6) ; *[gbr 'dn 'nh]* (II B 5).

(ii) As present tense copula : *kl zy rḥm h' ly,* " anyone who is a friend of mine " (III 8) ; *gbr 'dn h' ['nh],* " I am an ally " (I B 24).

(iii) As the remote demonstrative : See below (I A [33] ; I B [34] ; I C 22).

(b) *Suffixal forms :* There are many instances of the pronominal suffix on nouns, expressing a genitival relationship, and on prepositions (see Morphology, I 1 b ; II 1). What is striking here is the lack of the prospective or the resumptive suffix. The only forms which call for some comment here are the suffixes which appear on verbal forms. These are of two sorts mainly :

(i) Object suffixes : *lhmtty,* " to kill me " (II B [8] ; III 11,15) ; *'l t'šqny,* " you shall not try to hinder me " (III 20). Similarly : *ysbn<y>* (I B 28) ; *yqpy,* " those surrounding me " (I B 29) ; *'srh* (III 18) ; *yhwnnh* (II B 16) ; *y'brnh* (III 17) ; *yqtlnh* (I B 27) ; *tšryh* (III 18) ; *tkwh,* " strike it " (3 sg. fem., III 13) ; *lḥbzthm* (II B 7) ; *thskrhm* (III 2) ; *trqhm* (III 6) ; *'rqhm* (III 6).

(ii) Genitival suffixes : *ḫlph,* " his successor " (if the form is participial, III 22 [see note *ad loc.*]) ; *qrqy,* " my fugitive " (*qāriqī,* III 19) ; *qrqhm* (III 19).

(2) DEMONSTRATIVE

The demonstrative pronoun is either used absolutely as such or in a form of apposition modifying a noun in the emphatic state.

(a) *Absolute usage :* *ltmšl by bz' wltršh ly 'lyh,* " you must not (try to) dominate me in this (respect) nor assert your authority over me concerning it," the pronoun refers to " road " in the preceding clause (III 9).

(b) *Attributive usage :* Here the pronoun functions almost like an adjective, agreeing in gender and number with the noun in the emphatic state which precedes.   Thus,

['yk zy] *ygzr 'gl' znh,* " just as this calf is cut in two " (I A 40). Similarly: *spr' znh* (I A [6]; I B [8],[23],28,33; II B [9],[18]; II C [14]; III [4],14,17,[23]); *bnṣb' znh* (I C 17); *gnb' znh* (I A 36); *š'wt' z'* (I A 35,37,[42]); *nbš' z'* (I A [36]?); *byr' [h]'* (I B [34]); *'š[' h]'* (I C 22); *qr[yt' h']* (I A [33]); *'dy' 'ln* (I A 7bis; I B [7], [8],[11],24,38; II B [14]; III 7,9,19,20,27); *spry' 'ln* (II C [2],9); *tšbr qšt' wḥṣy' 'ln,* " (just as this) bow and these arrows are broken " (I A 38; the expression is not elegant here, for the sentence begins with the fem. sg. verb with which *qšt'* agrees, but then follows the plur. with the demonstrative is added, as a sort of afterthought).

(3) DETERMINATIVE-RELATIVE

The pronoun *zy* is found in these texts most frequently in a relative use, either alone (as a simple or general relative) or in combination with other words.

(a) *Simple Relative :* The pronoun in this case is preceded by an antecedent to which the *zy*-clause really acts as an appositive. In the clause itself the pronoun may have different functions.

(i) *zy* as subject of a verbal clause: *'m bnwh zy ysqn b'šrh,* " with his sons who will come after him " (I A 5; cf. I C 3); *kl mh mlk zy [ysq wymlk],* " any king who will come up and rule " (I B 2; cf. III 28).   Similarly: *zy ymlkn* (I B 22); *zy ysb* (I B 34); *zy y'l wylqḥ* (I B 35); *zy y'wrn* (II B 4); *zy y'z mnk* (II B 20); *kl gbr zy yb'h rwḥ 'pwh* (III 2); *zy yšb 'l khs'y* (III 17).

(ii) *zy* as subject of a nominal clause: *'dy' zy bspr' znh,* " the treaty which is in this inscription " (I B [23],28,33; II B [9], 18; II C 13; III 4,14,17,23); *zy bnṣb' znh,* " which is on this stele " (I C 17).   Similarly: *wkl zy bh* (I C 22); *kl zy rḥm h' ly* (III 8); *zy bydy* (III 5,10,13); *[kl mh] zy špr wkl mh zy ṭ[b]* (III 29).

(iii) *zy* as object of the verbal clause: *'dy' 'ln zy gzr br g'yh*, " this treaty which Bir-Ga'yah concluded " (I A 7). Similarly: *'dy 'lhn hm zy śmw 'lhn* (I B 6); *zy 'bdw* (II B [2]).

(iv) *zy* used with adverbial force: *bywm zy y'b[d] kn*, " on any day on which he will do so " (I C 20). Similarly: *bywm zy 'lhn* ... (I B 31); *bkl mh zy ymwt* (III 16).

(b) *General Relative* : The pronoun in this case functions doubly, in the main clause and in the relative clause itself. Thus *wy'mr lzy lyd'*, " and should he say to someone who does not understand " (II C 8). Similarly: *hn hšb zy ly 'hšb [zy lh]*, " if he has restored mine, I shall return his " (III 20). In this last instance the form *zy ly* almost functions like the later common possessive pronoun. But possibly it retains here its basic meaning, " that which is to me."

(c) *Combinatory usage* : The pronoun *zy* also is found with various prepositions or adverbs, composing with them what appears to be a separate conjunction. Thus *'n zy*, " where ": *bty 'lhy' 'n zy y[r]śmn*, " the bethels, where they are written " (II C 3).
'yk(h) zy, " just as ": *'yk zy tšbr qšt' whṣy' 'ln*, " just as (this) bow and these arrows are broken " (I A 38). Similarly: I A 35,37, 39,[39],[40],[41]. *kzy*, " when ": *wkzy ḥbzw 'lhn byt ['by]*, " and when the gods struck my father's house " (III 24). *mzy*, " as long as ": *mzy ymlk 'šr*, " as long as Asshur rules " (I A 25).
In two instances the simple *zy* has a nuance which may have developed from some combined usage: *zy 'dn ḥy[n hm]*, " because it is a living pact " (I B 41 [but the reading and interpretation are not certain here]); *[z]y kl lḥ[yh ltt'bd 'l] byt m[t''l]*, " that no evil may be done against the house of Matî'el " (I C 6).

(d) *Determinative usage* : In two instances the pronoun *zy* seems to function in the manner of the determinative pronoun which is so common in later Aramaic; it seems to express a genitival relationship and be a substitute for a construct chain. Thus *w[m]lkn [zy sḥr]ty*, " and as for kings of my vicinity " (III 19); *wkl mlky' zy sḥrty*, " now as for all the kings of my vicinity " (III 7). In both cases the expression is found in a *casus pendens*, and one may wonder whether this had something to do with the use of *zy* here. Possibly we should also include II A 12 (*zy byt*).

(4) INDEFINITE

We include here the following pronouns: *'ḥrn, kl, mn, mh.*

(a) *'ḥrn,* " another." It occurs only as the object of the preposition *l* (III 24).

(b) *kl,* " all." The form is either construct or suffixal.

(i) Construct: *kl 'lhy 'dy',* " all the gods of the treaty " (I B 23; II B 9,18; II C 13; III 4,14,16,23); *kl 'lhy rḥbh* (I A 10); *kl '[lhy ktk]* (I A 12); *kl mlky 'rpd* (II B [3]; II C 15); *kl mlky'* (I B 22; III 7); *kl zy ysb* (I B 34; cf. I C 22; III 8); *kl 'ly 'rm* (I A 6); *kl 'll byt mlk* (I A 6); *[kl 'lhy']* (I B 8); *kl [b'l] ḥṣy'* (I B 29); *kl nbš* (I B [40]); *kl lḥ[yh]* (I C 6); *bkl rbrby ...* (II A 7); *kl rbwh* (II C 15); *kl gbr zy* (III 1); *lkl ḥpṣy* (III 8); possibly II B 12.

A special case of this construct use is found with *mh*; the combined *kl mh* forming an indefinite pronoun, " any at all." For references, see Morphology, I 4.

(ii) Suffixal form: One clear instance of it is found in I A 5, *'m 'rm klh,* " with all Aram," lit. " with Aram, all of it." The same form is restored in I B 4. Cf. " The Syntax of *kl, kl'* in the Aramaic Texts from Egypt and in Biblical Aramaic," *Bibl* 38 (1957) 170-84, esp. 183-84.

(c) *mn :* Actually this pronoun means " who ? " and is an interrogative. But in these texts it is found only as a general relative or an indefinite pronoun. As the former it is found in I C 16 (*wmn lyṣr*); [*wmn y*]*'mr* (II C 1); *mn yš'* (III 26), where it functions as a subject in the relative clause; in II B 9 (*yqtl mn yqtl,* " let him kill whomever he would kill ") it is the object. More frequently it is found as an indefinite; then it is combined with *ḥd.* It precedes the noun it modifies, which may be either plural or a collective singular. Thus, *mn ḥd mlk,* " some king " (I B 30); *mn ḥd byt 'by,* " anyone of my father's household " (III 9); *mn ḥd bny,* " anyone of my sons " (II B [7]; III 10). Similarly: *mn ḥd 'ḥy* (III 9); *mn ḥd ngdy* (III 10); *mn ḥd pqdy* (III 10); *mn ḥd 'my'* (III 10); *mn ḥd śn'y* (III 10).

(d) *mh,* " what ? " This pronoun occurs in its interrogative function in I B 26 (*mh t['bd],* "what are you going to do?"). Otherwise it is used as an indefinite (either combined with *kl* and preceding a singular noun; see b above) or preceding *zy* (III 16,29,[29]) or as a general relative (I C 1; III 3).

(5) NUMERAL

Only two numbers occur in these texts, *ḥd* (" one ") and *šb'* (" seven "). Aside from the instances of *mn ḥd* mentioned above, the cst. *ḥd* occurs frequently; it functions either as the subject or object of a verb. Thus, as subject: *ḥd mlkn* (I B 26,28); *ḥd śn'y* (I B 26); *ḥd pqdy* (III 4,[13]); *ḥd 'ḥy* (III 4,13); *ḥd srsy* (III 4); *ḥd 'bdy* (III 13); *ḥd 'm'* (III 13). As object of a verb: *ḥd 'ḥwh* (III 17). As object of a preposition: *'l ḥd mlky 'rpd* (III 1); *'l ḥd srsy* (I B 45). The absolute masc. *ḥd* occurs only in III 22, as the subject of a verb (*wyqm ḥd [dmy]*, " someone will avenge my blood "). Its fem. counterpart is used similarly in I B 8 (*w'l tštq ḥdh mn mly spr'*). The suffixal form *ḥdhm* functions as the subject of a verb (I B 45) and as the object of a preposition (III 19).

The numeral *šb'*, found only in this masc. form, precedes in these texts feminine nouns, which may be either singular or plural. Thus, *šb' ssyh*, " seven mares " (I A 22), acting as the subject of a plural verb. Similarly: *šb' šwrh* (I A [22]; II A [1]); *šb' bkth* (I A 24; II A [3]); but *šb' š'n yhynqn* (I A 23; II A 1); [*šb' 'zn*] (II A [2]); *šb' [mhy]nqn* (I A 21). As an adverbial construction we find *šb' šnn*, " for seven years," (I A 27ter; II A [5],[6]).

II. Nouns

(1) APPOSITION : This feature includes the juxtaposition of a noun with either another noun or a pronoun. Thus *mh ktbt '[nh mt']'l lzkrn lbry*, " what I, Matî'el, have written (is to act) as a reminder for my son " (I C 2); *'m mt''l br 'trsmk*, " with Matî'el, the son of 'Attarsamak " (I A 1,3,14; I B 13); *'dy br g'yh mlk ktk*, " the treaty of Bir Ga'yah, the king of KTK " (I A 1,[15]). See further *mlk* (I A 1,3,[13],[14]; I B [1],7). If the words are not dittographical, then *mlkt ḥl* (I A 25) also belongs here.

(2) NOMINA RECTA : This usage consists of the juxtaposition of two nouns, the former of which (*nomen regens*) is sometimes modified in form to express its state of relationship. The dependent noun is the *nomen rectum* and in almost all cases in these texts it expresses a genitival relation. Thus *mn ḥd byt 'by*, " any one of my father's household " (III 10, *'by* is the *nomen rectum*); *lkl 'lhy 'dy'*, " all the gods of the treaty " (I B 23,33; II B [9],[18]; II C [13]; III 4, [14],17,23); *mlky 'rpd*, " the kings of Arpad " (II C 15; I B [41]; II B [3]; III 1,3,16,27). The *nomen rectum* can be a proper name, or a common noun which is either suffixal, emphatic, or absolute (e.g., I B 6,24; III 16).

Similarly: *'by* (II B 8; III [24],[25],25); *'dm* (I A 10); *'ḥy* (III 4,9,13,[21]); *'ḥwḥ* (III 17); *'lḥn* (I B 6); *'lḥy'* (I B [8]; II C 3,7,[10]); *'nš* (III 16); *'pwḥ* (III 2); *'ryḥ* (II A 9); *'rm* (I A 6); *'rnb* (I A 33); *'rpd* (I A [1],3,4bis,[12],[14bis]; I B [1],4,[5],[6]); *byr'* (I B [34bis]); *byty* (I B 40,44); *bry* (I C 3; III 1,12bis,15,[26]); *brk* (III 12,15); *brh* (I C 8; II C 14; III 25); *bny* (II B [7],13; III 10,21); *brd* (I A [26]); *btn* (I A 32); *br g'yh* (I A 1,2,[2],13, [15]; I B 1,[2],[7]); *gbr* (III 1); *gš* (I A 16; I B 3,11; II B 10); *dbḥḥ* (I A 31); *ḥbr* (I A [4]); *ḥwḥ* (I A 31); *ḥl* (I A 25bis; II A [4]); *ḥpṣy* (III 8); *ḥṣy'* (I B 29); *ḥrn* (II B 12); *knr* (I A 29); *l'wyn* (? I B 30); *lḥyh* (I C [6]); *lḥm* (I A 24; II A [3]); *mlk* (I A 6); *mlkn* (I B 26,28); *mlky'* (I B 22; III 7); *mlky* (I C [6]); *mrq* (I A 29); *mt''l* (I A 2,3,[38],41,[42]; I B 1,2; I C [7]); *ngdy* (III 10); *nmrh* (I A 31; II A [9]); *spr'* (I B 8; I C 17); *srsy* (I B 45; III 5); *'bdy* (III 13); *'dn* (I B 24; II B [5]); *'lb* (II C 10); *'m'* (III 5,13); *'my'* (III 10); *'my* (III 21); *'ml* (I A 26); *'qh* (I A 33); *'qry* (III 12,[21]); *'qrk* (III 15); *'qrh* (I A [2],41); *'qrb* (I A 31); *'trsmk* (I A 1,3,14; I B [1],[14]); *pqdy* (III 4,[10],13); *ṣby* (I A 33); *ṣdh* (I A 33); *ṣy* (I A [32]); *ṣll* (II B 10; I B 3); *ṣ'qh* (I A [29]); *rbwh* (I A 39,[41]; II C 15); *śn'y* (I B 26; II B 14; III 10,11; *š'wt'* (I A 39,[42]); *š'l* (I A 33); *šrn* (I A 33); *ṯṯh* (I A 6); *rḥbh* (I A 10); *ktk* (I A 1,3,4,[12],[15]; I B 4bis,5); *ḥlb* (I A [10]).

(3) CONSTRUCT CHAIN AS NOMEN RECTUM: This is in reality a special form of the preceding noun function, a compounded construct chain in which one or more nouns in the construct state depend on the preceding construct. Thus *'m kl 'll byt mlk,* "with everyone entering the royal palace" (I A 6: three constructs); *'w mn ḥd byt 'by,* "or anyone of my father's household" (III 9); *'dy b'ly ktk,* "the treaty of the lords of KTK" (I A 4; cf. I B [5]).

Similarly: *kl 'lhy rḥbh* (I A 10); *kl '[lhy ktk w'lhy 'r]pd* (I A 12); *'dy '[lhy 'rpd] w'dy 'lhy ktk* (I B 5); *lkl 'lhy 'dy'* (I B 23; II B [9],[18]; II C [13]; III 4,14,17, 3); *šybt by[t 'by]* (III 24); *kl b'l ḥṣy'* (I B [29]); *d[m b]r bry* (III 12); *lbb br brk* (III 15); *['] dy bny br g'yh* (I A 2ter; I B 1,[1]); *mn ḥd mlk l'wyn* (I B 30?); *kl* (or *ḥd*) *mlky 'rpd* (II B [3]; II C 15; III 1,[3]); *lbb mlky 'rpd* (III 16); *ṯby mlk br g'yh* (I B 6); *[lk]l nbš byty* (I B 40); *kl 'ly 'rm* (I A 6); *'m 'qr kl mh mlk* (I B 2).

(4) NOUN SUBJECT IN A NOMINAL SENTENCE: Thus, *ptḥḥ ly 'rḥ',* "the road shall be open to me" (III 9); *[wtl'y]m wkpryh wb 'lyh wgblh l'by,* "and Tal'ayim and its villages, its lords, and its territory belong to my father" (III 23).

Similarly: *ṭby* (I B 6); *nbš'* (I A [36]); *nṣb'* (I A [6]); *'dn* (I B 41); *'dy* (I A 1bis,2,3,[3],4bis; I B 1bis,[4],4,5); *qryh* (III 12).

(5) Noun Predicate in a Nominal Sentence: *gbr 'dn h'* ['nh], " I am an ally " (I B 24; cf. II B [5]); *wb'mh hml mrq whm[wn ṣ']qh wyllh*, " but among its people let there rather be the din of affliction and the noise of crying and lamentation " (I A 29). See further: *'dy'* (I A 7); *śhdn* (I A 12); *nbšh* (I A 37); *ṭb* (III 3,22,29); *rḥm* (III 8); *špr* (III 29).

(6) Noun Subject of a Verb, Which Either Precedes or Follows: *wyšlḥn 'lhn mn kl mh 'kl b'rpd*, " and may (the) gods send every sort of devourer against Arpad " (I A 30); *zy śmw 'lhn*, " which gods have concluded " (I B 6); *wšb' bkth yhkn bšṭ lḥm*, " and should seven hens (?) go in search of food " (I A 24). Similarly: *ḥwh* (I A 29,32); *'lhn* (I C 15,21; II B 2; III 24bis); *'rbh* (I A 27); *'śmh* (II A [4]); *br* (III 12,16,[26]); *bry* (I B 25; II B [6],8; III [17], [26]); *brk* (III 2,11); *brh* (II C 11); *bnth* (I A [35]); *bny* (I A [16]); *bnwh* (I B [21]; II B 2b); *gbr* (I A 39); *gbrt* (I A [42]); *hylk* (I B [28]); *ḥṣy'* (I A 38); *ḥṣr* (I A 28); *yrq* (I A 28); *mlky* (I B 41); *mlkth* (I A 25; II A [4]); *nbšk* (I B 39); *nšy* (I A 41ter, [42]); *ss* (I A 31); *ssyh* (I A 22); *'gl'* (I A 40); *'dy* (I B 6); *'zn* (II A [2]); *'mh* (I B [21]; II B 3); *'qr* (I A 15; III 3); *'qry* (I B 25; II B [6]; III 26); *'qrk* (I B [32]; III 3,12); *pm* (I A [30], 31bis; II A 9ter); *qbrh* (II A [4]); *ql* (I A 29); *qml* (I A 31); *qryt'* (I A [33]); *qšt'* (I A 38); *rbwh* (I A 40; II B 3); *ś'n* (I A 23; II A [2]); *śwrh* (II A [1]; I A 23); *š'wt'* (I A 35,37); *šršh* (I C [24]); *twy* (I A 28); *twl'h* (I A 27); *tl* (I A 32); *tl'ym* (III 25); *tw'm* (I A 34); *šrn* (I A 34); *mrbh* (I A 34); *mzh* (I A 34); *mdr'* (I A 34); *mblh* (I A 34); *'dm* (I A 35); *'rnh* (I A [34]); *'rpd* (I A 32,35); *'śr* (I A 25); *bynn* (I A 34); *byt'l* (I A 34); *ḥzz* (I A 35); *'nrt* (I A 38); *br g'yh* (I A [7]); *hdd* (I A [25],36,38); *mt''l* (I A 14,[24],[37],[39],40; I B 21; II B [2]). In one instance the noun subject of a following verb is preceded by the prefixed negative: *wl'š yhwnnh*, " and let no one oppress him " (II B 16).

(7) Noun as Direct Object of Verbs:

(a) *With the Perfect.* *wkzy ḥbzw 'lhn byt* ['by], " and when (the) gods struck my father's house " (III 24); *hšbw 'lhn šybt by[t 'by]*, " (the) gods have brought about the return of my father's house " (III 24). See also I A 7.

(b) *With the Imperfect.* In three instances the direct object precedes the verb: *wpgr 'rb' m'l pgr*, " and I shall pile corpse upon corpse " (I B 30) ; *w'dy'* [*'ln kl 'lhy'*] *yṣrn,* " all the gods will guard this treaty " (I B 7) ; see I B [25]. Otherwise it either follows the verb immediately or the verb and the subject. Thus, *wšb' ssyh whynqn 'l,* " should seven mares suckle a colt " (I A 22 ; see II A [1]) ; *wyzr' bhn hdd mlḥ wšḥlyn,* " and may Hadad sow in them salt and watercress " (I A 36) ; *w'l yrt šr[š]h 'šm,* " and may his scion not inherit a name " (I C 25). Similarly : *š't* (I A 21) ; *šdyhn* (I A [21]) ; *'lym* (I A 22) ; *'gl* (I A 23 ; II A [1]) ; *'mr* (I A 23 ; II A [2]) ; *'bny* (I A [26]) ; *qšt* (I A [38],39) ; *'dy'* (I B 24) ; *yd* (I B 25,[25],[27]) ; *ydh* (I B 27) ; *lḥmy* (I B 38) ; *lḥm* (I B 38,39 ; III 5,7) ; *mlḥ* (I B [41]) ; *ṭbt'* (I C [4], 19) ; *mly* (I C 17) ; *'š* (I C 21) ; *byth* (I C 22) ; *tḥtyth* (I C 23) ; *gdh* (II A 2) ; *r'šy* (II B [8] ; III 11) ; *spry'* (II C [4]) ; *ktk* (II C 5) ; *mlkh* (II C 5) ; *mt''l* (II C 14) ; *brh* (II C 14) ; *br* (II C 14) ; *'qrh* (II C 15) ; *'mhm* (II C 16) ; *rwḥ* (III 2) ; *mly'* (III 2) ; *nbšhm* (III 5,6) ; *ml'ky* (III 8) ; *ml'kh* (III 8) ; *dmy* (III 11,[22]) ; *dm* (III 12bis,[12]) ; *'qrh* (III 13) ; *śgbwh* (III 13) ; *mwddwh* (III 14) ; *lšnk* (III 17) ; *lšn* (III 21) ; *mrmt* (III 22) ; *mlk* (III 28).

(c)   *With the Imperative.*   *qtlw 'ḥk 'w 'srh,* " kill your brother or imprison him " (III 18) ; *qtlw mr'km,* " kill your lord " (III 21). Similarly : *spry'* (II C 9) ; *'ynykm* (I A 13).

(d)   *With the Infinitive.*   The direct object of the infinitive always follows the verb (contrast the Biblical Aramaic usage, cf. *BLA* §85c). Thus *lmšlḥ yd bmy by[r'],* " to raise a hand against the water of the well " (I B 34). Similarly : *'šmhm* (II B 7) ; *byty* (I B [32]) ; *br* (III 15) ; *bry* (III 11) ; *spry'* (II C 2,[6]) ; *'dy* (I A 13) ; *'qry* (I B [32] ; III 11,16). See III 4 f.

(8)   NOUNS AS PREDICATES IN VERBAL SENTENCES : Thus, *wthwy 'rpd tl,* " and may Arpad become a mound " (I A 32) ; [*yhwh*] *'lh qq btn,* " may they become towards it the throat of a serpent " (I A 32) ; *whwy ḥlph,* " and be his successor " (III 22).

(9)   NOUN OBJECT OF PREPOSITIONS : Thus, *kl mh lḥyh b'rq wbšmyn,* " every sort of evil on earth and in heaven " (I A 26) ; *wyqḥ mn 'rqy 'w mn mqny,* " and he will take some of my land or some of my possessions " (I B 27).

Similarly : I A 1,2,3,4,5ter,[5bis],[6],8quater,[8ter],9quater,[9bis] 10bis,[10] ; 11ter,[11ter],12ter,[13],[14],15,[15],24,25ter,26bis,28,29bis, 30ter,32,[32],35,37,[37],42 ; I B 1,2bis,3ter,[3],4,[4],5bis,[7bis],8,9ter, [9bis],[10],10ter,11,12bis,13,21,22,[23],[25bis],26,27bis,[28],28,30,[30], 31bis,32,33bis,34,36,38,40bis,42,45 ; I C 2,3,[3],[4],5,[6],7,[8bis],[9], 15,16,17,18,20bis,[24] ; II A [3],3,[4ter] ; II B [2bis],5,[5bis],6bis,

[6bis],[7],[8],[9],11,12,13bis,14,[14],[18] ; II C 2,7,9,10,13,16,17 ; III 1quinquies,2ter,3ter,4,5bis,6,7bis,[7],8,9,10,11,12,13bis,14quater,15ter, 16,[16],17bis,19,20,21ter,[21],22,[22],23bis,24,[24],25quater,[25],26ter [26],27.

(10) NOUN USED AS AN ADVERB : *wšbʿ šnn yʾkl ʾrbh*, " for seven years may the locust devour (Arpad) " (I A 27) ; *wyhkn ḥlb*, " and should they go to Aleppo " (III 5). Similarly : I A 27,[27] ; II A 5,6.

(11) NOUN IN CASUS PENDENS CONSTRUCTION : This is clear in two cases : *wkl mlkyʾ zy sḥrty ʾw kl zy rḥm hʾ ly*, " and as for all the kings of my vicinity or anyone who is a friend of mine " (III 7) ; *w[m]lkn [zy sḥr]ty*, " and as for kings of my vicinity " (III 19). Possibly also I B 34 (*wbyrʾ [h]ʾ kl zy ysb*).

(12) NOUNS DEPENDENT ON ZY AS SUBSTITUTE FOR THE CONSTRUCT CHAIN : There are only two instances of this use and both occur in the *casus pendens* construction mentioned in §11 above.

(13) NOUNS USED IN ATTRIBUTION : These nouns may also be called adjectives ; they follow the noun they modify and agree in gender, number, and state. Thus, *wymll mln lḥyt lʿly*, " and should he utter evil words against me " (III 2) ; *zy ʿdn ḥy[n hm]*, " because it is a living pact " (I B 41). See also *rb* (I B 7) ; *rbt* (I A [35]).

III. Verbs

(1) USES OF THE PERFECT

(a) *In main clauses :*

(i) To express the historical past : *šbt tlʾym*, " Talʾayim returned " (III 25) ; *hšbw ʾlhn šybt by[t ʾby]*, " the gods brought about the return of my father's house " (III 24). Similarly : *hwt lʾhrn* (III [24]) ; *n[ṣbʾ ʿm sprʾ z]nh śm* (I A 7) ; *kh ʾmrn [wkh k]tbn* (I C 1).

(ii) To express the future perfect in the apodosis of a condition : *šqrt bʿdyʾ*, " you will have been false to the treaty " (I B 38,[27],[36] ; III [9],19,20,27) ; *šqrtm* (II B 14 ; III 7) ; *šqrt lkl ʾlhy ʿdyʾ*, " you will have been false to all the gods of the treaty " (I B 23 ; II B 9 ; III 4,16,23) ; *šqrt* (I B [33] ; II B [17] ; III 14).

(b) *In subordinate clauses :*

(i) Relative : To express past time. Thus *zy gzr br gʼyh*, " which Bir-Gaʼyah has concluded " (I A 7) ; *zy śmw ʼlhn* (I B 6) ; *zy ʻbdw ʼlhn* (II B 2) ; *mh ktbt ʼ[nh mtʻ]ʼl lzkrn lbry* (I C 2).

(ii) Temporal : To express past time. *kzy ḥbzw ʼlhn byt ʼby*, " when the gods struck my father's house " (III 24).

(iii) Conditional : To express the future perfect, with the imperfect in the main clause : *hn hšb zy ly ʼhšb [zy lh]*, " if he has restored mine, I shall return his " (III 20).

(2) Uses of the Imperfect

(a) *In main clauses :*

(i) To express the future in a direct utterance or quotation : *ʼhld mn mlwh*, " I shall efface some of its words " (I C 18). Similarly : *ʼhpk ṭbʼ wʼśm [l]lḥyt* (I C 19) ; *mh t[ʻbd]* (I B 26) ; *ʼšmʻ lbr gʼyh* (II B [5]) ; *[ʼšb ʼl krsʼ] ʼby* (II B [7]) ; *ʼhʼbd spryʼ* (II C 4) ; *ʼhbd ʼyt ktk* (II C 5) ; *ʼnh ʼgr ʼgr* (II C 8) ; *wpgr ʼrbʼ mʻl pgr* (I B 30) ; *ʼʻbd lhm* (III 3).

(ii) To express the future stipulations in the treaty : *rqh trqhm wthšbhm ly*, " you must placate them and return them to me " (III 6). It is obvious that the nuance of " must " is derived from the treaty-context much more than from the verb-form itself, which does not really differ from the preceding class of uses. Similarly : *tbʻh* (I B 39) ; *ygbr* (? II B 19) ; *lygzrn mlh* (I B 41) ; *lykhl lprq* (I B [34]) ; *[ltk]hl ltśʼ* (I B 39) ; *wʼkhl* (I B 33) ; *plʼkhl lʼšlḥ* (II B 6) ; *[l]tqh mlyʼ mn ydh* (III 2) ; *yqm ḥd [dmy]* (III 22) ; *[yśʼ]n kl ʼlh[y] ʻdyʼ* (II C [13]) ; *ʻqrk yskr lʼqry* (III 3) ; *thskrhm* (III 2) ; *yhskr* (III 3) ; *yhskrn* (III 3) ; *yʻzz qlbt byty* (I B 44) ; *yšḥdn* (? III 28).

(iii) To express the present : *wybʻ wyzqn*, " for he (i.e., my father) is babbling and grows old " (II B 8).

(iii) To express the jussive : *yqtl mn yqtl*, " let him kill whomever he would kill " (II B 8) ; see also I B [9], [ytšmʻn].

(iv) To express prohibitions (either negative commands or negative jussives) ; *ʼl tpnw bʼšrh*, " do not return to his region " (III 7) ; *ʼl tštq ḥdh mn mly sprʼ znh*, " let not one of the words of this inscription be silent " (I B 8). Similarly : *[ʼl] tšryh* (III 18) ; *ʼl tʻšqny* (III 20) ; *ʼl tʼmr* (I A 36) ; *ltmšl by* (III 9) ; *lthrm nbšhm* (III 5) ; *ltršh ly ʻlyh* (III 9) ; *ltšlḥ lšn bbyty* (III 21) ; *wlʼš yhwnnh* (II B 16).

(v) To express wishes: *thwy 'rpd tl*, " may Arpad become a mound " (I A 32); *'l thry*, " may she not conceive " (I A 21); *yzr' bhn hdd mlḥ wšḥlyn*, " may Hadad sow in them salt and weeds " (I A 36). Similarly: *yśb'* (I A 22bis,23bis; II A [1],1,[2bis]); *yhrgn* (I A 24; II A [3]); *thwy* (I A 25; II A [4],6); *ysk* (I A [25],26); *ysq* (I A [27]); *ypq* (I A 28); *ytšm'* (I A 29); *yšlḥn* (I A 30); *yštḥṭ* (I A [32]); *t'mr* (I A 33); *yhww* (I A [31]); *yṣrn* (I B 8); *y'bdw* (I C [5]); *yṣrw* (I C 15); *yhpkw* (I C 21); *yśmw* (I C 23); *yrt* (I C 24); *ytnšy* (II A [4]); *yhwh* (II A 4); *ymt* (II C [10]); *y'kl* (I A 27,[30]; II A [9]); *t'kl* (I A 27).

To these wishes we should probably relate the use of the future apodosis in conditional sentences, which express the treaty stipulations, or in comparative sentences. Thus, with *kn* correlative to *'yk zy*: *kn tqd 'rpd*, " so may Arpad be burned "; or is it simply, " so will Arpad be burned "? *kn yqd mtî'l*, " so may Matî'el be burned " (I A 37). Similarly: *yšbr* (I A 38); *y'r* (I A 39); *ygzr* (I A 40); *ygzrn* (I A 40); *y'rrn* (I A 41); *yqḥn* (I A 42); *tgzr* (I B 43). In conditions: *['nh l'khl l'šlḥ yd] bk*, " I shall not be able to raise a hand against you " (I B 24); *lykhl bry [l]yšlḥ yd bbrk* (I B 25); *y'th ḥ[ylk]*, " your army must come " (I B 28). Similarly: *wtqp yqpy wtnt' ly* (I B 29); *lts[k l]hm lḥm* (III 5); *lt'mr lhm* (III 5); *'t t'th wtqm dmy ... wbrk y'th yqm dm bry ... wbr brk y'th yqm d[m b]r bry w'qr y'th yqm dm 'qry* (III 11-12); *nkh tkwh bḥrb* (III 13); *nkh tkh 'y<t>h* (III 13); *ltšlḥ lšnk bnyhm wt'mr lh* (III 17-18); *lyqtl wly'sr* (III 18); *'hšb* (III 20).

(vi) Finite Complement. The imperfect is used instead of an infinitive as a complement to the verb *khl*; it appears in the same form as the main verb itself and is simply juxtaposed without any coordinating conjunction. Thus, *pl'khl l'šlḥ y[d bk]*, " then I shall not be able to raise a hand against you " (literally, I shall not be able, I shall not send, II B 6); cf. I B [24]; *lykhl bry [l]yšlḥ yd bbrk* (I B 25); *[lyk]hl ltś' lḥm* (I B 39). Contrast I B 34.

In this connection, in which note is taken of the asyndetic coordination of similar verbs, one should also recall that this phenomenon turns up in another context, where the introductory verb is scarcely modal. Thus, *wbrk y'th yqm dm bry mn śn'wh wbr brk y'th yqm d[m b]r bry w'qrk y'th yqm dm 'qry*, " your son must come and avenge the blood of my son from his enemies; your grandson must come and avenge the blood of my grandson; your offspring must come and avenge the blood of my offspring " (III 11-12).

(b)   *In subordinate clauses :*

(i) Temporal: *'d 'hk 'nh w'rqhm,* "until I come and
placate them" (III 6); *mzy ymlk 'šr,* "as long as Asshur rules"
(I A 25). Should one include here the expression in III 8, *w'šlḥ*
ml'ky ... *'w yšlḥ ml'kh?*

(ii) Comparative: *'yk zy tqd š'wt' z' b'š,* "just as this wax
is burned by fire" (I A 35,37). Similarly: *tšbr* (I A 38); *y'r* (I A
39); *ygzr* (I A 40); *t'rr* (I A [40]); *tqḥ* (I A [42]); *ymḥ'* (I A 42).

(iii) Simple Relative: *kl gbr zy yb'h rwḥ 'pwh,* "any man
who rants" (III 2); *bkl mh zy ymwt br 'nš,* "in whatever way a
man shall die" (III 16). Similarly: *bry zy yšb 'l khs'y* (III 17);
zy ysqn b'šrh (I A 5; I C 4); *zy [ysq wymlk] b'šrh* (I B [3]); *zy*
ymlkn b'rpd (I B 22); *kl zy ysb* (I B 34); *zy y'l wylqḥ* (I B 35);
bywm zy y'bd kn (I C 20); *zy y'wrn* (II B 4); *zy y'z mnk* (II B 20);
'n zy yršmn (II C 3).

(iv) Compound Relative: *yqtl mn yqtl,* "let him kill whomever he would kill" (II B 9). Similarly: *mn lyṣr mly spr' ... wy'mr*
(I C 17); *... wymll 'ly ...* to *wymll mln* (III 2); *mn yš'* (? III 26); *[mn*
y]'mr lhldt (II C [1]).

(v) Conditional (protasis): *whn yšqr mt''l ... lbr g'yh,* " and
if Matî'el ... should be false to ... Bir-Ga'yah" (I A 14; cf. I A 15,24,
[16]; II A 3); *[whn tšm'n wtš]lmn 'dy' 'ln wt'mr,* "and if you obey
and fulfill this treaty and say ..." (I B 24).

Similarly: *[whn mlh ymll] 'ly ḥd mlkn ... wt'mr* (I B 26); *wyqtlnh*
wyšlḥ ydh wyqḥ mn 'rqy (I B 27); *whn y'th ḥd mlkn wysbn<y>* (I B
28); *lt'th ... lt'twn ... ly'th* (I B 31-32); *tšlḥ* (I B 37); *whn lthb lḥmy...*
wltsk (I B 38); *phn tšm'* (II B 4); *hn t'mr bnbšk wt'št blbb[k]* (II
B 5); *whn y'mr mn ḥd bny ... wyb'h* (II B 7-8); *hn yhwnh* (II B 16);
hn tb'h (II B 17); *whn yqrq mny qrq ḥd ... wyhkn ḥlb* (III 4-5); *whn*
ly[šb]n b'rqk (III 6); *whn thrm nbšhm mny wtsk lhm lḥm wt'mr* (III
6-7); *whn ... wy'bh* (III 9-11); *hn 'yty yqtln* (III 11); *whn ysq 'l*
lbbk wtš' 'l śptyk ... wysq ... wyš' ... 'w hn ysq ... wyš' ... whn ysq 'l lbb mlky
'rpd (III 14-16); *whn yrb bry ... 'w y'brnh ... whn rqh trqh bnyhm* (III
17-19); *[whn t]'bd mrmt* (III 22); *w[hn yrb bry ...]* (III 26).

The conditional nuance of the imperfect is also to be noted; it
is not introduced by the conjunction *hn,* but occurs only with the
conjunction *w-.* Thus, *[w]yhynqn 'lym wšb' mhynqn ymšḥ[n šdyhn],*
"and should seven nurses anoint their breasts and nurse a young
boy" (I A 21-22); *wšb' ssyh yhynqn 'l,* "and should seven mares
suckle a colt" (I A 22; cf. *yhynqn,* I A 23bis; II A [1bis,2]). Similarly: *yhkn* (I A 24; II A [3]); *wlyšm' mt''l* (I B 21; II B [2];

cf. *lyšmʿn*, I B [21-22]; II B 2b,3bis); *wyqrq ḥdhm wyʾth* (I B 45); *wyzḥl hʾ mn ld ... wyʾmr* (II C 6-8).

   (vi) Consecutive: *wlythzh yrq, wly[thzh] ʾḥwh* "so that no green may be seen, that its vegetation may not be seen" (I A 28).

(3) Use of the Imperative

   The imperative expresses a command. Thus, *pqḥw ʿynykm lḥzyh ʿdy br gʾyh*, "open your eyes (O gods) to gaze upon the treaty" (I A 13). Similarly: *ld* (II C 9); *rqw* (III 6); *šbw* (III 7); *ʾsrh* (III 18); *qtl* (III 18); *qtlw* (III 21); *hwy* (III 22).

(4) Use of the Infinitive

   (a) *Complementary*: The infinitive is used as a complement to modal verbs. Thus, *lyk[ḥl l]prq wlmšlḥ yd bmy by[rʾ]*, "he will not be able to destroy (it) or raise a hand against the water of (that) well" (I B 34). See also II C 2 (*lhldt*).

   (b) *Epexegetical*: This infinitive explains the function of a preceding expression. Thus, *wybʿh rʾšy lhmtty wlhmtt bry*, "seeks my head to kill me and to kill my son" (III 11). Similarly: *lhmtty* (II B [8]; III 15); *lhmtt* (III 15,16).

   (c) *Final*: *pqḥw ʿynykm lḥzyh ʿdy br gʾyh*, "open your eyes (O gods) to gaze upon the treaty of Bir-Gaʾyah" (I A 13). Similarly: *lśgb* (I B 32bis); *lʿbdt* (I B 36); *lhbzthm* (II B 7).

   (d) *Intensive*: This use of the infinitive is Cannanite and corresponds to the Hebr. infinitive absolute; it precedes the verb, is of the same root as the main verb which it modifies, but not necessarily in the same conjugation. Thus, *hskr thskrhm*, "you must hand them over" (III 2). Similarly: *mwt* (? I B 30); *ʾgr ʾgr* (II C 8); *nkh tkwh* (III 12); *nkh tkh* (III 13); *rqh trqhm* (III 6, 18).

   (e) *Object of a Preposition*: *wyzḥl hʾ mn ld spr[y]ʾ mn bty ʾlhyʾ*, "and should that man be frightened from effacing the inscriptions from the bethels" (II C 6).

   (f) *Position of the Infinitive*: In eleven cases the direct object follows the infinitive (I A 13; I B 32bis, 34, 36; II B 7; II C 2, 6; III 11, 15, 16); possibly it preceded in I B 33-34. See J. Carmignac, *Revue de Qumran* 5 (1965-66) 506-07.

(5) Uses of the Participle

   (a) *Predicative*: In a nominal sentence the participle serves as the predicate. Thus *ptḥh ly ʾrḥʾ*, "the road shall be open to me"

(III 8). Similarly: *lzy lyd'* (II C 8, " to someone who does not understand ").

(b) *Substantive* : The verbal adjective is used as a noun. Thus, *tqp yqpy*, " you must surround those who surround me " (I B 29) ; *mhynqn*, " nurses " (I A [21]). Similarly: *'ll* (I A 6) ; *qrq* (III 4) ; *qrqy* (III 19) ; *qrqhm* (III 19) ; *ḥlph* (III 22) ; [z]n[yh], " a harlot " (I A 41).

IV. Adverbs

Under this heading we include those words which are not declined in any way and are simply juxtaposed to other words, for the most part verbs, in order to express modifications of time, place, manner, relation, or negation.

(1) Time

Only one instance of an adverb of time is found in these texts : *wk't hšbw 'lhn šybt by*[*t 'by*], " now however the gods have brought about the return of my father's house " (III 24). The adverb *k't* is actually compound (prep. *k* + noun *'t*, " time ") ; it should be considered also from the standpoint of compounds (see below, § 6).

(2) Place

An adverb of place is found in III 6, *rqw šm 'd 'hk*, " placate (them) there until I come." The interrogative adverb of place, *'n*, " where ", is found in II C 3, in composition with *zy*, to form an indefinite pronominal expression.

(3) Manner

The majority of the adverbial expressions in these texts denote manner. Thus, *kh 'mrn* [*wkh k*]*tbn*, " thus we have spoken and thus we have written " (I C 1) ; *kn tgzr 'pl'* (I B 43) ; *bywm zy y'b*[*d*] *kn*, " on the day he will do so " (I C 21). The adverb *kn* often appears correlated to *'yk zy*, " just as ... so " : *'yk zy tqd š'wt' z' b'š kn tqd 'rpd*, " just as this wax is burned by fire, so may Arpad be burned " (I A 35). Similarly: I A 37,38,39,40,41,42. Another adverb of manner is *hn*, which is always combined with the prefixed negative adverb *l-* in the expression, *whn lhn*, " and if not so." Thus, *whn lhn šqrtm lkl 'lhy 'dy'*, " and if (you do) not (do) so, (then) you (will) have been false to all the gods of the treaty " (III 4). Similarly: I B 36 ; III

9,14,20.   The expression is elliptical.   Two other adverbial expressions which probably belong here are : *kym* (III 1), which intensifies the following noun construction (*kl gbr zy*) ; and *lmgn*, " with impunity " (II C 4), if this word is rightly understood.

(4)   RELATION

It is not easy to say just where one should classify the *signum accusativi* ; should it be classed here or as a preposition? The clear example of it in these texts is the form *'yt*, both with and without suffixes.   It is used only sporadically, and it is not easy to say just what force was attributed to it.   It occurs before proper names and definite common nouns used as direct objects of verbs ; it also occurs with pronominal objects.

Thus, *'hbd 'yt ktk w'yt mlkh*, " I shall destroy KTK and its king " (II C 5) ; *'yt Mtʻʾl wbrh* (II C 14, the verb is unfortunately lost) ; *wybʻh bry '[yt r'šy]* (II B [8]) ; *lšgb 'yt ʻqr[y]* (I B 32).   There is one example of *l-* which is possibly so used : *ltbt['] yʻbd[w tht] šmš'*, " may they make good relations under the sun " (I C 4).

Two examples of the suffixal form of *'yt* occur : *'y[t]y* (III 11) and *'y<t>h* (III 13).

(5)   NEGATION

(a)   The most common form of the negative adverb is that of the prefixed *l-*.   Not only is it prefixed to the adverb *hn*, " so " (see above), but to an adjective (*ltb h' mk*, " he is not better than you ", III 22 ; cf. *lydʻ* [II C 8]), and most frequently to verbs (usually the impf.) : *wlythzh yrq*, " so that no green may be seen " (I A 28 ; the nuance here seems to be that of result, and not of a negative wish, which usually is introduced by *'l*).   Similarly : *wlyšmʻ mtʻʾl*, " and should M. not obey " (I B 21) ; I B [21],[22],[24bis],25,[25], 31,[32bis],34,38bis,39,[39],41 : I C [7],17 ; II B [2],2b,3ter,6bis,17 ; III 5ter,6,9bis,17,18bis,19,21).   There is one peculiar use of this prefixed negative adverb : *wl'š yhwnnh*, " and let no one oppress him " (II B 16).   The text is not certain here and one may wonder if it is rightly interpreted.

(b)   The negative *'l* is used with the impf. either to express a negative wish or a negative stipulation (jussive or prohibition).

(i)   Wish : *w'l yšbʻ*, " and may it not be sated " (I A 22). Similarly I A 22,23,[23] ; II A [1bis],[2],2.   *w'l yhrgn* (I A 24 ; II A [3]) ; *w'l t'mr* (I A 33,36) ; *w'l thry* (I A 21) ; *w'l ypq hṣr* (I A 28) ; *w'l yrt* (I C 24).

(ii) Stipulations: *w'l tštq ḥdh mn mly spr'*, " let not one of the words of this inscription be silent " (I B 8). Similarly: *w'l ytšmʿ ql knr* (I A 29); *w'l tpnw* (III 7); *w['l] tšryh* (III 18); *[w']l tʿšqny* (III 20).

(6) ADVERBS IN COMPOSITION: Here we list simply those forms which are found joined with other words: *'yk* or *'ykh*, used with *zy* (I A 35,37,38,39,[39],[40],[41]); *'n*, used with *zy* (II C 3); and *kʿt* (III 24).

V. Prepositions

Being a word expressive of relationship, the preposition functions in these texts most frequently as an adverbial modifier of the sentence as a whole or of the verb. Thus *yšlḥ ml'kh 'ly*, " he will send his messenger to me " (III 8); *yzrʿ bhn hdd mlḥ*, " may Hadad sow in them salt " (I A 36); *thwy mlkth kmlkt ḥl*, " may his kingdom become like a kingdom of sand " (II A [4]); *šqrtm lkl 'lhy ʿdy'*, " you will have been false to all the gods of the treaty " (I B 23). Examples of such a relationship could be multiplied indefinitely. Much more significant, however, are the following instances of prepositional usage:

(1) THE RELATING OF AN INFINITIVE TO A VERB: This may be either an expression of purpose or explanation. Thus, expressing purpose, *pqḥw ʿynykm lḥzyk ʿdy br g'yh*, " open your eyes, to gaze upon the treaty of Bir-Ga'yah " (I A 13). Similarly: *lśgb* (I B 32bis); *lḥbzthm wl'bdt* (II B 7); *[l]'bdt* (I B 36?); The epexegetical infinitive is so introduced in *wyb'h r'šy lhmtty wlhmmt bry*, " and seeks my head to kill me and to kill my son " (III 11). Similarly: III 15,16. The complementary infinitive is likewise so introduced: *lyk[hl l]prq wlmšlḥ yd*, " he will not be able to destroy (it) or raise a hand against (it) " (I B 34); cf. II C 2. In one instance the prep. *mn* is found introducing an infinitive too: *wyzḥl h' mn ld spry'*, " and that man shall be frightened from effacing the inscriptions " (II C 6).

(2) THE INTRODUCING OF A PREDICATIVE PREPOSITIONAL PHRASE IN A NOMINAL SENTENCE: Thus *mh ktbt '[nh mtʿ]'l lzkrn lbry*, " what I have written is (to act) as a reminder for my son " (I C 2); *ʿdy' zy bspr' znh*, " the treaty which is in this inscription " (I B [23],28, 33; I C 17,[22]; II B [9],18; II C 13; III 4,14,17). Similarly: III 3,5,10,13,20,[20],23bis.

(3) THE MODIFICATION OF A NOUN: Thus *ʿdy br g'yh ... 'm mtʿ'l*, " the treaty of Bir-Ga'yah with Matîʿel " (I A 1). Similarly: I A 2,3bis,4,5ter,6,[13]; I B 1,2bis,3ter,4bis,5,11; possibly also II B 12.

VI. Conjunctions

These words are used to express various inter-sentence relationships. Here we may list the following types of such relationship which occur in these texts:

(1) SIMPLE RELATIVE CLAUSES, in which the clause acts as an appositive to a noun antecedent. Thus *yhpkw 'lhn 'š[' h]' wbyth wkl zy [b]h*, " may (the) gods upset that man and his house and all that is in it " (I C 21-22); *w'dy 'lhn hm zy śmw 'lhn*, " and this is the treaty of gods which gods have set up " (I B 6). See further the examples under Syntax, I 3 a.

(2) GENERAL RELATIVE CLAUSES, in which the pronoun-conjunction has a double function. Thus *mh ṭb b'yny ''bd 'lhm*, " what is good in my sight I shall do to them " (III 3). See further the examples under Syntax, I 3 b, I 4 d.

(3) TEMPORAL CLAUSES: Thus *wkzy ḥbzw 'lhn byt ['by h' h]wt l'ḥrn*, " when (the) gods struck my father's house, it (i.e., Tal'ayim) came to belong to another " (III 24); *thwy mlkth kmlkt ḥl, mlkt ḥl, mzy ymlk 'šr*, " and may his kingdom become a kingdom of sand, a kingdom of sand, as long as Asshur reigns " (I A 25); *rqw šm 'd 'hk w'rqhm*, " placate (them) there until I come and placate them " (III 6). Cf. II B 19.

(4) CAUSAL CLAUSE: Thus *whwy ḥlph ky lṭb h' mk*, " and be his successor for he is not better than you " (III 22).

(5) DIRECT QUOTATIONS: These are introduced without any conjunctions; their nature of an utterance is indicated merely by a preceding verb of saying. Thus *[whn tšm'n wtš]lmn 'dy' 'ln wt'mr gbr 'dn h' ['nh l'khl l'šlḥ yd] bk*, " but if you obey and fulfill this treaty and say, ' I am an ally,' (then) I shall not be able to raise a hand against you " (I B 24); *[wt'mr bnbšk y]qtl mn yqtl, šqrtm lkl 'lh[y 'dy' zy bspr' znh]*, " and (if) you say in your soul, ' Let him kill whomever he would kill,' (then) you will have been false to all the gods of the treaty which is in this inscription " (II B 8-9). Similarly: I B 26; I C 18,19; II B 5-6,7; II C 4-5,8,9; III 5,7,18,21-22.

(6) ADVERSATIVE CLAUSE: On one occasion *p-* occurs with apparently this nuance: *phn tšm' nḥt m[...*, " but if you obey, (may) tranquillity .... " (II B 4).

(7) CONDITIONAL CLAUSES: These clauses are introduced either by *hn* or by *w-* and occur in the following forms:

(a) *Elliptical conditions :*

In this category belongs the expression *whn lhn*, " and if not so."
Thus, *whn lhn šqrtm lkl 'lhy 'dy' zy bspr' [znh]*, " and if (you do) not
(do) so, then you will have been false to all the gods of the treaty
which is in this inscription " (III 3-4).   In each instance (see I B 36 ;
III 9,14,20) the perfect in the apodosis has a future perfect nuance.

(b) *Future conditions :* By and large, these express the
stipulations of the treaties.   Thus, *whn yšqr mt"l br 'trsmk ml[k 'rpd
lbrg'yh mlk ktk*, " and if Matî'el, the son of 'Attarsamak, the king of
Arpad should be false to Bir-Ga'yah, the king of KTK, ..." (the
apodosis is lost, I A 14-15) ; *whn y'th ḥd mlkn wysbn<y> y'th ḥ[ylk
'ly 'm] kl [b'l] ḥṣy'*, " if one of (the) kings comes and surrounds <me>,
[your] ar[my] must come [to me with] every arch[er] " (I B 28).
Similarly : I A [16],24 ; I B [23],[25],[32],38 ; II A [3] ; II B 4,5,
[7],16,17 ; III 4,6bis,11,14,15,16,17,18,19,[22],[26].   Only in III 20 do
we find a future perfect nuance expressed in the protasis, *hn hšb zy
ly 'hšb [zy lh]*, " if he has restored mine, I shall return [his]. "   In
two instances the protasis is a nominal clause, *whn qryh h' nkh tkwh
bḥrb*, " and if it is a city, you must strike it with a sword " (III
12) ; *whn ḥd 'hy h' ... nkh tkh 'y<t>h*, " if it is one of my brothers...,
you must strike him " (III 13).   The context is broken in the following instances : I B 31,37,43 ; III 27.

The sole problematical sentence in this regard is found in III 9-
11.   It begins with *whn*, which is followed by a long list of coordinated
subjects, before the verb is introduced to which *w-* is prefixed.   It
has been suggested that this is *waw* of the apodosis, but this is not
possible, since *wyb'h* is actually the verb in the protasis.   We really
have anacoluthon here.   Possibly the construction is influenced by the
conditional use of the conjunction *w-*, which is found elsewhere in
these texts (see below, 8 d iii).   The only instance of a conjunction
introducing the apodosis in these inscriptions is apparently *p-* in II
B 6, *[w]hn t'mr bnbšk wt'št blbb[k gbr 'dn 'nh w'šm' lbr g'yh] wbnwh
w'qrh pl'khl l'šlḥ y[d bk]*," " and if you say in your soul and think
in your mind, ' I am an ally and I shall obey Bir-Ga'yah] and his
sons and his offspring,' *then* I shall not be able to raise a hand
against you."

(8) Coordination

The conjunctions *'w* and *w-* are used frequently throughout these
texts as a means of coordination.

(a) *The Coordination of Nouns :* Thus, *ḥd 'hy h' 'w ḥd 'bdy
'w ḥd pqdy 'w ḥd 'm' zy bydy*, " it is one of my brothers or one of

my slaves or one of my officials or one of the people who are under
my control" (III 13); *'dy br g'yh mlk ktk 'm mt''l br 'trsmk mlk*
'm 'qr mt''l br 'trsmk mlk 'rpd w'dy ktk 'm ['dy] 'rpd w'dy b'ly ktk
'm 'dy b'ly 'rpd w'dy ḥb[r ..., " the treaty of Bir-Ga'yah, king of
KTK, with Matî'el, the son of 'Attarsamak, the king of Arpad; and
the treaty of the sons of Bir-Ga'yah with the sons of Matî'el; and
the treaty of the grandsons of Bir-Ga'yah and his offspring with the
offspring of Matî'el, the son of 'Attarsamak, the king of Arpad; and
the treaty of KTK with the treaty of Arpad; and the treaty of the
lords of KTK with the treaty of the lords of Arpad; and the treaty
of the union of ..." (I A 1-4). The nouns so coordinated are often
subjects of verbs, objects of verbs, objects of prepositions, and even
occasionally *nomina recta* (*kl 'lhy rḥbh w'dm*, I A 10; *[lrbq ṣy w]ṣby*
wš'l w'rnb wšrn wṣdh, I A 33), and proper names (*wqdm mrdk wzrpnt*,
I A 8). See further I A 6,7,8ter,[8],9bis,[9],10,11,[11],12bis,31,[33],
34octies,[34],35ter,36bis,37,38bis; I B 7,[9],11,12; 1 C [8bis],22; II
B 2,6bis,[6bis],13; II C 11,14,15; III 11,13bis,14,21,23ter,[23],26bis.
In one instance the nouns are introduced by coordinated *signa accu-*
sativi (*'yt ktk w'yt mlkh*, II C 5).

(b) *The Coordination of Verbs :* These are coordinated within
the same clause either by the use of *'w* or *w-*. Thus *qtl 'ḥk 'w 'srh*,
" kill your brother or imprison him" (III 18); *wyqrq ḥdhm wy'th*,
" and one of them shall flee and come" (I B 45). Similarly: I A
[21]; I B [3],35,38; I C 19; II B 7bis,8; III 6,8,11,17.

(c) *The Coordination of Phrases :* This is of two sorts in
these inscriptions, the coordination of a construct chain or the coordination of prepositional phrases.

(i) Coordinated construct chains : *mn ḥd 'ḥy 'w mn ḥd*
byt 'by, " any one of my brothers or any one of my father's household" (III 9); *[p]m ḥwh wpm 'qrb wpm dbḥh wpm nmrh wss wqml...,*
" the mouth of a snake and the mouth of a scorpion and the mouth
of a bear and the mouth of a panther, and a moth and a louse,
and ..." (I A 31). See further for *'w :* I B 26, III 4bis,5,8,10quin-
quies; for *w- :* I A [12],26,29,30,39,41bis; I B 1bis,[4],4,5,[6],29; I
C 22; II A 9bis; II B 10bis; II C 15bis,16; III 9,21bis,[21],29.

(ii) Coordinated prepositional phrases : *'w 'l bny 'w 'l*
'qr[y], " or against my sons or against my offspring" (III 22); *[qdm*
...]wmlš wqdm mrdk wzrpnt wqdm nb' wt[šmt wqdm 'r wnś]k wqdm
nrgl wls wqdm šmš wnr wqdm s[..], " in the presence of ... and Mullesh,
and in the presence of Marduk and Zarpanit, and in the presence of
Nabu and Tashmet, and in the presence of 'Ir and Nusk, and in the
presence of Nergal and Laṣ, and in the presence of Shamash and Nur,

and in the presence of S[in ...] " (I A 7-9). Similarly for 'w : I B 27,45 ; III 1sexties,8,22 ; for w- : I A 5ter,6,[9],10,[10],11ter,[11],12, [24],25,26,29,30 ; I B 2,3ter,5,10,[10],34,40bis,[40] ; I C [3],16 ; II A 3,[4] ; II B [2] ; II C 16 ; III 11,23,25ter.

One usage in particular must be cited here : [mn] 'rqw w'd y'd[y w]bz, mn lbnn w'd yb[rdw wmn dmś]q w'd 'rw wm..w [wm]n bq't w'd ktk, " from 'Arqu to Ya'di and BZ, from Lebanon to Yabrud, from Damascus to 'Aru and M..W, and from the Valley to KTK " (I B 9-10).

(d) *The Coordination of Clauses:* Only one instance of this coordination can be cited with the conjunction 'w : 'w hn following up an introductory whn (III 14-15). The vast majority of cases introduced by w- are either the continuation of main clauses (such as I A 6,7,26,27,28, etc.) or the continuation of subordinate clauses (especially conditions, such as II B 8 ; III 14,15, etc.). Special note should be made of the following uses :

(i) The introduction of conditional clauses by *whn* : Thus, whn yśqr mt''l br 'trsmk ml[k 'rpd lbr g'yh mlk ktk wh]n yśqr 'qr mt''l [l'qr br g'yh ...], " Now if Matî'el, the son of 'Attarsamak, the king of Arpad should be false to Bir-Ga'yah, the king of KTK, and if the offspring of Matî'el should be false to the offspring of Bir-Ga'yah " (I A 14-15). Similarly : I A [16],24 ; I B [23],[24],[25],28,31,[32], 36,37,38,43 ; II A [3] ; II B [4],7 ; III 3,4,6bis,7,[9],12,13,14bis,16,17, [18],19,20,[22],25,27.

(ii) The introduction of comparative clauses by *w'yk zy* : See I A 38,39,[39],[40],[41].

(iii) At times the simple *w-* seems to have conditional force. Thus wlyśm' mt''l, " and should Matî'el not obey " (I B 21) ; wt'mr gbr 'dn h' ['nh], " and should you say, ' I am an ally,' " (I B 24). See further I B [22] ; III 19,20. A more developed use of this case may be found in the curses : wśb' ssyh yhynqn 'l w'l yś[b' wśb'] śwrh yhynqn 'gl w'l yśb', " and should seven mares suckle a colt, may it not be sated ; and should seven cows give suck to a calf, may it not be sated " (I A 22-23). Of course, literally the verbs are simply coordinated : " and seven mares shall suckle a colt and it shall not be sated," etc. See further I A 21,24 ; II A [1]-3.

GLOSSARY

(The references in square brackets [ ] indicate that some part of the word concerned has been restored. But since the degree of certainty or probability for the restoration varies considerably, one should consult the passage before discounting it.)

'b ("father"): 'by, II B 8; III 10,23,[24],[25],25.

'bd ("destroy"): 'bdt (Pael inf.), I B 36; II B 7; 'h'bd (Haph. impf.), II C 4; 'hbd, II C 5.

'bn ("stone"): 'bny, I A [26].

'gr ("reward"): Peal inf. and impf., II C 8,8.

'w ("or"): I B 26,27,35,45; I C 19; III 1sexies,4bis,5,8ter,9, 10quinquies,13ter,15,17,18,22bis

'zl ("go"): t'zl, I B 39.

'ḥ ("brother"): 'ḥk, III 18; 'ḥy ("my brothers"), III 4,9,13, [21]; 'ḥwh ("his brothers"), III 17.

'ḥw ("vegetation"): 'ḥwh (3 sg. fem. suff.), I A 29,32.

'ḥrn ("another"): III 24.

'yt (sign of the accusative): I B 32; II B [8]; II C 5bis,14; III [11], <13>.

'yk ("just as," always used with zy): I A 35,38,39,[39],[40], [41].

'ykh ("just as," used with zy): I A 37.

'kl ("eat"): y'kl, I A 27,[30]; II A [9]; t'kl, I A 27; 'kl (act. ptc.), I A 30.

'l (= 'al, "not"): I A 21,22bis, 23,[23],24,28,29,33,36; I B 8; I C 24; II A [1bis],[2],2,[3]; III 7,[18],[20].

'l (= 'el, "to"): I B [29]; II B 13?; III 1ter,[8],8,19,20.

'lh ("god"): 'lhn, I A 30; I B 6bis,31; I C 15,21; II B 2; III 24bis; 'lhy, I A 10,[12bis]; I B 5,[5],23,33; II B [9],[18]; II C [13]; III 4,14,17,23; 'lhy', I B [8]; II C 3,7,[10].

'l n ("these"): I A 7bis,38; I B [7],[8],[11],24,38; II B [14]; II C [2],9; III 7,9,19,20,27.

'mr ("say"): 'mrn, I C 1; y'mr, I C 18; II B [7]; II C [1], [4],7,[8]; t'mr (2 sg. masc. impf. Peal), I A 36; I B 24, 26; II B 5,[8]; III 5,7,18,21; t'mr (3 sg. fem. impf. Yuqtal), I A 33.

'mr ("lamb"): I A 23; II A [2].

'n ("where"): II C 3.

'nh ("I"): I B [24]; I C [2]; II B [5]; II C 8; III 6.

'nš ("man"): III 16.

'sr ("bind, imprison"): y'sr, III

18; *'srh* (impv. + 3 sg. masc. suff.), III 18.

'p (" nostrils, face "): *'pwh*, III 2; *'pyh*, I A 42.

'pl' (?): I B 43.

'rbh (" locust "): I A 27.

'rḥ (" road "): *'rḥ'*, III 9.

'ryh (" lion "): II A 9.

'rnb (" hare "): I A 33.

'rq (" land "): I A [11],26; *'rqy*, I B 27; *'rqk*, III 6; *'rqh*, I A 28; II A 8.

'š (= *'iš*, " man "): II B 16; *'š'*, I C 21.

'š (= *'eš*, " fire "): I A 35,[37], 37.

'šm (" name "): I C 25; *'šmh*, II A [4]; *'šmhm*, II B 7.

'šr (" place "): *'šry*, I C [4]; *'šrh*, I A [5]; I B 3; III 7; *'šrkm*, III 5.

'šrt (" sanctuary "): *'šrthm*, I B 11.

't (" you," sg. masc.): I B [39]; III 11,20.

'th (" come "): *y'th*, I B 28bis, 32,45; II B 13; III 11,12bis, 20; *t'th*, I B 31; III 11; *t'twn*, I B [32].

'tm (" you," pl. masc.): I B [31].

b (" in, on, among," expressing place or time): I A 5,26bis, 29bis,30bis,36; I B 3,12,22,[23], 28,30,31,33,36,41; I C 4,17,20, [22]; II A 7; II B 2,[2],5bis, [8],[9],12,16,18; II C 13; III 2,3,4,5,6,7,9bis,10,13,14,16,17,21 23; (" by, with," expressing manner, instrument): I A 24, 35,37,[37]; I B 31,32; II A [3]; II C 10; III 13,14; (" toward, against "): I B 25ter,

[27],[28],34,38; II B [6ter], [14]; III 7,9,19,20,27.

byn (" between "): *bnyhm*, III 18bis,19.

byr (" well "): I B [34]; *byr'*: I B 34,[34].

byt (" house, household "): I A 6; I B 3,[11]; I C [6],7; II A 12; II B 10bis; III 9,24, [24],[25]; *byty*, I B [32],40, 44; III 21; *bytk*, I B 40; *byth*, I C 16,22; III [24]; *bytkm*, I B 21; *bty* (cst. pl.), II C 2,7, 9; *btyhm*, II C 16.

bkth (" hen "): I A 24; II A [3].

b'h (" seek "): *yb'h*, II B 8; III 11; *tb'h* I B 39; II B 17; *.b'h*, I B 35.

b'h (" rant "): *yb'h*, III 2.

b'l (" lord "): *b'l* (cst), I B [29]; *b'ly*, I A 4bis; I B 4,[5]; *b'lyh*, III 23,26.

br (" son "): *br* (cst.), I A 1,3, 14; I B 13; I C [3],[8]; II C 14; III 1,12,[12],15bis,16,25, [26]; *br* (in a proper name): I A 1,2bis,7,13,[14],[15]; I B 1,[2],[7]; II A 3; II B [5]; III [25]; *bry* I B 25,27,45; I C 3bis; II B [6],8,13; III 1bis, 3,11,12bis,15,[17],[26bis]; *brk*, I B [25],41; II B [6]; III 1,2, 11,12,15; *brh*, I A 25; I C [8], 8; II A [4]; II C 11,14bis; III 25bis; *bny* (cst. pl.): I A 2ter, [16]; I B 1bis,[1],[2],3; II B 13; III 21ter,[21]; *bny* (1 sg. suff. on pl.); II B [7], 13; III 10,21,22; *bnwh*, I A 5; I B [21]; II B 2b,6.

brd (" hail "): I A [26].

brh (" daughter "): I A [35].

btn (" serpent "): I A 32.

gbl (" territory ") :　III 23.

gbr (" surpass ") :　*ygbr*, II B 19.

gbr (" man ") :　*gbr* (abs.), III 1 ;
　gbr (cst.), I A 39 ; I B 24 ; II
　B [5].

gbrt (" woman ") :　I A [42].

gdh (" kid ") :　II A 2.

gzr (" cut, conclude ") :　I A 7 ;
　ygzr, I A 40bis ; *tgzr*, I B 43 ;
　ygzrn, I A 40 ; I B [41].

gnb (?) :　I A 36.

dbhh (" bear ") :　I A 31.

dm (" blood ") :　*dm* (cst.), III
　12bis, [12] ; *dmy*, III 11, [22].

h' (= hū', " he ") :　I B 24 ; III
　8,13,22 ; (used as a demonstra-
　tive), ; I C 22 ; II C 6, [10].

h' (= hī', " she, it ") :　I A 37 ;
　III 12, [24] ; I B [34], 42bis ?
　(used as a demonstrative) I A
　[33] ; I B [34].

hw' (" be ") :　*hwt*, III [24] ;
　yhwh, II A 4 ; *thwy*, I A 25,
　32 ; II A [4],6 ; *yhww*, I A
　[31] ; *hwy* (impv. sg. Peal),
　III 22.

hwk (" go ") :　*'hk*, III 6 ; *yhkn*,
　I A 24 ; II A [3] ; III 5.

hm (" they ") :　I B 6, [42].

hmwn (" noise ") :　I A [29].

hml (" din ") :　I A 29.

hn (" so," adv.) :　I B 36 ; III 4,
　9,14,20.

hn (" if," conj.) :　I A 14, [15],
　[16],24 ; I B [23], [25],28,31,
　[32],36,37,38,43 ; II A [3] ; II
　B 4,5, [7],16,17 ; III 4bis,6bis,
　9bis,11,12,13,14bis,15,16,17,18,
　19,20bis, [22], [26],27.

hpk (" upset ") :　*'hpk*, I C 19 ;
　yhpkw I C 21.

hrg (" kill ") :　I A 24 ; II A [3].

hrh (" conceive ") :　*thry*, I A 21.

w- (" and ") :　I A [1],2, [2],3,
　4bis,5ter,6ter,7bis,8quinquies,
　[8bis],9quinquies, [9bis],10ter,
　[10],11quater, [11bis],12ter, [12]
　14, [15], [16],21bis, [21],22ter,
　[22],23ter,24ter, [24],25,26ter,
　27ter,28ter,29ter,30ter,31sexies,
　32, [32],33septies, [33],34octies,
　[34],35ter,36quater,37,38ter,
　39bis, [39],40, [40],41bis, [41],42,
　[42] ; I B 1bis,2, [3],3ter, [4],4,
　5bis, [6],7ter,8,9bis, [9bis],10ter,
　[10bis],11,12,21, [21bis], [22],
　[23], [24],24,25bis, [25],26, [26],
　27ter,28bis,29ter,30bis,31bis,
　[32],33bis,34bis, [35],35,36,37,
　38bis, [39],39bis,40bis, [40],41,43,
　45bis ; I C [1], [3], [8bis],16bis,
　18,19,22bis,23,24 ; II A [1ter],
　1,2, [2bis], [3ter],3, [4bis],4, [5],
　[6],8bis,9bis, [9] ; II B 2, [2bis],
　2b,3bis, [4],5, [5],6bis, [6bis],
　7ter,8ter, [8],10ter,11,12,13,16,
　17 ; II C [1],3,4,5,6,7,8,10,11,
　14bis,15ter,16bis ; III 1,
　2bis,3ter,4,5ter,6quater,7quater,
　8,9bis, [9],10,11quater,12ter,
　13ter,14quater,15bis,16bis,17,
　18ter, [18],19quater,20bis, [20],
　21quinquies, [21],22bis, [22],
　23quater, [23],24bis,25quinquies
　26ter, [26],27,28,29.

z' (" this," fem. sg.) :　I A 35,
　[36],37, [42] ; III 9.

zhl (" be frightened ") :　*yzhl*, II
　C 6.

zy (" who, which," rel. pron.) :　I

A 5,7: I B 2,6,22,[23],28,31, 33,34,35bis; I C 3,17,20,22; II A 12; II B [2],4,[9],18,20; II C 3,8,13; III 2,4,5,8,10,13,14, 16,17bis,20,[20],23,28,[29],29; (used with *'yk* or *'ykh,* " just as ") : I A 35,37,38,39,[39],[40], [41]; *zy* (" of ") ; III 7,[19]; " because, that ", I B 41; I C [6]; see also *kzy, mzy.*

zkrn (" reminder ") : I C 2.

zn' (" be a harlot ") : *znyh,* I A [41].

znh (" this," masc. sg.) : I A [6], 36,40,; I B [8],[23],28,33,[37]; I C 17; II B [9],[18]; II C [14]; III [4],14,17,[23].

zqn (" be old ") : *yzqn,* II B 8.

zrʻ (" sow ") : *yzrʻ,* I A 36.

ḥbz (Pael, " destroy ") : *ḥbzw,* III 24; *ḥbzthm,* II B 7.

ḥbr (" union ") : I A [4].

ḥd (" one ") : *ḥd* (abs.), III 22; *ḥd* (cst.), I B 26bis,28,30,45; II B [7]; III 1,[3],4ter,5,9bis, 10quinquies,13ter,[13],17; *ḥdh* (abs. fem.), I B 8; *ḥdhm,* I B 45; III 19.

ḥwh (" snake ") : I A 31.

ḥz' (" see ") : *ythzh* ('Ithpeel), I A 28,[28]; *ḥzyh* (Pael inf.), I A 13.

ḥy (" living, alive ") : I B [41].

ḥyl (" army ") : *ḥylk* I B [28], 31; *ḥylkm,* I B 32.

ḥl (" sand ") : I A 25bis; II A [4].

ḥlp (" successor ") : *ḥlph* (with 3 sg. masc. suffix), III 22.

ḥpṣ (" business ") : *ḥpṣy,* III 8.

ḥṣ (" arrow ") : *ḥṣy',* I A 38; I B 29.

ḥṣr (" grass ") : I A 28.

ḥrb (" sword ") : III 13,14.

ḥrn (" wrath ") : II B 12.

ṭb (= ṭūb, " happiness ") : *ṭby* (cst. pl.), I B 6.

ṭb (" good ") : III 3,22,[29].

ṭbt (" good [treaty] relations ") : *ṭbt',* I C [4],19; II B 2.

ṭll (?) : I B 42.

yd (" hand ") : *yd* (abs.) I B [25], 25,[27],34; II B [6]; *yd* (cst.), II B 14; III 11; *ydh* (" his hand "), I B 27; III 2; *ydy* (" my hands "), III 2,5,10,13.

ydʻ (" know ") : *ydʻ* (ptc.), II C 8.

yhb (" give ") : *thb,* I B 38.

ywm (" day ") : *ywm* (abs.), I A 12; I B 31; I C 20; *ywm* (cst.), II B 12; *ywmh* (" his day "), I C 15; *ywmyhm,* II C 17.

yllh (" lamentation ") : I A 30.

yn' (" oppress ") : *yhwnh* (impf. Haph.), II B 16; *yhwnnh* (energic impf. Haph. with suff.), II B 16.

ynq (" suck ") : *yhynqn* (impf. Haph.), I A 22bis,23bis; II A [1bis],[2bis]; *mhynqn* (" nurses," fem. pl. Haph. ptc.), I A [21].

yqd (" burn ") : *yqd* (impf. Peal), I A 37; *tqd,* I A 35bis,37.

yqp (" surround "?) : *tqp,* I B 29; *yqpy,* I B 29.

yrq (" green ") : I A 28.

yrt (" inherit ") : I C 24.

yšb (" sit, dwell ") : *yšb* (impf. Peal), III 17; *'šb,* II B [7]; *yšbn,* III [6]; *šbw* (impv. pl.), III 7.

yšmn (" desolation ") : I A 32.

k (" like, as ") : I A 25 ; II A [4]. See also *kzy, k't.*

kh (" thus ") : I C 1,[1].

khl (" be able ") : *ykhl,* I B 25, [34] ; *tkhl,* I B [39] ; *'khl,* I B [24],33 ; II B 6.

khs' (" throne," variant of *krs'*) : *khs'y,* III 17.

kzy (" when ") : III 24.

ky (" for ") : III 22.

kym (" indeed " ?) : III 1.

kl (" all ") : *kl* (cst.), I A 6bis, 10,12 ; I B [8],22,23,29,34,[40] ; I C 6,22 ; II A 7 ; II B [3],9, 12,18 ; II C 13,15bis ; III 1,4, 7,8bis,14,16,23 ; *kl mh,* I A 26bis,30 ; I B 2,[26],29 ; III 16, 28,[29],29 ; *klh* (3 sg. fem. suff.), I A 5 ; I B [4].

kn (" so ") : I A 35,37,38,39,40, 41,42 ; I B 43 ; I C 21.

knr (" lyre ") : I A 29.

k't (" now ") : III 24.

kpr (" village ") : *kpryh,* III 23, 26.

krs' (" throne ") : II B [7].

ktb (" write ") : *ktbt* (1 sg. pf. Peal), I C 2 ; *ktbn,* 1 C [1].

l- (" to, for ") : I A 13,[14],[15], [24],25,32bis ; I B [7],13,21, 23bis,26,32bis,[33],[34],34,[36], 40ter,[40],42 ; I C 2,3,[3],[6], [20],[23] ; II A 3bis,[4] ; II B [5],7,[8],9,12,18 ; II C 2,4,7 ; III 2,3bis,4,7,8bis,11bis,14,15bis, 16bis,23ter,24,25quater ; *ly,* I B 29,37,38 ; III 3,6,8,9bis,20 ; *lk,* I B 39 ; II B 19 ; *lh,* III 18,[20] ; *lhm,* III 3,[5],5,7bis, 21.

l- (sign of accusative ?) : I C 4.

l- (" not," prefixed neg. adv.) : I A 28bis ; I B 21,[21bis],[22], [24bis],25,[25],31,[32bis],34, 38bis,39,[39],41 ; I C [7],17 ; II B [2],2b,3ter,6bis,16,17 ; II C 8 ; III 5ter,6,9bis,17,18bis, 19,21,22 ; *lhn* (" not so ") : I B 36 ; III 4,9,14,20.

lbb (" heart ") : *lbb* (cst.), III 15bis,[16] ; *lbbk,* II B [5] ; III 14.

lhn : see *l-* (" not ") above.

lwd (" efface ") : *ld* (Peal impv.) : II C 9 ; *ld* (inf.), II C 6 ; *'hld* (1 sg. impf. Haph.), I C 18 ; *hldt* (Haph. inf.), II C 2.

lhy (" evil ") : *lhyh* (fem. sg. abs.), I A 26 ; I C [6] ; *lhyt* (fem. pl. abs.), I C 20 ; III 2.

lhm (" bread, food ") : I A 24 ; I B 38,39 ; II A [3] ; III 5,7 ; *lhmy,* I B 38.

lhṣ (" oppression ") : II C 10.

lylh (" night ") : I A 12.

lqh (" take ") : *ylqh,* I B 35bis ; *yqh,* I B 27 ; *tqh,* I A [42] ; III 2 ; *yqhn,* I A 42.

lšn (" tongue ") : III 21 ; *lšnk,* III 17.

mgn (" with impunity " ?) : II C [4].

mh (" what ") : I B 26 ; I C 1 ; III 3 ; *kl mh,* I A 26bis,30 ; I B 2,26,29 ; III 16,28,[29],29.

mwdd (" friend ") : *mwddwh,* III 14.

mwt (" die ") : *ymt,* II C [10] ; *ymwt,* III 16 ; *mwt* (inf. ?), I B 30 ; *hmtt* (Haph. inf.), III 11, 15,16 ; *hmtty* (with suffix), II B [8] ; III 11,15.

mzy (" as long as ") : I A 25.

mḫ' (" strike ") : *ymḫ'*, I A 42.

myn (" water ") : *my*, I B 33,34.

ml'k (" messenger, ambassador ") : *ml'ky*, III 8 ; *ml'kh*, III 8.

mlh (" word ") : I B [25],[41] ; *mly* (cst. pl.), I B 8 ; I C 17 ; *mln*, III 2 ; *mly'* III 2 ; *mlwh*, I C 18.

mlḥ (" salt ") : I A 36.

mlk (" rule, reign ") : *ymlk*, I A 25 ; I B [3] ; *ymlkn*, I B 22.

mlk (" king ") : I A 6 ; I B 2,7, 26 ; III 28 ; *mlk* (cst. sg.), I A 1bis,3,[13],[14],[15] ; I B [1], 30 ; *mlk'*, I B [35] ; *mlkh* (3 sg. fem. suff.), II C 5 ; *mlkn*, I B 26,28 ; III [19] ; *mlky* (cst. pl.), I A [5] ; I B 41 ; II B [3] ; II C 15 ; III 1,[3],16,[27] ; *mlky'*, I B 22 ; III 7.

mlk (= mulk, " kingdom ") : I B 6 ; *mlky*, I C [6].

mlkt (" kingdom ") : *mlkt* (cst. sg.), I A 25bis ; II A [4] ; *mlkth* (3 sg. masc. suff.), I A 25 ; II A [4].

mll (" speak ") : *ymll*, I B [26] ; III [1],2.

mn (= man, " whoever ") : I C 16 ; II B 9 ; II C [1] ; III 26 ; *mn ḥd* (" any one "), I B 30 ; II B [7] ; III 9bis,10quinquies.

mn (= min, " from ") : I A 20? , 30 ; I B 8,[9],9,[10bis],27bis ; I C 15,16,18 ; II B 14 ; II C 2, 6,7,9,16bis ; III 2,11,12 ; *mny*, III 4,6,7 ; *mnk*, II B 20 ; *mk* (= *m<n>k* ?), III 22 ; *mnhm*, I B 41 ; *m-* (before laryngeal), I B 7,30. See also *mzy*.

m'yn (" spring ") : *m'ynn*, I A 12.

m'l (" above, upon ") : I B 30.

mṣlh (" abyss ") : I A [11].

mqnh (" possessions ") : *mqny*, I B 27.

mr' (" lord ") : *mr'km*, III 21.

mrmt (" treachery ") : III 22.

mrq (" affliction ") : I A 29.

mšḥ (" anoint ") : *ymšḥn*, I A [21].

mšl (" dominate ") : *tmšl*, III 9.

nb' (" babble ") : *yb'*, II B 8.

nbš (" soul ") : I B 40 ; *nbš'*, I A [36] ; *nbšy*, I B 40 ; *nbšk*, I B 39,42 ; II B 5,[8] ; *nbšh*, I A 37 ; *nbšhm*, III 5,6.

ngd (" officer ") : *ngdy*, III 10.

nḥt (" tranquillity ") : II B 4.

nkh (" strike ") : *tkh*, III 13 ; *tkwh*, III 13 ; *nkh* (Peal inf.), III 12,13.

nmrh (" panther ") : I A 31 ; II A [9].

nsk (" pour out ") : *ysk*, I A [25], 26 ; *tsk*, I B 38 ; III [5],7.

npq (" come forth ") : *ypq*, I A 28.

nṣb (" stele ") : *nṣb'* I A [6] ; I C 17.

nṣr (" guard, protect ") : *yṣr*, I C 17 ; *yṣrn*, I B 8 ; *yṣrw*, I C 15.

nqm (" avenge ") : *yqm*, III 12ter, 22 ; *tqm*, III 11.

nš' (" lift, take, bring ") : *yš'*, III 15,16,26 ; *tš'*, I B 39 ; III 14 ; *yš'n*, II C [13] ; *.š'*, I B [38].

nš' (" forget ") : *ytnšy*, II A [4].

nšn, (" women ") : *nšy* (cst. pl.), I A 41ter,[42].

nt' (" draw " ?) : *tnt'*, I B 29.

sbb (" surround ") : *ysb*, I B 34 ; *ysbn<y>*, I B 28.

shrt (" vicinity ") : *shrty*, III 7, [19].

skr (" hand over ") : *yskr* (Aphel impf.), III 3 ; *yhskr* (Haph. impf.), III 3 ; *yhskrn*, III 3 ; *thskrhm*, III 2 ; *hskr* (Haph. inf.), III 2.

slq (" come up, ascend ") : *ysq*, I A [27] ; I B [3] ; III 14,15bis, 16 ; *ysqn*, I A 5 ; I C 4.

ss (" moth ') : I A 31.

ssyh (" mare ") : I A 22.

spr (" inscription ") : *spr'*, I A [6] ; I B 8,[23],28,33 ; I C 17 ; II B [9],[18] ; II C 13 ; III 4, 14,17,23 ; *spry'*, II C 2,[4],[6], [9].

srs (" courtier, eunuch ") : *srsy*, I B 45 ; III 5.

'bd (" do, make ") : *'bdw*, II B 2 ; *y'bd*, I C [20] ; *t'bd*, I B [26] ; III [22] ; *''bd*, III 3 ; *y'bdw*, I C [5] ; *tt'bd*, I C [7].

'bd (" servant ") : *'bdy*, III 13.

'br (" pass on, by ") : *y'brnh* (Aphel impf.), III 17.

'gl (" calf ") : I A 23 ; II A [1] ; *'gl'*, I A 40.

'd (" up to, until," prep.) : I B 9bis,10 ; I C [8] ; III [24],25.

'd (" until," conj.) : II B 19? ; III 6.

'dn (" treaty ") : *'dn*, I B 24,41 ; II B [5] ; *'dy*, I A 1bis,2,3,[3], 4ter,13 ; I B 1bis,[4bis],4bis, 5bis,6 ; *'dy'*, I A 7bis ; I B [7], 7,11,23,24,[28],33,38 ; II B 2, [9],[14],[18] ; II C [13] ; III 4, 7,9,[14],17,19,20,23,27.

'wr (" be blind ") : *y'r* ('Ophal impf.), I A 39bis.

'wr (" be watchful ") : *y'wrn*, II B 4.

'zh (" she-goat ") : *'zn*, II A [2].

'zz (" be strong ") : *y'z*, II B 20 ; *y'zz* (Pael impf.), I B 44.

'yn (" eye ") : *'yny*, III 3 ; *'ynykm* I A 13.

'l (" upon, against, concerning ") : I A 26,28,42 ; I B 44,[45], 45 ; I C [7] ; II B [7],11 ; III 1ter,5,14bis,15ter,16bis,17,22bis, [26] ; *'ly*, I B 26 ; III [1],2, 22 ; *'lyh*, III [9] ; *'lh*, I A 32. See also *m'l*.

'l (" colt ") : I A 22 ; II A [1].

'lb (" torment ") : II C 10.

'ly (" upper ") : I A 6.

'lym (" young boy ") : I A 22.

'lyt (" upper part ") : I C [24].

'll (" enter ") : *y'l*, I B 35 ; *'ll* (act. ptc.), I A 6.

'lm (" eternity ") : I C [9] ; III 24,25 ; *'lmn*, I B [7].

'm (= 'am, " people ") : *'m'*, III 5,13 ; *'mh*, I A 29,30 ; I B 5, 11,[21] ; II B [2],3 ; *'mhm*, II C 16 ; *'my'*, III 10 ; *'my*, III 21.

'm (= 'im, " with ") : I A 1,2, 3bis,4,5ter,[5],6,[6],[13] ; I B 1,2bis,3ter,4bis,5bis,11,[29] ; III [26] ; *'my*, I B 33 ; *'mk*, I B 43.

'ml (" trouble ") : I A 26.

'qh (" magpie ") : I A 33.

'qr (" offspring ") : I A 3,15,[15] ; I B 2bis ; III 3 ; *'qry*, I B 25, [32] ; II B [6] ; III 1,3,11,12, 16,[21],[22],26 ; *'qrk*, I B [25], [32] ; II B [6] ; III 1,3,12,15, [26] ; *'qrh*, I A [2],25,41 ; II A [4] ; II B 6 ; II C 15 ; III 13,25.

ʿqrb (" scorpion "): I A 31.

ʿrr (" strip naked "): tʿrr, I A [40]; yʿrrn, I A 41.

ʿšq (" oppress, wrong "): tʿšqny, III 20.

ʿšt (" think "): tʿšt, II B 5.

ʿt : see kʿt.

p- (" and, but "): II B 4,6.

pgr (" corpse "): I B 30bis; II B 11bis.

pm (" mouth "): I A [30],31ter; II A 9ter.

pnh (" turn, return "): tpnw, III 7.

pqd (" official "): pqdy (1 sg. suffix on pl.), III 4,[10],13.

pqḥ (" open [the eyes] "): pqḥw, I A 13.

prq (" destroy "): prq (Peal inf.), I B 34.

ptḥ (" open "): ptḥḥ (fem. sg. pass. ptc.), III 8.

ṣby (" gazelle "): I A 33.

ṣdh (" owl "): I A 33.

ṣy (" desert animal "): I A [32].

ṣʿqh (" crying "): I A [29]; II A [8].

qbr (" grave "): qbrh, II A [4].

qdm (" before, in the presence of "): I A [7],8bis,[8],9ter,[9], 10,[10],11ter,[11],12.

ql (" voice "): I A 29.

qlbt (?): I B 44.

qml (" louse "): I A 31.

qq (" throat "): I A 32.

qryh (" town, city "): III 12; qryt, I B 36; qrytʾ, I A [33].

qrq (" flee "): yqrq, I B 45; III 4,19bis; qrq (ptc., " fugitive "):

III 4; qrqy, III 19; qrqhm, III 19.

qšt (" bow "): I A [38],39; qštʾ, I A 38.

qtl (" kill "): qtlw (impv. pl.), III 21; yqtl, II B [8],9; III 18; yqtln, III 11; yqtlnh, I B 27.

rʾš (" head "): rʾšy, II B [8]; III 11.

rb (" great "): rb, I B 7; rbt, I A [35]; rbwh (" his nobles "): I A 39,40,[41]; II B 3; II C 15; rbrby, II A 7.

rbʾ (" multiply "): ʾrbʾ, I B 30.

rbq (" to house "): rbq, I A [32].

rwḥ (" breath "): III 2.

rwm (" raise, lift up "): thrm, III 5,6.

rḥm (" friend "): III 8.

ryb (" quarrel "): III 17,26, [26bis].

rqh (" please "): rqh (Peal inf.), III 6,18; trqh (2 sg. masc. Pael impf.), III 18,19; trqhm, III 6; ʾrqhm, III 6; rqw (Pael impv.), III 6. Pael: " placate."

ršh (" assert authority "): tršh, III 9.

ršm (" write "): yršmn, II C [3].

śʾt (" ewe "): I A 21; śʾn, I A 23; II A [2].

śbʿ (" be sated "): yśbʿ, I A 22, [22],23,[23]; II A [1],1,[2bis].

śgb (" strengthen "): I B 32bis.

śgb (" noble "): śgbwh, III 13.

śhd, (" witness "): śhdn, I A 12.

śym (" place, set up "): śm, I A 7; śmw, I B 6; ʾśm, I C 19; yśmw, I C 23.

śnʾ (" enemy "): śnʾy, I B 26;

II B 14; III 10,11; *śn'wh*, III 12.

śpt ("lip"): *śptyk*, III 14; *śptwh*, III 15,16.

šbʿ ("seven"): I A 21,22,[22], 23,24,27ter; II A [1],1,[2],[3], [5],[6].

šbr ("break, shatter"): *yšbr*, I A 38; *tšbr*, I A 38.

šd ("breast"): *šdyhn*, I A [21].

šwb ("return"): *šbt*, III 25; *hšb*, III 20; *hšbw*, III 24; *'hšb*, III 20; *thšbhm*, III 6.

šwrh ("cow"): I A 23; II A [1].

šḥd ("bribe"): *yšḥdn*, III 28.

šḥṭ ("destroy"): *yštḥṭ*, I A [32].

šḥlyn ("watercress, weeds"): I A 36.

šṭ ("search"): I A 24; II A [3].

šybt ("return"): III 24.

šyt ("thorns"): II A 5.

šlʾ ("stay quietly"): *šlw*, III 5.

šlḥ ("send"): *yšlḥ*, I B 25,[26], 27; III 8; *tšlḥ*, I B 37; III 17,21; *'šlḥ*, I B [24]; II B 6; III 8; *yšlḥn*, I A 30; *mšlḥ*, I B 34.

šlm ("peace"): III 8.

šlm ("fulfill"): *tšlmn* (Aph. impf.), I B [24].

šm ("there"): III 6.

šmyn ("heaven"): I A [11],26; I B 7.

šmʿ ("hear, obey"): *yšmʿ*, I B 21,[21]; II B [2],3; *tšmʿ*, II B 4; *'šmʾ*, II B [5]; *yšmʿn*, I B [21],[22]; II B 2b; 3,[3]; *tšmʿn*, I B [24]; *ytšmʿ*, I A 29; *ytšmʿn*, I B [9].

šmr (?): II B 15.

šmš ("sun"): *šmšʾ*, I C 5.

šnh ("year"): *šnn*, I A 27bis, [27]; II A 5,6.

šʿwt ("wax"): *šʿwtʾ*, I A 35,37, 39,[42].

šʿl ("fox"): I A 33.

špr ("beautiful"): III 29.

šqr ("be false to"): *šqrt* (Pael pf.), I B [27],[33],[36],38; II B [17]; III [9],14,19,20,27; *šqrtm*, I B 23; II B 9,14; III 4,7,16,[23]; *yšqr*, I A 14,15, 24; II A [3]; *yšqrn*, I A [16].

šry ("loose, let go free"): *tšryh*, III 18.

šrn ("wildcat"): I A 33.

šrš ("scion"): *šršh*, I C [24].

štq ("be silent"): *tštq*, I B 8.

twy (?): I A 28.

twlʿh ("worm"): I A 27.

tḥt ("under"): I C [5]; *tḥtkm* ("your place"), III [7].

tḥty ("lower"): *tḥth*, I A 6.

tḥtyt ("lower part"): *tḥtyth*, I C 23.

tl ("mound, tell"): I A 32.

PROPER NAMES

1. Of Persons and Gods

'l ('El): I A 11.
'nrt ('Inurta): I A 38.
'r ('Ir): I A [8].

br g'yh (Bir-Ga'yah): I A 1,2,[2], [7],13,[14],[15]; I B 1,[2],[7]; II A 3; II B [5]; III [25].

gš (Gush): I A 16; I B 3,11; II B 10.

hdd (Hadad): I A [10],[25],36, 38.

zrpnt (Zarpanit): I A 8.

kd'h (Kadi'ah?): I A 10.

lṣ (Laṣ): I A 9.

mlš (Mullesh): I A 8.
mrdk (Marduk): I A 8.
mt''l (Matî'el): I A 1,2,3,[13],

14,15,[24],37,[37],[38],[39],40, 41,[42]; I B 1,2,13,21; I C [2], [7]; II B [2]; II C 14.

nb' (Nabu'): I A 8.
nkl (Nikkal): I A [9].
nkr (Nikkar): I A 10.
nr (Nur): I A 9.
nrgl (Nergal): I A 9.
nšk (Nusk): I A [8].

sbt (Sibitti): I A 11.
sn (Sin): I A [9].

'lyn ('Elyan): I A 11.
'trsmk ('Attarsamak): I A 1,3, 14; I B [1],[14].

ṣll (ṢLL): I B 3; II B 10.

šmš (Shamash): I A 9.

tšmt (Tashmet): I A [8].

2. Of Places

'dm ('Adam?): I A 35; in I A 10 *'dm*[ ].
'rm ('Aram): I A 5,6; I B [3].
'rnh ('Arneh): I A [34].
'rpd ('Arpad): I A [1],3,4bis, [12],[14bis],26,29,30,32,35; I B

[1],4,[5],[6],22,[30],[41]; II B [2],[3]; II C 15; III 1,3,16,27.
'šr ('Asshur): I A 25.

bz (BZ): I B 9.
bynn (BYNN): I A 34.

byt'l (Beth'el) : I A 34.
bq't (the Valley) : I B 10.

dmśq (Damascus) : I B [10].

ḥzz (Ḥazaz) : I A 35.
ḥlb (Aleppo) : I A [10] ; III 5.

y'dy (Ya'di) : I B [9].
ybrdw (Yabrud) : I B [9].

ktk (KTK) : I A 1,3,4,[12],[15] ;
  I B 4bis,5,10 ; II C 5.

l'wyn (?) : I B 30.
lbkh (?) : I B 35.

lbnn (Lebanon) : I B 9.
mblh (MBLH) : I A 34.
mdr' (MDF) : I A 34.
mzh (MZL) : I A 34.
mṣr (Muṣr) : I A 5 ; I B 12.
mrbh (MRBH) : I A 34 ; I B 12.

'rw ('RW) : I B 10.
'rqw ('Arqu) : I B 9.

rḥbh (Raḥbah) : I A 10.

šrn (Sharun) : I A 34.

tw'm (Tu'im) : I A 34.
tl'ym (Tal'ayim) : III [23],25,26.

INDICES

I. Index of Subjects

(Numbers in Roman type-face refer to pages.)

13

II. Index of Modern Scholars

III. Index of Scripture References

IV. Index of Other Northwest Semitic Texts

| | Mesha C. 840 | Kilamuwa | Zakir | Hadad Beginning of the 8th cent. | Sefire Middle of the 8th cent. | Karatepe Second half of the 8th cent. | Panammu C. 730 | Bir-RKB End of the 8th cent. |
		End of the 9th cent.						
א								
ב								
ג								
ד								
ה								
ו								
ז								
ח								
ט								
י								
כ								
ל								
מ								
נ								
ס								
ע								
פ								
צ								
ק								
ר								
ש								
ת								

PLATE I: Comparative Table of the Scripts of the Main Northwest Semitic Inscriptions of the 9th-8th Centuries B.C.

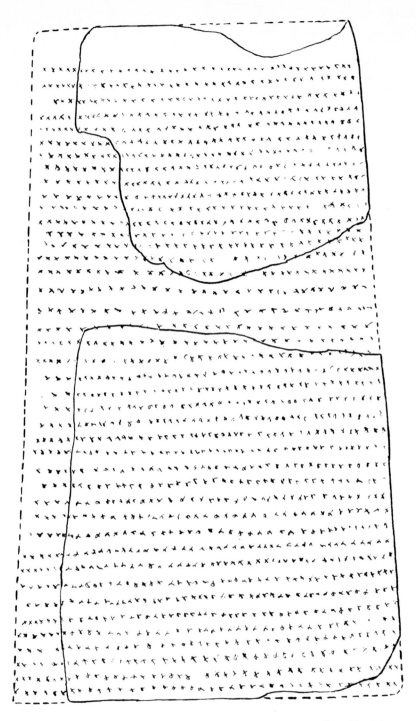

PLATE II: Stele I — Diagram Showing the Relative Position
of the Fragments

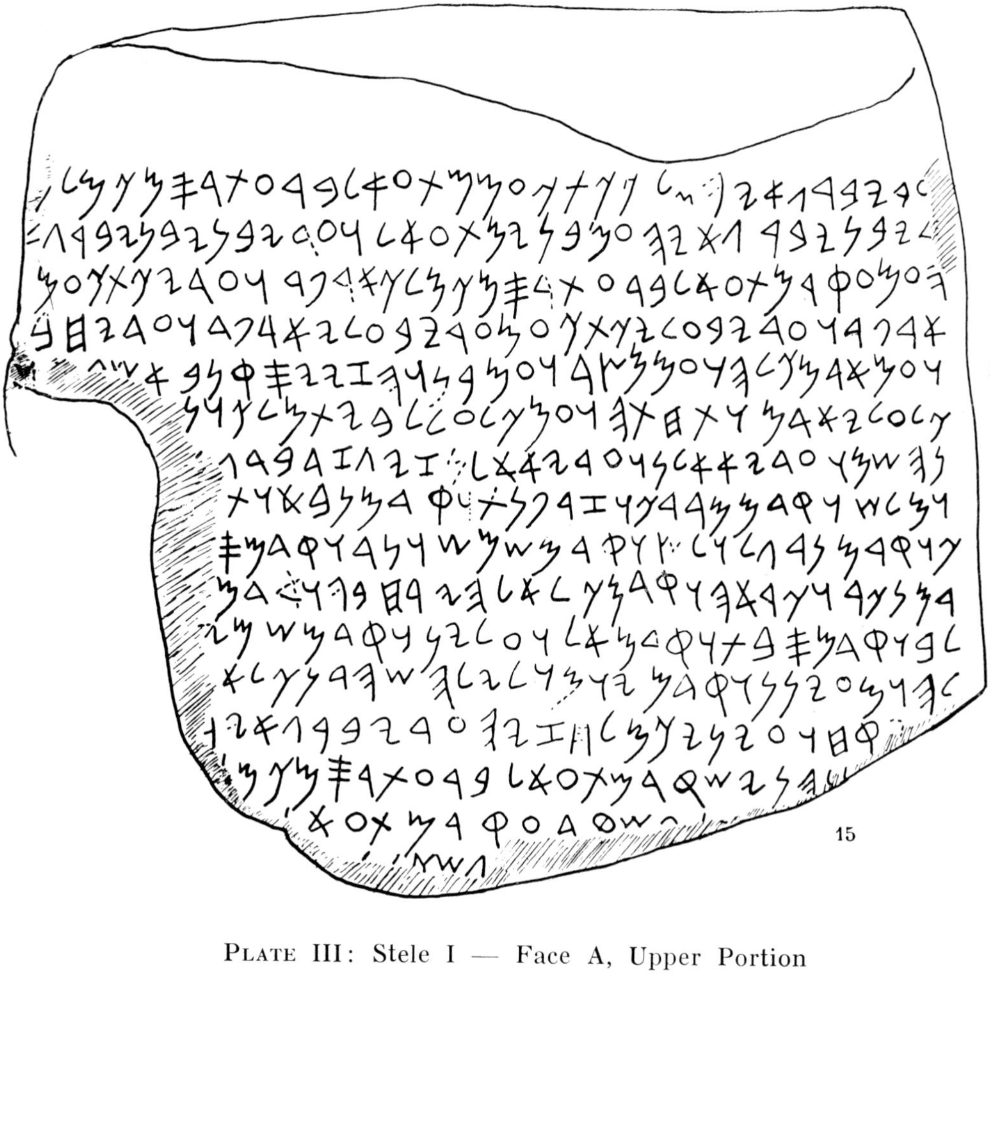

PLATE III: Stele I — Face A, Upper Portion

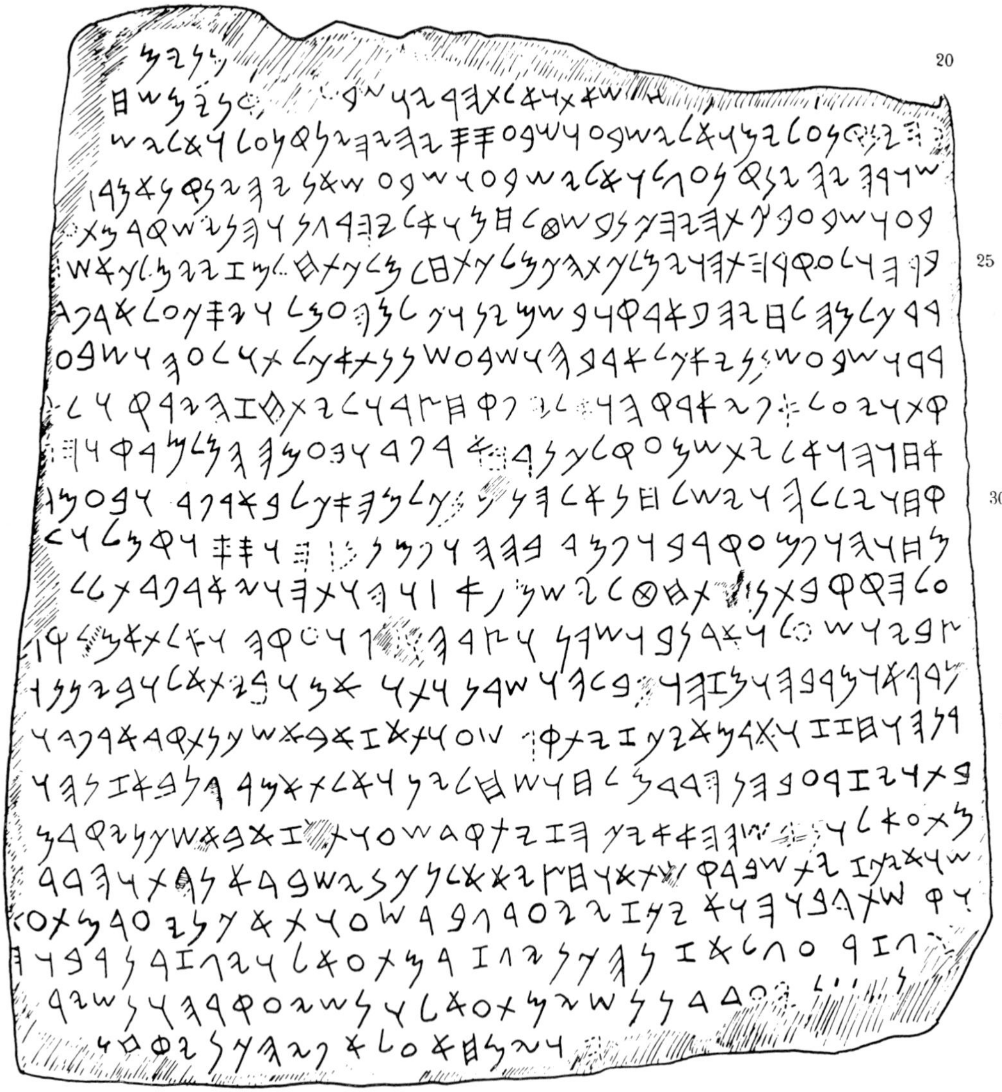

Plate IV: Stele I — Face A, Lower Portion

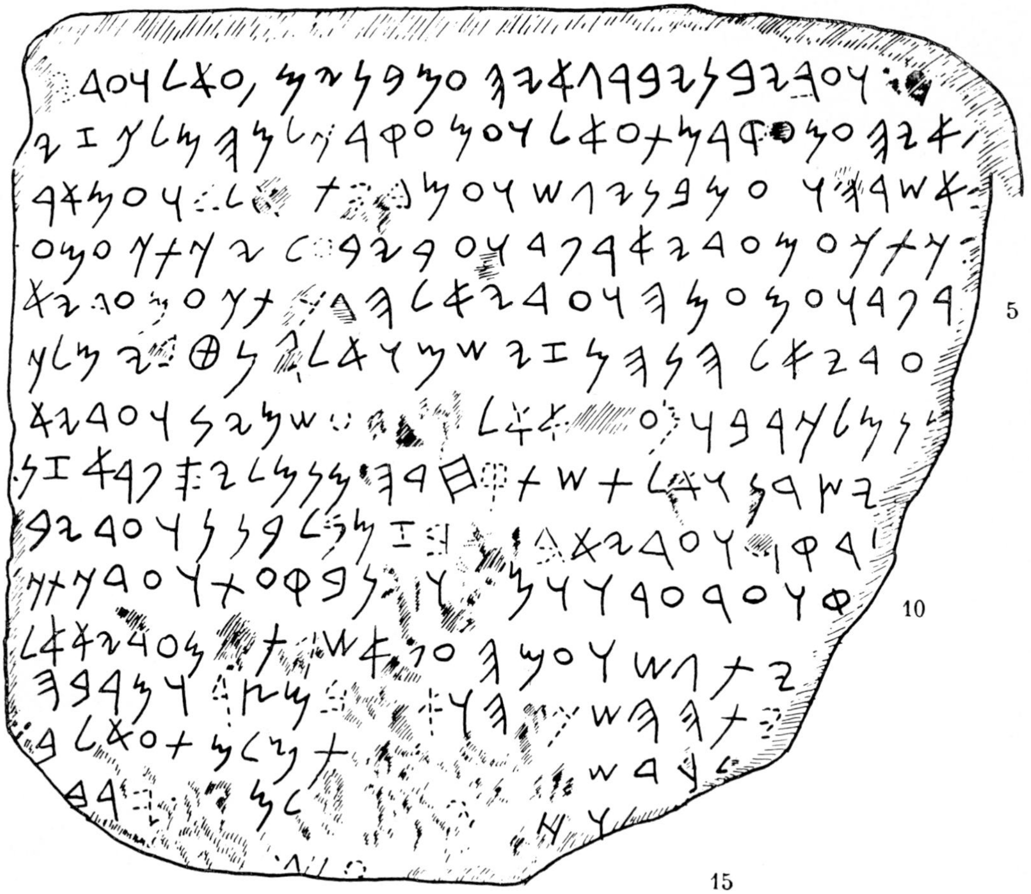

PLATE V: Stele I — Face B, Upper Portion

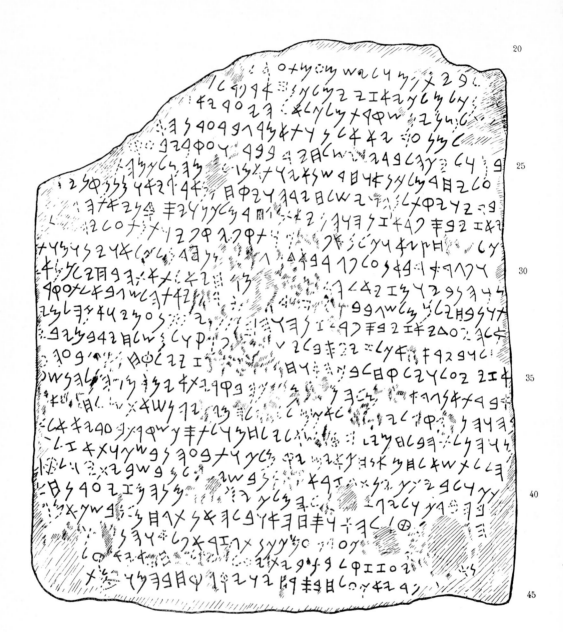

PLATE VI: Stele I — Face B, Lower Portion

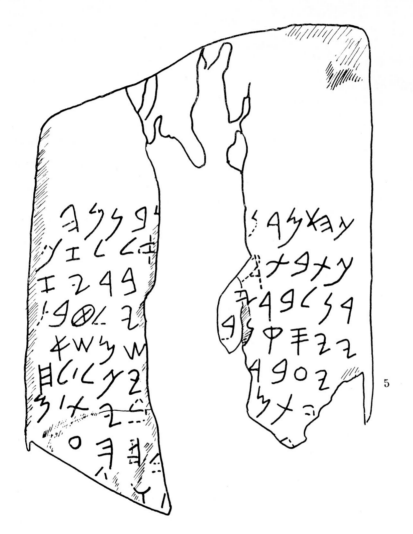

PLATE VII: Stele I — Face C, Upper Portion

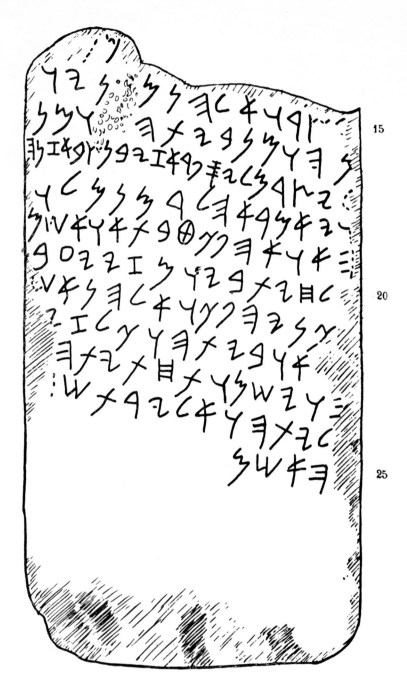

PLATE VIII: Stele I — Face C, Lower Portion

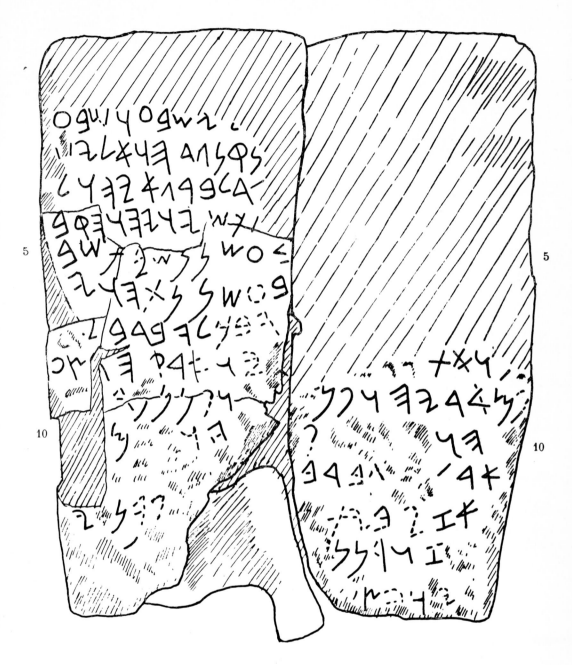

PLATE IX: Stele II — Face A

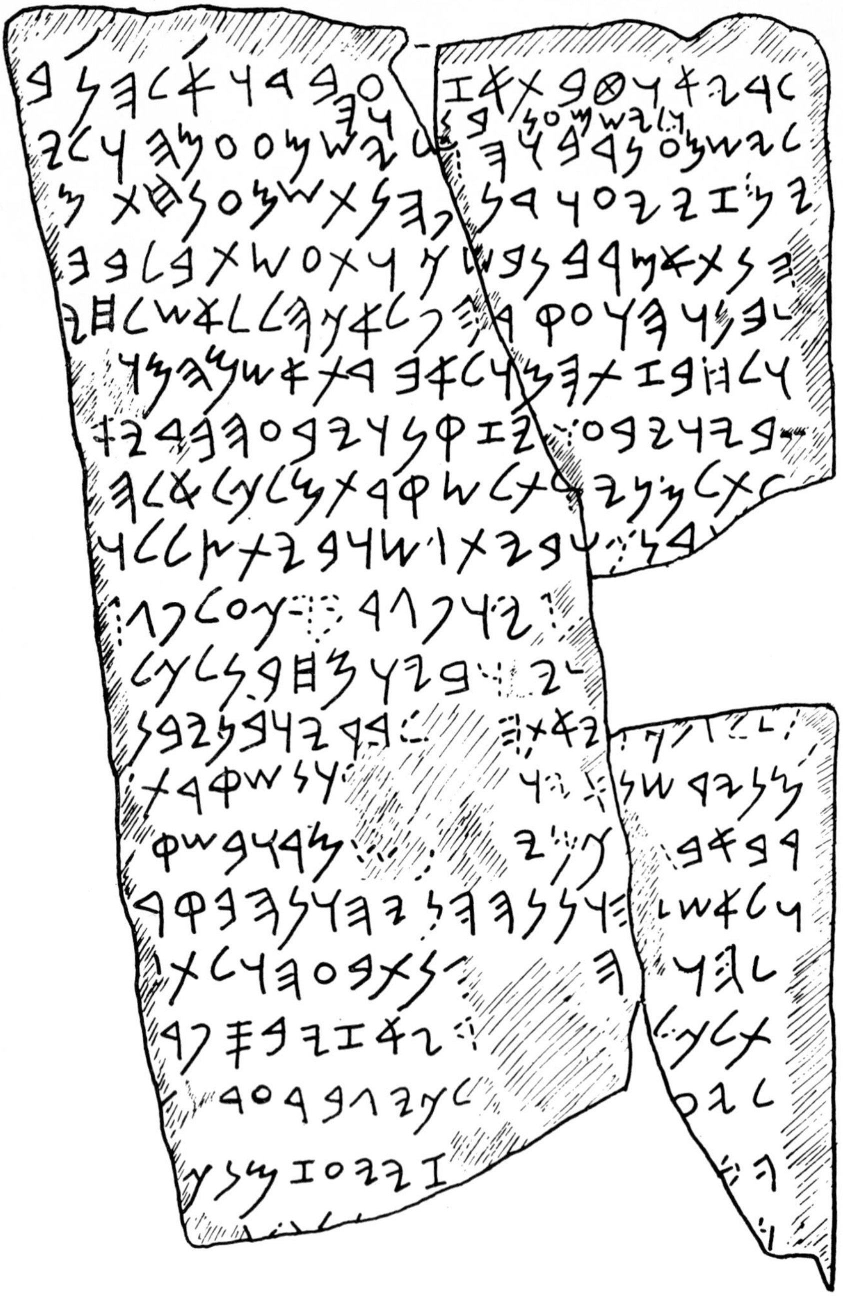

PLATE X: Stele II — Face B

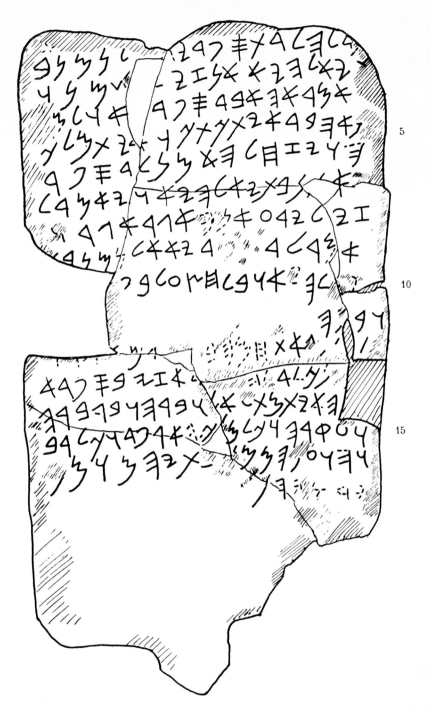

5

10

15

PLATE XI: Stele II -- Face C

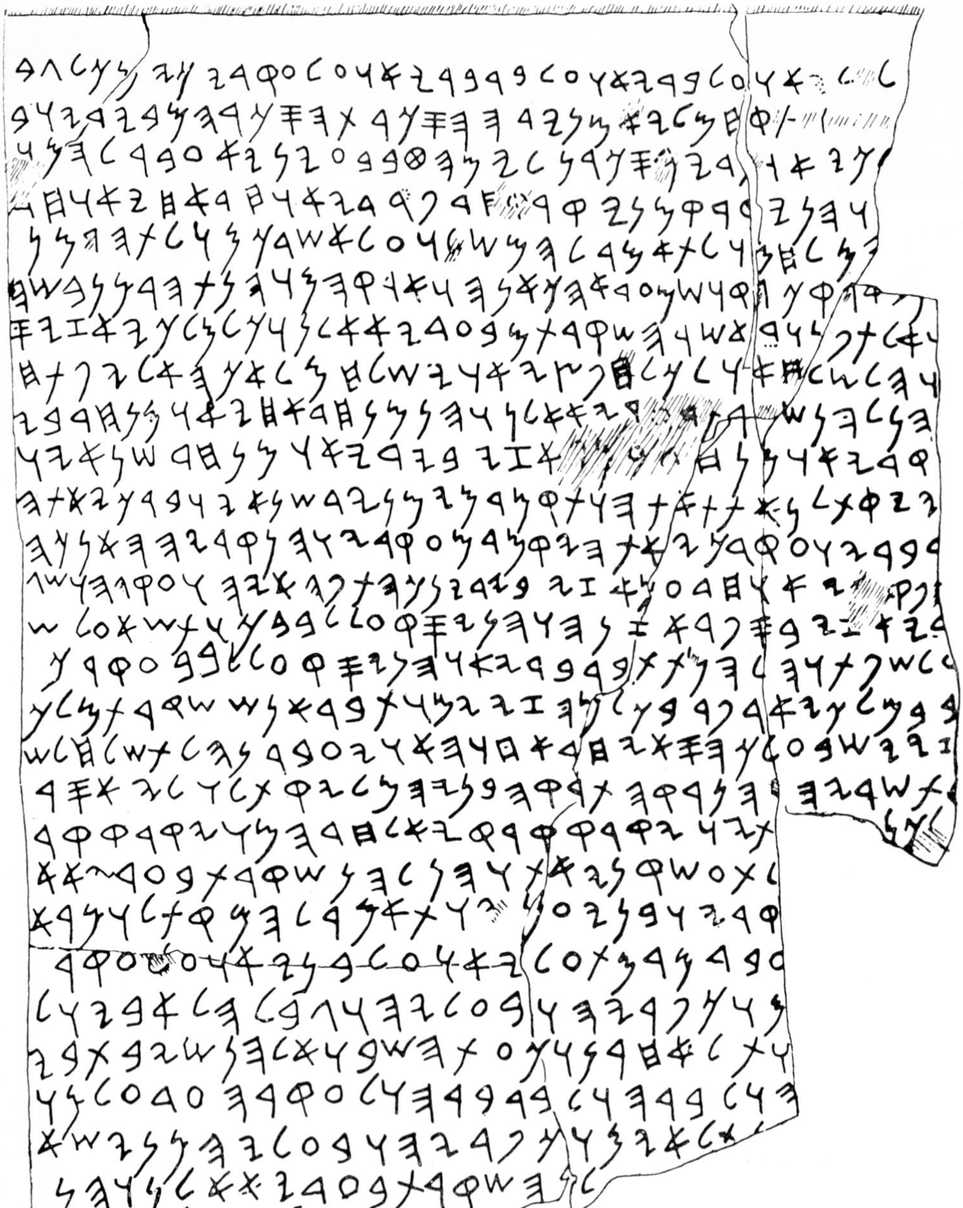

PLATE XII: Stele III — Left Side

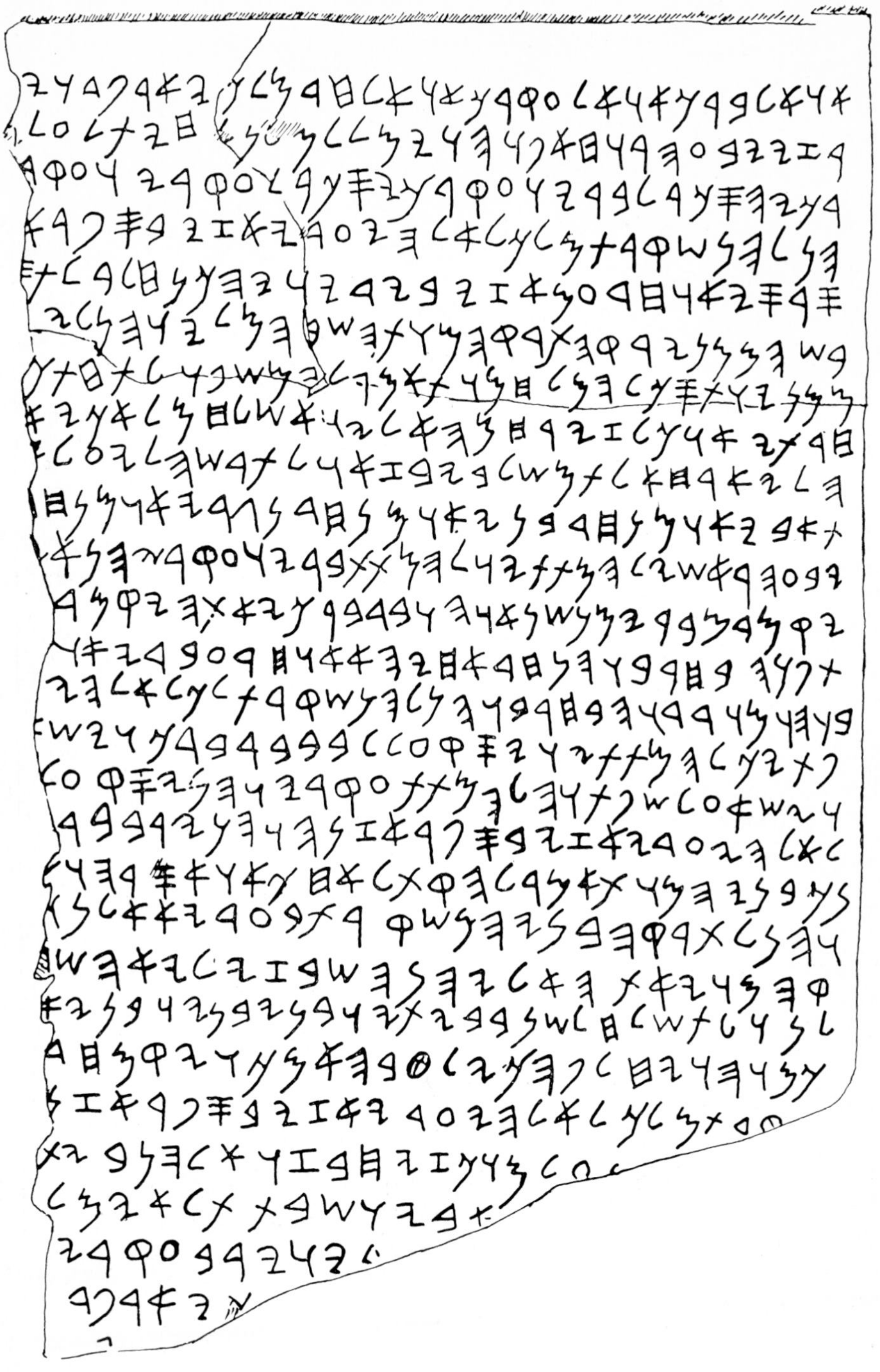

PLATE XIII: Stele III — Right Side

PLATE XIV: Stele I A (a-b) — Photographic Reproduction

PLATE XV: Stele I B (b) — Photographic Reproduction

PLATE XVI: Stele II B — Photographic Reproduction

PLATE XVII : Stele III — Photographic Reproduction

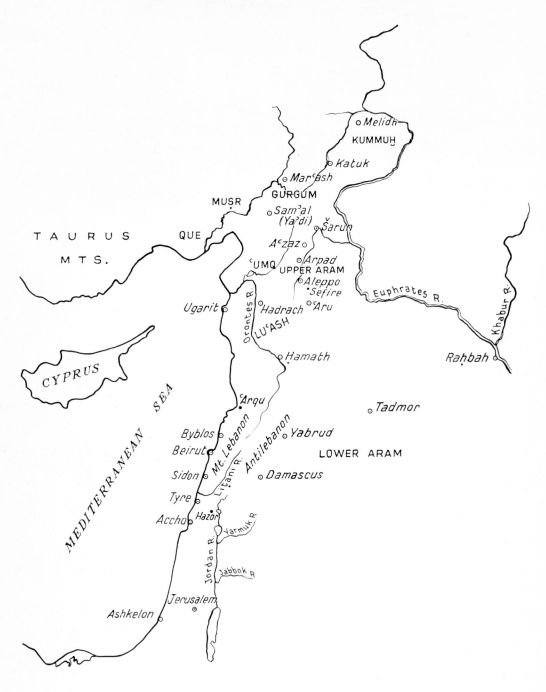

PLATE XVIII: Map of the Ancient Near East with reference to the Sefîre
Inscriptions